SURVIVING AS A TEACHER:
THE LEGAL DIMENSION

FRED HARTMEISTER, J.D., Ed.D.

Precept Press

Division of Bonus Books, Inc., Chicago

99   98   97   96   95   5   4   3   2   1

Library of Congress Cataloging-in-Publication Data

Hartmeister, Fred.
      Surviving as a teacher : the legal dimension / Fred Hartmeister.
          p.   cm.
      Includes bibliographical references and index.
      ISBN 0-944496-43-1 (pbk.) : $18.95
      1. Teachers—Legal status, laws, etc.—United States. I. Title.
KF4175.Z9H37   1995
344.73'078—dc20
[347.30478]   95-1452
                                                              CIP

Precept Press
Division of Bonus Books, Inc.
160 East Illinois Street
Chicago, Illinois 60611

Cover design by Wendy Hudgins
Printed in the United States of America

To
my mother, Mildred M. Hartmeister,
and
my father, Joel T. Hartmeister (1915-1990)

Contents

Foreword

In the big-inning, *Brown v. Board of Education of Topeka* became the opening pitch in what was to become a whole new ball game in public education. Since that seminal call in 1954, other equally devastating pitches have struck out many time-honored practices so that today, playing the game to its finish for the teacher or school administrator may well depend on how well each understands and practices the new rules under which the game must be played.

When the predecessor to this book first appeared, *How to Survive in Teaching: The Legal Dimension*, it was the first of its kind and was intended to meet a need theretofore thought unnecessary. Designed to inform both the beginning and the experienced teacher, it caught on immediately. Modeled on the dialectic methodology of Socrates (who skillfully asked questions and sought to build concepts from precepts), the book has been widely used as both a classroom text and as an individualized tutorial. In time, it went through five printings. Upon the retirement of the original author, a rush of additional pitches made the book obsolete. A dormant period followed. The publishers sought someone with legal knowledge and a background in educational law to revive the book and again bring it up-to-date.

Needed was a person experienced in teaching, administration and law with added innings at the university level. Such a person would need to interpret anew for another generation of practitioners their legal rights and liabilities under the present rules of the game. This would require one who not only knew the law but also knew the problems faced by those who were to put it into practice.

Fortunately, the task, though daunting, was one well-fitted to the qualifications of Dr. Fredric J. Hartmeister. As an Assistant Professor of Educational Leadership at Texas Tech University, Dr. Hartmeister accepted the challenge and *Surviving as a Teacher: The Legal Dimension* is the welcome result.

Dr. Hartmeister's qualifications begin impressively with his J.D. (1990) and Ed.D. (1986) degrees from the University of Wyoming, by way of an M.B.A. (1979) from the University of Denver and a B.S. in Elementary Education (1973) from Valparaiso University. In addition, he has served in a wide range of professional positions including a stint as a staff attorney and law clerk for the Chief Justice of the Wyoming Supreme Court. A switch-hitter between the law and educational arenas, Dr. Hartmeister also has experience as a public school teacher and elementary school principal. His list of legal publications and national presentations are equally impressive. At Texas Tech University, he teaches courses in educational law and educational policy.

In bringing my original text up-to-date, Dr. Hartmeister has rendered a real and valuable service to the educational profession. *Surviving as a Teacher: The Legal Dimension* meets a serious need to enable those who teach and those who administer the nation's schools to keep abreast of the game's new rules. My hope is that today's reader can find this book as useful as its predecessor was when it first crossed the plate and broke into print.

Denver, Colorado   M. Chester Nolte
August 1994   Professor of Education Emeritus
                         University of Denver

Preface

As indicated in the foreword written by my dear friend Dr. M. Chester ("Chet") Nolte, this book is intended to serve as a helpful, handy, easy-to-understand legal resource for secondary and elementary school teachers and prospective teachers. It has a dual purpose in that: (1) it can be used as a text in undergraduate education classes for those preparing to become teachers; and (2) it provides a basic review of legal issues and topics for the experienced or veteran teachers who simply wish to become more familiar with general legal principles that impact contemporary education and the teaching profession. It must be noted, however, that this book is not intended to take the place of obtaining more specific legal advice when circumstances dictate. In other words, a teacher should not rely on this book in lieu of consulting with an attorney. More particularly, anyone perusing this book must realize that it only covers the tip of the school law iceberg. There are many different situations and eventualities that may arise in the everyday professional life of a teacher that cannot fit within the pages of a single volume.

Unlike many other legal texts, this book is not heavily footnoted or "legalistic." This is to ensure readability and to emphasize the significance of the legal concepts being discussed. Consequently, case names, citations and other pertinent references are included within the text so that readers may quickly and easily identify sources and make connections between circumstances and outcomes.

Although this book has a slightly different title from Dr. Nolte's original book (*How to Survive in Teaching: The Legal Dimension*), it is essentially an updated version of that same text. The question and answer format has been retained since it has proven to be popular with readers and professors as an informal—and informed—way to provide a basic understanding of "school law" and, at the same time, answer many frequently-asked questions shared by those in the education profession. The chapter structure has been modified rather significantly. More cases have been added at the beginning of each chapter to stimulate thought and discussion. Since nearly all of these "case descriptions" are taken from reported court opinions in actual cases, they are conducive to "case study" or "problems-based" classroom instruction that contemporary readers will find to be relevant, informative, and "real." Cases have been carefully selected to provide broad exposure to a variety of legal issues and principles—yet most of the cases should also make the reader stop and think, "What would I do in this situation?" From this kind of vicarious exposure to problems encountered by others in the teaching profession, it is hoped that history—and the often distasteful experience of resolving a problem via litigation—will not necessarily need to repeat itself.

This book would not have been possible without the able assistance, patience and understanding of many people whom I would like to acknowledge and thank: Dr. Chet Nolte (who, it goes without saying, made this opportunity possible); Dr. Maurice Wear and Dr. Stan Cole as well as Mr. Robert Cohn, Esq. (the professors who taught me school law during my years as a graduate student); Drs. William Sparkman, Charles Reavis, Mary John O'Hair, and Joseph Claudet (my colleagues in the Educational Leadership Program at Texas Tech University); several unnamed fellow members and close friends in the National Organization on Legal Problems of Education (NOLPE); all of the graduate students and prospective administrators that I have had the pleasure of working with during my first year as a professor at Texas Tech University; Ms. Margaret Graham and Ms. Kay Gleghorn (the very able typists in the College of Education typing pool at Texas Tech University); Sharon Blackburn and several other members of the library staff at the Texas Tech University Law Library; and the staff at Precept Press in Chicago. Last—and quite the opposite of least—I wish to thank my beautiful wife Becky for her many endearing qualities including boundless energy and patience, expert legal advice, research assistance, computer expertise, good humor and overall support. As a practicing attorney in her own right, she made the culmination of this project possible.

Lubbock, Texas
September 1994

Fred Hartmeister
Assistant Professor of Education
Texas Tech University

Chapter One

From Classroom to Courtroom

A ninth-grade government class teacher received the following written reprimand from his principal:

> After completing the investigation of the alleged incident in your period 3 class on March 30, 1989, I find it necessary to write you this letter of reprimand. The investigation revealed that you displayed poor judgment in your comment "making out" on the tennis court. Informing your students of an alleged incident of one of your tennis players "making out" with a female student on the tennis courts during the lunch period was an inappropriate topic for comment in a classroom setting.
>
> In the future you will need to refrain from commenting on any items which might reflect negatively on individual members of our student body. *Miles v. Denver Public Schools*, 944 F.2d 773, 774-75 (10th Cir. 1991).

The *Miles* case started when Mr. Miles, the ninth-grade teacher, responded to a student's question about how the quality of the school had declined since 1967. The student requested specifics, and the teacher replied that in the past "there were not so many pop cans laying around and school discipline was better." He added, "I don't think in 1967 you would have seen two students making out on the tennis court." This comment referred to an alleged incident that occurred the previous day. The rumor throughout the school was that two students had been observed having sexual intercourse on the tennis court during the lunch hour. The teacher had heard the rumor from a colleague, but did not seek to confirm or verify the authenticity before responding to his student's question in class.

The teacher's comments led parents of the alleged participants in the tennis court tryst to complain to the principal, who met with the teacher and other individuals. The teacher was then placed on paid administrative leave for four days, and he wrote to the principal apologizing for his "bad judgment." During this time, the principal investigated and then issued the reprimand letter quoted above.

After the teacher was reinstated, he filed a civil rights lawsuit. The lawsuit claimed that the teacher's free speech rights were "chilled" by his having been put on administrative leave and by having the letter of reprimand placed in his file. The United States District Court for the District of Colorado ruled in favor of the school district. The teacher then appealed to the Tenth Circuit Court of Appeals.

To decide the case on appeal, the Tenth Circuit considered the facts and circumstances under the light of various standards adopted over time by the United States Supreme Court. The standards balance the interests of government (the school district in this case) to provide a safe and orderly educational environment against the rights of individuals (the ninth-grade teacher Miles) to speak out—in this case in a public school classroom.

To determine if the teacher's speech in this case was constitutionally protected, the court followed a 1988 United States Supreme Court decision in *Hazelwood School District v. Kuhlmeier*, 484 U.S. 260 (1988). *Hazelwood* involved a high school principal's decision to eliminate two pages from the school newspaper being prepared for publication by students in a journalism class. The excised articles dealt with teenage pregnancy and the impact of divorce on students. After concluding that the school newspaper was not a "public forum" in the traditional sense of a "free press," the Court in *Hazelwood* held:

> that educators do not offend the first amendment by exercising editorial control over school-sponsored expression 'so long as their actions are reasonably related to legitimate pedagogical concerns.' *Id.* at 273.

In applying the *Hazelwood* standard to the facts in *Miles*, the Tenth Circuit found that the school district acted appropriately in suspending and reprimanding the teacher for his comments. The court looked at the facts and concluded that the ninth-grade classroom was not a public forum and that the teacher's comments should be treated as school-sponsored expression since they were uttered in a traditional classroom setting. Next, the court examined the school's motives to see if its actions in dealing with the teacher were "reasonably related to legitimate pedagogical interests." After finding legitimacy in the school's stated interest of preventing a teacher from spreading unsubstantiated and embarrassing rumors about students to their peers and a desire to have teachers exhibit professionalism and sound judgment, the court held that the school's response to the teacher's comments was appropriate. The court concluded that it would "not intervene with the authority of the school officials to select among alternative forms of discipline." The school district's course of action in sanctioning the teacher was affirmed. *Miles*, 944 F.2d at 778-79.

If you are a teacher or plan on becoming one in the future and the circumstances described in the above case do not touch a chord of familiarity or give a sense of "that could happen to me," then perhaps it should! The facts in the *Miles* case (named for John G. Miles, the government teacher and plaintiff who filed the lawsuit) are not extraordinary. It does not stretch the imagination to see that this is exactly the sort of thing that might happen to a teacher anywhere in this country on any given school day. Although the teaching profession remains a higher calling, perhaps now more than ever before, teachers and others in the education profession encounter frequent and significant risks. By comparison, a mere four-day suspension with pay seems almost insignificant. The perils many teachers face from day-to-day are diverse and practically limitless. Free speech issues are abundant, and students now carry and use weapons to threaten and harm teachers. Unsubstantiated charges of sexual molestation are sometimes brought against teachers who did nothing more than impose appropriate discipline. The uncertainty of funding sources for school operations and ensuring employment security for dedicated educators are two more wide-ranging perils. Many of the cases discussed in this book attest to the fact that teaching is increasingly becoming a precarious profession—not just physically or emotionally but legally as well. While this represents an unfortunate sign of the times, it is something about which we cannot afford to be ill-prepared.

As a teacher, you cannot learn to avoid lawsuits or handle your job coolly and professionally until you understand the nature and scope of the legal problems you may face. That is the purpose of this book—to expose you to examples and situations from actual court cases so that you can learn to minimize risks and become aware of how to defend yourself against needless litigation and the possibility of losing your good name or personal assets.

To begin, it is important to recognize that the *Miles* case you just read about happened in Colorado in 1989. The United States District Court for the District of Colorado granted summary judgment on behalf of the school district on March 27, 1990. In effect, that meant that the federal district court dismissed the lawsuit filed by Mr. Miles against the Denver Public School District. The court failed to recognize any substantial rights claimed by the teacher which would entitle him to recover monetary damages or obtain injunctive relief from the school district. That ruling by the trial court is cited in legal literature as *Miles v. Denver Public Schools*, 733 F.Supp. 1410 (D.Colo. 1990).

The teacher's appeal to the Tenth Circuit Court of Appeals, which is described in detail in this introduction, is cited as *Miles v. Denver Public Schools*, 944 F.2d 773 (10th Cir. 1991). It took about two and a half years for this case to move from the March 30, 1989, events in Mr. Miles' classroom to the Tenth Circuit's ruling in favor of the school district on Sept. 11, 1991.

The numbers and abbreviations in the case citation have

special significance. For example, the first number (944) is the volume number of the publication; F.2d is the citation for the Federal Reporter Second Series (volumes of reported court cases from West Publishing Co.); the following number (773) is the page in that volume where the case begins. If you visit a law school or county bar association law library, ask the librarian how to find Volume 944 of the Federal Reporter 2nd (F. 2d). By turning to page 773 of that volume you will find the appellate court's opinion in the *Miles* case. As you have probably surmised, the parenthetical information at the end of the citation (10th Cir. 1991) indicates which federal circuit court of appeals reviewed the *Miles* case on appeal as well as the year in which the court issued its decision in the case. The Federal Reporter contains all published United States Circuit Court of Appeals decisions.

The same applies to the lower court's decision on this case, which was affirmed by the Tenth Circuit Court in the opinion discussed above. The case was originally filed in the United States District Court for the District of Colorado, and that court's original ruling in the case is cited as *Miles v. Denver Public Schools*, 733 F.Supp. 1410 (D.Colo. 1990). That case will be found in Volume 733 of the Federal Supplement Reporter (referred to as F.Supp.) beginning on page 1410. There you will find the memorandum opinion and order granting the school district's motion for summary judgment as decided by the federal district court judge in Colorado. A comparable type of citation system is used for cases decided by the United States Supreme Court as well as all published opinions from the state court systems in all fifty states.

Questions and Answers that Demand Your Attention

Why a book on the legal dimensions of teaching?

There are four primary reasons why this book should be important to you as a classroom teacher. First, lawsuits in which a teacher is either a *plaintiff* (person filing a civil lawsuit) or a *defendant* (person being sued and against whom recovery is sought in a civil suit, or the accused in a criminal case) are proliferating at an alarming and troublesome rate. Second, your preparation for teaching probably did not include much, if any, substantive information about your legal rights and responsibilities. Third, the teaching profession has been changed considerably by what the United States Supreme Court and all the other courts in our country have ruled regarding individual rights and school district obligations. Finally, Congress and the fifty state legislatures are constantly enacting new legislation that impacts education in general and the role of teachers in particular. As a result of such new legislation, a huge volume of administrative rules and regulations are generated by federal and state agencies to "flesh out" the legislative mandates.

This book's two main objectives are to help you become aware of your legal rights and responsibilities so that: (1) you may avoid violating others' constitutionally and statutorily protected rights in your daily work in the classroom; and (2) you will know how to assert your own personal and professional employment rights as a teacher. With both of these objectives the ultimate goal is to minimize the risks of becoming involved in litigation.

What is the "target audience" for this book?

This book is intended to serve as both a pre-service and an in-service resource for elementary and secondary school teachers. It can be used as a classroom text for undergraduate education students, and it is just as useful when read on an individual basis. Prospective student teachers who may not have covered some of the legal aspects of the teaching experience in their coursework can use this book to become better informed as to the rights and duties they will share with others in the education profession. The text can also serve as a refresher for experienced teachers who recognize the need to stay up-to-date with regard to the legalities affecting the profession.

Will this volume alleviate the need for an attorney?

No, of course not. This book is designed to give a classroom teacher a general and practical knowledge of school law. Just as any other professional person needs to know the law, this book is intended to make you aware of your legal rights and responsibilities as a teacher. With a careful eye on the risks of oversimplification, the author attempts to provide a resource that is legally accurate and will serve as a guide or starting point for teachers without being overly technical. While this volume is informative and will make you reflect on your legal relationships with students, parents, other teachers, administrators and the board of education, it cannot replace the need for a competent attorney when potential litigation arises.

How is this book organized?

There are five broad legal areas that teachers must be aware of in order to survive and thrive in the classroom. Each of these areas encompasses a chapter in this book:

Employment Issues:

Before, During, and After	Chapter 2
Freedom of Expression	Chapter 3
Student Issues	Chapter 4
Torts and Liability	Chapter 5
Collective Bargaining	Chapter 6

In addition to these general legal concerns, the final chapter (Chapter 7) deals with the teacher's role in the attorney/client relationship. The appendices contain the amendments to the United States Constitution, an alphabetical listing of cases cited within this book, and a table listing the states within the federal judicial circuit courts of appeal. There is also an index and glossary to assist you in finding and understanding legal concepts and definitions. *A most important point to remember is that answers to your specific legal questions may differ in your state depending on the laws and court decisions there.*

How can a teacher become more aware of the new rules under which schools are now operating?

An obvious (and somewhat self-serving) way is to read this volume in its entirety. Another is to check those articles in current professional journals and periodicals that cover educational law. For example, there is a column in the *Kappan* (published by Phi Delta Kappa) called "Courtside" by Dr. Perry Zirkel (a professor of law and education at Lehigh University) that discusses a different prominent case or legal issue each month. Daily newspapers and weekly news magazines frequently carry stories related to the emerging body of law, particularly decisions of the United States Supreme Court. There may be statewide media publicity on legislative actions related to teachers, students or boards of education. A favorite convention topic for teachers is how these legal changes affect the teaching profession and life in the classroom. A visit to a law school or county bar association library will provide first-hand information on the cases cited in this text. Attendance in a law class for teachers and administrators offered by a college of education at a local university would be most helpful in staying apprised of changes affecting school law. Above all, it is important to remember that the law seldom remains static or unchanged. Also, keep in mind that the concept of "school law" encompasses constitutional protections, legislative enactments (usually called statutes) and administrative agency rules and regulations (i.e., regulations implemented by a state board of education or the United States Department of Education). In this regard, "school law" is far more than just the massive volume of judicial opinions written by the courts.

Why aren't all of the cases in this book brand new?

Several of the cases discussed in this text are many years old. But an old case can still be good law. Although some of the facts and situations may seem slightly dated, the cases have been selected to illustrate the legal principles and doctrines upon which "school law" is grounded. For this reason, the age of a case is of minor significance—rather, the key is how each case exemplifies contemporary legal issues about which teachers need to be aware. Note, however, that more recently decided cases may change the law—either by reversing, over-ruling or modifying a previous decision made by a lower court in the same case or by deciding new legal issues that had not been previously litigated or resolved. The bottom line is to re-member that school law—like most law—is not set in stone. Rather, in many ways, it is a dynamic and somewhat fluid body of statutes, judicial opinions, administrative rules and regula-tions, and constitutional protections.

Before we get into particulars, here are six case excerpts or "descriptions" taken from actual reported cases from around the country that illustrate what can happen to a class-room teacher who ends up in a courtroom. You might want to go to a law library and read the entire case to get the full fla-vor of the facts and circumstances from which the case arose, as well as a more expansive description of the court's reason-ing. The outcome of each case is given at the end of the chap-ter so you have the opportunity to contemplate and discuss each case before knowing what the court decided.

Case Descriptions

Case No. 1: "Just cause" for termination?

A fourth-grade teacher had taught in a public school district for several years. After being under surveillance for some time, she was arrested in 1989 for shoplifting. Criminal charges were filed. The school district superintendent gave the teacher no-tice of his recommendation to terminate her employment con-tract based on the impact of her actions and that her conduct did "not reflect the role model necessary to be an effective el-ementary teacher." The school board agreed with the superin-tendent that the teacher was no longer an effective teacher or role model and terminated her employment for "just cause." In a trial following her termination, the teacher blamed her conduct on the result of a "medically induced mania" from taking medication, and contended that a mental illness or disability does not rise to the level of "just cause" for termination. She admitted that she had stolen clothing a number of times; further, she had signed a form at the store although she claimed memory loss with regard to some of the charges. Expert medical testimony differed as to whether she knew right from wrong at the time she shoplifted. However, testimony from other teachers and parents pointed out additional occurrences of inappropriate behavior with students and that these incidents did not establish her as a good role model. Did the school board have just cause to terminate or was the teacher simply unable to help herself due to her disability?

Case No. 2: A teacher should teach

Teachers unions and a public school system had reached an agreement which allowed the teachers who were elected president of the employee organizations to apply for a year-long leave of absence. The teacher who had been president of one teachers' union for the past seven years sought a one-year leave for the 1991-1992 school year. She had received the leave for each of the previous seven years, during which time the union paid her salary and provided her benefits, and she had continued to accrue seniority and retirement benefits as if she were in the classroom. The school administration had always retained full discretion to grant or refuse to grant the one-year leave, and in 1991 her request was denied by the superintendent and the school board. (No other teacher had been granted this type of leave status for more than two years.)

The teacher was convinced that her leave was denied because she had publicly been critical of the administration and the board. She filed suit claiming violation of her First Amendment rights of free speech and association and violation of equal protection under the Fourteenth Amendment. Do you think the teacher should have received a leave of absence for an eighth year, or was the denial of leave justified?

Case No. 3: From teaching high school English to teaching fifth grade

A high school English teacher was granted a one-year leave of absence by the school board. Pursuant to a state statute, the teacher expected to be placed in "the same or a comparable position upon return from leave." However, upon her return she was assigned to teach a fifth-grade elementary class even though she was not certified to do so. The teacher declined to accept the fifth-grade position, and she was eventually discharged, following which she sued the school district. Why do you suppose the school board did this? Was it an abuse of the school board's discretion or was it permissible?

Case No. 4: Birds of a feather

A non-tenured teacher's contract was not renewed and she brought suit in federal district court claiming denial of her civil rights. The school board gave as its reasons for not renewing her contract that she lacked discipline in the classroom, that she was untidy, and that her teaching methods were inadequate. The teacher said that in reality the school board was acting in bad faith—that she was really being non-renewed because of lack of church attendance, her physical size, the location of her trailer, and how she conducted her personal life. She sought back pay, punitive damages, and attorney's fees. Her case was tried to a jury. Do you think that the teacher was unconstitutionally dismissed?

Case No. 5: Give them a hand

After negotiations for renewal of a collectively bargained employment agreement failed, teachers went on strike in violation of a state law. Letters were sent by the school board to striking teachers, inviting them to return to work or else be discharged. While a few returned to work, some eighty-eight teachers refused and were called before the school board. Following abbreviated hearings the teachers were dismissed one at a time at twenty-minute intervals. Claiming the school board was not an impartial tribunal and that it had denied them due process of law, the eighty-eight teachers brought an action in federal court to have their jobs restored. The case finally reached the United States Supreme Court. Do you think the teachers received due process of law? Was the school board biased because it had previously been negotiating against the teachers? Should the Supreme Court allow the firings to stand on the grounds that the teachers had violated the law?

Case No. 6: How far does neglect of duty extend?

Oregon statutes provide that a permanent teacher may be dismissed for "neglect of duty" which refers to a teacher's obligation to the employing district, her students and others. A permanent contract teacher who had taught satisfactorily for eleven years was dismissed for "neglect of duty" based on the teacher's failure to take appropriate measures in response to her husband's use of the family home for selling marijuana. The teacher maintained that though she opposed drug use, she was unable to prevent her husband's misuse of the house. She urged him to get counseling but was afraid to push him further because he might leave (they had two young children) and she feared he might react violently. The State's Fair Dismissal Appeals Board reversed her dismissal, concluding that the teacher's conduct did not constitute "neglect of duty." The school district appealed. Who do you think prevailed?

The Teacher and the Law

What is meant by "the law" in the United States?

The term is generic and applies to the complete collection of rules which govern our society. Law may either be written or unwritten. Written law generally includes Congressional acts, state statutory enactments, city council ordinances, and board of education policies which result from actions of the legislative branch of government. On the other hand, *common law* (which is sometimes unwritten) dates back over centuries and consists of court decisions and rulings, recognized customs, attorney general opinions, and proclamations or orders emanating from the executive branch of government. Taken together, all of these sources comprise what is generally referred to as "the law."

What has been the trend in "school law?"

Since 1954 when the United States Supreme Court decided *Brown v. Board of Education of Topeka*, 347 U.S. 483 (1954), much of what is considered "school law" is of the judge-made variety. For example, between 1953 and 1969, the United States Supreme Court under Chief Justice Earl Warren decided approximately three dozen cases dealing with educational issues. Since then the Supreme Court under Chief Justices Warren Burger (1969 to 1986) and William Rehnquist (1986 to present) has not been far behind in deciding a comparable number of cases which involved schools or educational issues. Most recently, a large number of United States Supreme Court decisions have focused on special education and religious issues involving such things as school prayer and public funding for parochial and private school programs. In addition, the Court has also looked at such varied issues affecting teachers and teaching as school-based search and seizure, employment rights, sexual harassment and free speech issues.

Why is the number of lawsuits involving teachers increasing?

In a very real sense the legal problems facing teachers are the same problems shared by society at large. As society changes, so must laws change to accommodate newer values and to protect the rights of individuals. What was taken for granted for many years is no longer acceptable. Instead of expecting legislative bodies to implement change, people have turned to the courts—partly because it may be quicker, and partly because the model by which social change is to be handled has been radically revised.

Are teachers expected to know the law?

Yes. Teachers, like other American citizens, are expected to know and abide by the law. The courts will not accept ignorance of the law as an excuse or as a defense. This is not because all citizens already know the law, but rather because there is no way to refute such a claim. If courts allowed citizens to plead ignorance of the law, almost everyone would use this defense and there would be no legal accountability. In short, the price we must pay for our freedom is eternal vigilance against breaking the law. Said another way, the first duty of every citizen is to obey the law. Considering the tremendous influence teachers have over their students and the malleability of the young lives entrusted to their care, teachers have an amplified duty not only to know the law, but also to abide by it at all times.

What is the likelihood that a classroom teacher will be involved in a legal battle during her career?

The probability of a classroom teacher becoming personally entangled in a legal battle was remote throughout most of our nation's history. However, in the last twenty years or so, it has become somewhat more likely that anyone who makes teaching a career will eventually get involved in some fashion in at least one legal case. Among other possibilities, this job-related legal involvement may be as a plaintiff or defendant, as a party in a grievance proceeding, or as a witness in a trial or hearing which involves someone else.

In the question above, why was the teacher referred to as "her"?

Good question. When the author discusses hypothetical situations in order to illustrate principles of law, the pronouns "he," "she," "his," "hers," "himself" and "herself" are used in a generic sense without intent to place particular significance on either the masculine or feminine gender and solely for the purpose of avoiding awkward or unnecessarily complicated grammatical situations. Thus, the reference to "her" in the preceding question is intended to be gender-neutral. Regardless of gender, it is the role of being a *teacher* that is important; it is *teachers* to whom this book is mainly addressed (as opposed to principals, other administrators, school board members or students).

Do teachers need an attorney's legal expertise to stay out of "hot water"?

No, such a level of expertise is neither practical nor necessary. However, you do need to know enough law to spot potentially dangerous legal situations and to avoid needless litigation. This book, therefore, is not intended to make teachers into instant attorneys, but rather to assist you in meeting your legal obligations by providing you with some guidelines, thoughts and suggestions for day-to-day classroom activities. If and when necessary, you will still need to rely on an attorney knowledgeable about and experienced in school law. You might want to keep the name and telephone number of such an attorney handy just in case of an emergency. (More will be said in Chapter 7 as to your possible need for and relationship with an attorney.)

Why shouldn't a teacher act as his own attorney when a legal problem arises?

For the same reason you shouldn't do your own brain surgery! While you have the legal right to plead your own case in court, your potential loss is generally so substantial as to warrant hiring an attorney familiar with school law to represent you. There is an old and familiar saying that "one who acts as his own attorney has a fool for a client." You should find out what types of competent and qualified legal counsel may be available through your employing school district as well as through any professional education associations or unions to which you belong. Additionally, professional liability insurance coverage may be available under your homeowners insurance policy or other sources. You should also know of an attorney or firm that specializes in school cases. The complexity of the law involved in many facets of education cases is so great that even skilled attorneys have difficulty keeping abreast of ongoing changes. A courtroom is no place to demonstrate your own ignorance of the law.

Is going to court always the best way to solve a legal dispute?

In many cases, it is not. Regardless of the outcome, a lengthy court battle can be very costly in terms of dollars as well as emotions. Some issues take many years to reach a final determination. It is not uncommon for cases in which desegregation is involved to run twenty years or more and still remain unresolved. The actual time spent in court usually constitutes only a very small portion of the whole lawsuit process which may involve taking depositions of many potential witnesses, lengthy discovery requests and exchanging of documents, and other procedural battles between the attorneys where the persons named in the case will probably not even be present. Also, in a court battle the loser may have to pay court costs and attorneys' fees to the winning side. However, pointing out the potential disadvantages of litigation is not intended to dissuade you from sticking to your guns and pursuing a matter through proper legal channels when you believe that your cause is just and that a constitutional or other important issue is at stake.

What are the alternatives to going to court?

Negotiations, for one. Collective bargaining agreements almost universally contain grievance procedures for resolving questions which might otherwise end up immediately in court. In most cases, one can appeal such awards to a court of competent jurisdiction after the administrative procedure has been exhausted. In several states, educational issues are submitted to a hearing examiner who then turns over his findings to the commissioner of education. In other states, conflicts may be submitted to the county superintendent or to the state board of education. Finally, some states or individual school districts have policies for fact-finding, mediation or the arbitration of disputes between school personnel and the board of education.

What advantages might internal resolution of a grievance have over taking the matter to court?

There are at least three reasons why resolving personnel problems internally is often better than going to court. First, time; the deadlines to be met in grievance resolution may be shorter than the deadlines imposed for court proceedings—as a result, it takes less time to get a decision or settlement. Second, cost; labor relations practices in many negotiated agreements call for splitting the costs in half between the parties. Third, publicity; internal resolution is more likely to keep the matter confidential, whereas taking the matter to court will most likely put the matter on the record for the whole world to see. Keep in mind that courts will almost always expect the parties to have exhausted all available administrative remedies prior to bringing a case to court.

In which teaching areas do most legal cases arise?

Within the total volume of school law-related cases, it would appear that those involving teacher employment, dismissal and non-renewal issues comprise the largest "subgroup" of cases. Despite collectively bargained contracts in many states between school boards and teachers' associations or unions, issues related to probationary or tenure status, reduction in force, assignment-reassignment, and the First Amendment rights of freedom of expression and the right to privacy seem to be matters in which the parties involved often ask the courts to decide. Another area of particular concern to teachers involves personal and professional liability for student injuries. Each of these different issues are covered in separate chapters or sections in this text.

The State and Education

What is the legal status of public schools in this country?

Education is considered to be a state, rather than a federal, governmental function. Thus, state constitutions and state legislation provide for a system of publicly-supported, common-school education in all fifty states.

How did education become a state function rather than a federal one?

The United States Constitution does not say anything about how education is to be provided. Under the Tenth Amendment to the Constitution, "the powers not delegated to the United States by the Constitution, nor prohibited by it to the States, are reserved to the States respectively, or to the people." Thus, through the legislative branch of our representative form of government, education is a matter for the people in each of the fifty states to determine the type and extent of public school education that is desired. On occasion, however, the United States Congress does get involved with public education when it passes legislation governing such things as special education and categorical assistance programs. National performance standards, federal gun control legislation, and the prospect of constitutionally mandated school prayer efforts reflect other congressional ventures into controlling certain aspects of public education.

What is meant by "The American School System"?

Rather than a nationally unified educational "system," Americans have fifty separate and distinct school systems. However, there is a remarkable similarity between these disparate systems for the following reasons: (1) all are under the direct authority of the legislative branch of state government; (2) both students and teachers are quite mobile and carry ideas from state to state; and (3) the decisions of the United States Supreme Court are equally applicable to schools in all the various states. While there are some differences between the states, taken as a whole the fifty state systems for providing public education are more alike than different.

What limits on state power are imposed by the U.S. Constitution?

The United States Constitution—and particularly the first ten amendments to the Constitution which comprise the Bill of Rights—ensures that objectionable, governmental activities which infringe unjustly on the rights of individuals will be curtailed. This is true in the operation of public schools since they are one type of governmental institution. Unconstitutional state laws or actions of those responsible for education at the local or state levels will be invalidated by the courts under the United States Constitution. The Constitution protects individual rights and personal freedoms which often come into conflict in an educational setting. Since each state (which has the basic responsibility for providing public education) may not deprive a person of equal protection of the laws and also may not deprive any person of life, liberty or property without due process of law, a state must operate fairly in an attempt to nurture and enforce equality for all.

How much power do state legislatures exercise over education?

A state legislature is said to have *plenary* (complete) power over education within the state so long as it acts within the limits of the state and federal constitutions. For example, unless it would be prevented from doing so by a state constitutional provision, a legislature may eliminate school districts and operate all public schools directly if it chooses. While the legislature has plenary power, it goes without saying that this power must be exercised in a legal fashion. All legislated acts are subject to review by the courts.

What is the legal nature of a local school district?

School districts are *quasi*-corporations. As agencies or political subdivisions of the state, school districts have the purpose of carrying into effect educational policies of statewide interest. By contrast, municipal corporations, such as cities and towns, are usually not considered primary instruments of state policy but are created to help local groups of people to regulate and administer their own particular concerns.

How much power does a local school board exercise in running the schools?

For the most part, state legislatures delegate the day-to-day responsibility for providing elementary and secondary educational services to local school boards. The local boards are limited by the state's constitution, acts of Congress, and judicial decisions. In general, local school boards have three kinds of powers: (1) enumerated (listed) powers; (2) implied powers (meaning that the powers are assumed although not written down); and (3) necessary powers (such as the power to close the schools during an epidemic and to require vaccination as a condition of re-entry). At this time, Hawaii is the only state that does not follow the practice of using local school boards to manage public schools.

Are local school boards as powerful as they once were?

No. During most of our nation's history, local school boards were quite powerful. For years they enjoyed extensive legislative, executive, and judicial powers which they were allowed to exercise virtually without limitation or oversight. More recently, however, the extent of local school board discretion has been limited and narrowed by court actions, through mutual agreement with local teachers' unions, membership in voluntary associations such as the state's student activities association, and through statutes which tend to deprive local school boards of their autonomy and decision-making powers. In some respects, local school boards have much greater responsibility and accountablilty for solving social problems (desegregation, child care, and health concerns) than they have power or the financial resources to deal realistically with these issues.

What do most state constitutions say about free public education?

State constitutions use general wording in assigning to their legislative bodies responsibility for educating their citizens. For example, the Colorado Constitution (Art. IX, Sec. 2) provides for "a thorough and uniform system of free public education." The Texas Constitution (Art. VII, Sec. 1) says that it is the duty of the state legislature to establish, support and maintain "an efficient system of public free schools." These terms are arguably somewhat vague so the courts are often called upon to determine what the terms mean and how far a particular concept is meant to extend in different situations.

The Courts and Education

What is meant by the statement: "We are a litigious people"?

The statement means that Americans are overly inclined to go to court or to litigate rather than compromise or work things out in a less adversarial manner. Almost a century and a half ago, Alexis de Tocqueville noticed this tendency when he visited America. He observed that "scarcely any political question arises in the United States that is not resolved, sooner or later, into a judicial question." The statement is equally true today. Judge-made law probably plays a larger role in our society than in any other nation in the world.

What is meant by "judge-made" law?

The common law that results from court or judicial decisions is referred to as "judge-made" law. These decisions often result from a court having to interpret the meaning and scope of constitutional provisions and/or statutes passed by a legislature or Congress.

How do cases get to the United States Supreme Court for review?

By two routes: (1) on appeal, which is an automatic review by right; or (2) with a petition for *certiorari* (a discretionary review granted or denied by vote of the nine justices on the Court). Unlike an appeal of right, there is no guarantee that the Court will agree to hear and decide a case presented in a petition for *cer-*

tiorari. Nearly all education cases that reach the United States Supreme Court involve petitions for *certiorari.* The Court will decide to grant or deny *certiorari* on the basis of the significance of the legal issues involved and the likelihood that confusion exists in courts around the country as to the proper interpretations or applicability of an act or statute. The net effect of a denial of *certiorari* is to let stand the decision of the court immediately below, usually a federal circuit court of appeals or a state supreme court. The United States Supreme Court denies *certiorari* in many more cases than it grants. For example, in its 1992-93 term, the Court granted *certiorari* in a total of 163 cases while denying petitions in more than 6,100 cases.

Is judge-made law binding on teachers and students?

It depends on the jurisdiction of the court which decided the case. Decisions of the United States Supreme Court are binding on all citizens of the United States and its possessions. Individual state supreme court decisions normally apply only to individuals in that particular state. Federal district courts and circuit courts of appeal decisions usually apply only to the particular geographical area covered by that district or circuit.

You should become familiar with decisions of your state and federal courts in order to know the limits of your rights and responsibilities as a teacher. Ordinarily, a case decided in another state by a state court is not controlling in your state. However, if your state's courts have not decided a particular issue, a decision and the legal reasoning in a comparable case from another state might have a significant effect in persuading the judges in your state toward or against making a similar decision. The same is true of federal court decisions in a circuit other than your own. Where the circuit courts are not in agreement, the United States Supreme Court tends to settle the differences by granting *certiorari* and accepting the case or a group of related cases for review.

What is the current model for change in our social institutions?

When the Warren Court began handing down a significant volume of judge-made law in the 1950s, the United States Supreme Court instituted a model that has become the process we now often follow to deal with changing societal norms and modifying the law. This change process consists of three steps: (1) a minority individual or group of individuals goes to court and wins judicial recognition of a right guaranteed under the United States Constitution; (2) a period of time passes during which the general public must adjust to come into alignment with the Court's decision; and (3) eventually, the new value is accepted by the majority of people and enacted into law by Congress or by state legislatures.

What is meant by "judicial activism"?

Judicial activism is on one end of a continuum and "judicial restraint" is on the other. An "activist" judge or court is usually characterized as being willing to depart from precedent in order to effectuate new and progressive social policies. By comparison, "judicial restraint" implies strict adherence to existing law without indulging in or advocating personal views. Ever since it was decided that the United States Supreme Court could review governmental actions, the role of the courts has been to balance the powers of the executive and legislative branches and to prevent government from invading or submerging individual rights. Former Justice William O. Douglas put it succinctly in a 1970 speech: "Our Constitution . . . was not designed to do things for people . . . It was designed to take government off the backs of people." ARIC Press, *Newsweek* (Jan. 28, 1980). From time to time the pendulum swings from one extreme to the other depending on the membership of the Court and on which President is appointing judges of a like-mind with his philosophies.

Is there danger in allowing the courts to become too powerful?

Some people believe that on occasion the courts go too far and actually invade the realm reserved for the other two branches of government. Justices on the United States Supreme Court are not elected, but are appointed by the President with the approval of the United States Senate. They hold their positions for life. However, if the purpose of the balance-of-power concept is to prevent any one branch from becoming too powerful, it is necessary that each branch (including the United States Supreme Court) exercise its constitutionally granted powers in the interest of the general welfare. Justices must give reasons for their decisions, and these reasons are public records. Conceptually, an advantage is that a group decision probably produces a final judgment of greater breadth and depth that is susceptible to fewer extremes than most decisions made by individuals. At least some degree of control over judicial activism is possible through the selective executive appointment of new justices and the enactment of new laws by the legislative branch.

Should judges be making educational decisions?

Many people feel that educational decision making should be done as close to the problem as possible. They point to our nation's long history of local control of education to show that educational problems are best dealt with at the local level. On the other hand, many of the problems facing local school boards are national or statewide in scope; broad-based guidelines are therefore necessary to provide stability and predictability in the educational decision-making processes. Most courts tend to defer to local school boards with regard to academic matters. They recognize that local school boards, administrators and teachers are in a better position than judges to make most educational decisions. However, if local school boards misuse or fail to use their power, they tend to lose their power by default. This is particularly true in situations involving due process and other constitutionally protected rights. Finally, courts and judges often must decide an educational issue when no one else seems to be willing or able to resolve a problem legislatively or via negotiation.

The Federal Government and Education

Doesn't the federal constitution guarantee educational opportunity to all children?

No. That question was presented to the United States Supreme Court in *San Antonio School District v. Rodriguez*, 411 U.S. 1 (1973). The Court, by a 5-4 vote, held that so long as the state of Texas was providing minimal "schooling" to a child living in a poor district, it was not a violation of the equal protection clause of the Fourteenth Amendment to the United States Constitution to allow more prosperous districts to spend more per child per year on public education. Thus, by deduction, the educational birthright of each child must be found in the state constitution of that state in which the child lives.

Does that mean that some children will be educationally disadvantaged because of where they live?

Yes, at least at the present time in most states. The amount and quality of the state's minimal program for its children varies from state to state according to the benefits that each state sees fit to provide for its children. However, there is presently a very real effort within many states to equalize educational opportunity, or more precisely, to avoid discriminating between and among children because of factors such as the child's location of residence or the wealth of a particular school district. Although a state may be able to satisfy its constitutional obligation to provide a "minimal" opportunity for its children to receive a free public education, this issue continues to spawn numerous school finance cases. Consequently, school finance is an unsettled area that is under constant scrutiny.

Isn't the right to attend public schools a protected right under the United States Constitution?

Yes. In 1954 the United States Supreme Court said that the right to attend public schools is a protected right under the Fourteenth Amendment. "In these days, it is doubtful that any child may reasonably be expected to succeed in life if he is denied the opportunity of an education." *Brown v. Board of Education of Topeka*, 347 U.S. 483, 493 (1954). In Brown, the Court held that separate but equal facilities for the races are inherently unequal. "Where the State has undertaken to provide [education for all], the right to attend school is a right which must be made available to all on equal terms." *Id*. The state is therefore prohibited from discriminating within its borders and must provide equal treatment in the distribution of the benefits of education.

Do public school students have the same constitutionally protected rights that adults enjoy?

Yes, to a large extent. In 1969, the United States Supreme Court held that constitutional protections (e.g., freedom of speech, freedom of religion) are not just "freedoms" for adults. In *Tinker v. Des Moines Independent Community School District*, 393 U.S. 503, 506 (1969), the Court stated:

> First Amendment rights, applied in light of the special characteristics of the school environment, are available to teachers and students. It can hardly be argued that either students or teachers shed their constitutional rights to freedom of speech or expression at the schoolhouse gate.

Tinker went on to say:

> In our system, state-operated schools may not be enclaves of totalitarianism. School officials do not possess absolute authority over their students. Students in school as well as out of school are "persons" under our Constitution. *Id.* at 511.

Constitutional protections for children have thus been recognized as extending into the classroom. However, the scope of student rights is not without some limitations. For example, as noted in the introduction to this chapter, the United States Supreme Court ruled in 1988 that a high school principal has a right to exercise prior restraint over the content of a school-sponsored newspaper since the newspaper was not a "public forum" and the principal's actions were reasonably related to a valid educational purpose. *Hazelwood School District v. Kuhlmeier*, 484 U.S. 260 (1988). Thus, students do not enjoy quite the same expansive freedom of the press or free speech rights that are indigenous to the national media.

How has the United States Supreme Court's decision that children have the right to fair and equal treatment changed the way we run our schools?

More will be said in later chapters about the total effect such declarations have had on public education in the United States during the latter portion of this century. Suffice it to say at this point that the recognition of constitutional rights in the schools has dramatically changed how schools are managed. These changes extend to all concerned—teachers, pupils, parents, administrators, school board members, non-certificated employees and the general public served by the school. The relationships are not the same; they have been transformed. In effect, running the schools is and will continue to be "a whole new ball game."

Case Resolutions

Case No. 1: "Just cause" for termination? (see page 9)

In Iowa, as in some other states, just cause for termination of a teaching contract may be found as a result of mental or physical disability. Among the appropriate factors to be considered are "the nature and extent of the duties required by the contract, the character and duration of the illness, the needs of the employer and the extent to which the duties can be performed by another." In applying these criteria to this teacher's case, the school board specifically found she was not a good role model even before the shoplifting incident, and she lacked credibility in that her testimony about memory loss did not fit with medical testimony about her manic condition. Her status as a role model was permanently impaired in her employment at the school with no hope of being resurrected due to the small size of the district and the widespread knowledge about her conduct. There was just cause and the teacher's termination was affirmed by the Iowa Supreme Court. *Board of Directors of Lawton-Bronson v. Davies*, 489 N.W.2d 19 (Iowa 1992).

Case No. 2: A teacher should teach (see page 10)

The Court found that the school board's denial of the leave of absence was rationally related to a legitimate governmental purpose—that of

> seeing that teachers who remain on the school system's roster and accrue benefits, such as seniority, step increases in salary, and retirement benefits, actually teach; and it was rational for the Board to conclude that the skills of a teacher who has been out of the classroom for eight years have eroded. Thus, in this case, the School Board's interest in the welfare of the school children, in fairness to other teachers, and in the integrity of the school system was without a doubt rationally related to the ac-

tion taken by the School Board in denying [the teacher] an eighth consecutive year of leave of absence.

Accordingly, the teacher's equal protection claim failed, as did her First Amendment claims. She was unable to show legally sufficient evidence that her speaking critically of the school board was a motivating factor in the board's decision to deny the eighth year of leave. *Flickinger v. School Board of the City of Norfolk, Virginia*, 799 F.Supp. 586, 596 (E.D.Va. 1992).

Case No. 3: From teaching high school English to teaching fifth grade (see page 11)

This case began when the English teacher gave a well-deserved failing grade to the high-school basketball star which made him ineligible to play. The community responded by calling for the teacher's dismissal. She was intimidated by the principal into changing the failing grade to a D-minus, and someone even fired a bullet through the windshield of her car. Other types of harassment continued, and she sought psychiatric treatment. Eventually she was unable to perform her teaching duties. However, when she notified school officials, she was ordered to return to work. When she did not, she was suspended and ultimately discharged.

A court subsequently ruled she was wrongfully discharged and ordered reinstatement. She also received worker's compensation benefits for her disability resulting from the circumstances leading to discharge. Since she was not able to return to her reinstated position immediately, the school board granted her a one-year leave of absence. After the year passed, the teacher sought to return to work and at that point she was assigned to the fifth grade. In the final ruling in the teacher's favor, the Tennessee Supreme Court stated bluntly that the school officials' actions were "reprehensible." The law is clear that she must be reinstated to her position at the high school with all benefits. Although school officials need latitude to do what is best for their individual school systems, they must also observe state law. The school board lacked discretion to assign her to a different position.

This case was finally resolved upon the third appeal to the Supreme Court of Tennessee. Bottom line: the teacher was wrongfully discharged and the school board was ordered to reinstate the teacher and pay damages for wrongful discharge. *State ex rel. McGhee v. St. John*, 837 S.W.2d 596 (Tenn. 1992).

Case No. 4: Birds of a feather (see page 11)

The jury found for the teacher and awarded her $33,000 compensatory damages, $5,000 punitive damages, and $5,800 attorney fees. The judge upheld the *compensatory damages* (monetary award designed to make an injured party "whole") on the ground that a teacher "has the right to be free from unwarranted governmental intrusions into one's privacy." The court concluded that such right of privacy extends to the right to attend or not attend church, to determine one's own physical proportions, and to determine with whom one will associate. The judge, however, denied the award of *punitive damages* (damages awarded to punish a defendant in a civil case) and attorney fees on the grounds that although the school board members did invade the teacher's privacy, they had not acted maliciously in so doing. *Stoddard v. School District No. 1*, 429 F.Supp. 890 (D.Wyo. 1977).

Case No. 5: Give them a hand (see page 11)

The United States Supreme Court ruled (6-3) that the school board was within its rights in discharging the teachers. The Court said that teachers did not seek relief with *clean hands* since they had disobeyed Wisconsin law by striking illegally. Also, it is better for the judiciary to keep *hands off* in local school matters; the legislature has decided that schools are *in good hands* with local boards of education, which the courts should not try to second-guess. If teachers want to act like blue-collar *hands*, then they will be treated as such before the law. Nor was the school board automatically a biased tribunal just because it was familiar with the facts. The school board members did not have a personal or official stake in the matter sufficient to disqualify them from making the discharge decision as a hearing tribunal. The Court majority held that the striking teachers had breached their contracts and could not be heard to complain that they had been denied due process of law by their firing. *Hortonville Joint School District No. 1 v. Hortonville Education Association*, 426 U.S. 482 (1976).

Case No. 6: How far does neglect of duty extend? (see page 12)

"Neglect of duty" is a separate issue from the definition of what the duty is, and the neglect issue can center on "conflicting demands of a teacher's professional and personal life." However, the Appeals Board and the Oregon appellate court agreed that a teacher cannot simply avoid all conduct which might damage her effectiveness. Further, society considers that it is important to protect a teacher's rights in her personal life sometimes even at the expense of her effectiveness as a teacher. This teacher had a good employment record, and even if she could not separate herself from her husband's activities, dismissal was an excessive sanction. She was confronted with a no-win situation in which there was little she could do to salvage either her personal or her professional interests. The question of whether she neglected her duty could have been answered either way, and in this circumstance, the Appeals Board decision that she did not neglect her duty would not be disturbed. *Kari v. Jefferson County School District*, 852 P.2d 235 (Or.Ct.App. 1993); *rev. denied*, 862 P.2d 1305 (Or. 1993).

Chapter Two

Employment Issues: Before, During, and After

Teaching in a public school means going to work for the government. No one, no matter how well qualified, has an inherent right to obtain employment with the government. Unless it can be shown that a hiring decision was made arbitrarily, capriciously, or with a discriminatory motive, a school board is generally left to exercise its own discretion in selecting teachers from a pool of qualified applicants. In conjunction with the requirements for teacher certification set by the state, a local school board may also impose its own additional, reasonable and uniformly applied eligibility requirements for a teaching position. For example, the school board may require that a successful candidate for a teaching position will have completed certain college-level coursework that serves to supplement the state's minimum standards necessary to qualify for certification.

Once a teacher is hired, that person is entitled to substantially greater employment protection. On the basis of an unscientific survey of recent judicial opinions, the number of teacher employment and retention cases continues to outnumber litigated cases involving most other educational issues. Consequently, it is this area that is the focus of a major portion of this chapter.

Most of the laws governing teacher employment are legislatively enacted at the state level. General contract laws and administrative regulations promulgated by state agencies (i.e., state boards of education) combine with state legislation to create each state's teacher employment structure. On top of all this, a teacher's employment rights are further influenced by constitutional protections and civil rights legislation passed by Congress (e.g., Title VII of the Civil Rights Act of 1964, which prohibits employers from discriminating against employees on the basis of race, color, religion, sex or national origin). Finally, in many states the traditional school district/employer-teacher/employee relationship may be modified by collectively bargained agreements. Chapter 6 goes into greater detail on the subject of collective bargaining and the implications it holds for many in the education profession.

Although no single book could possibly cover every aspect of teacher employment, this chapter touches on a number of the more commonplace questions and issues that arise in this area. The chapter is divided into three sections: certification, contracting and tenure, and discrimination issues. It should also be noted that several additional employment-related issues are covered in other sections of this book. For example, "freedom of expression" cases involving teachers in Chapter 3 (i.e., teachers who faced employment sanctions after speaking out on matters of public concern or private interest) naturally overlap with employment concerns in this chapter. The following case descriptions are intended to highlight some of the legal concepts which are then discussed in greater detail.

Case Descriptions

Case No. 1: Avoid impulsive decisions

A tenured teacher submitted a letter of resignation which was accepted by the school board. One week later, the teacher sought to rescind, retract or withdraw his resignation, but the school board reaffirmed its acceptance of the resignation. In response, however, the school board did offer the teacher an opportunity to apply for re-employment while it investigated allegations of possible misconduct which led to the resignation in the first place. The school board reviewed the allegations and gave the teacher an opportunity to present evidence in his own behalf. During the proceedings the teacher admitted to conduct that reflected poor judgment. Thereafter, the school board found "no evidence of sexual harassment or sexual misbehavior that would merit the loss of this chosen livelihood which is teaching." The superintendent recommended that the teacher be re-employed and the school board rehired him as a non-tenured, *probationary* teacher. Two years later the teacher was notified that his contract would not be renewed. He requested a hearing which the school board denied since he was classified as a probationary employee. Do you think a teacher loses his tenure status by resigning and being rehired a short time later in the same school district for the next school year?

Case No. 2: How involved should a teacher get with a student?

A single, male, fourth-grade teacher was well thought of in his school and community since he began teaching in 1985. Along with teaching, he was involved with students outside of school when boys would come to his house to play games and sports or to get help with their homework. His principal was aware of these activities and raised concerns about them with the teacher. In 1988 and with his mother's permission, one young above-average student began spending a lot of time at the teacher's house. The boy's mother was unmarried, had four other children, primarily spoke Spanish and was illiterate in both Spanish and English. Within a year the boy was spending 90 percent of his time at the teacher's house and the teacher was making parental decisions on the boy's behalf. Eventually, the boy's mother gave temporary custody of the boy to the teacher. This lasted until one day in 1990 when the student disappeared. After the teacher found out that the boy's mother had taken him to Mexico, the teacher initiated court proceedings to re-obtain custody of the child. A court granted an order prohibiting the mother from taking the boy from the teacher's care and custody. Unfortunately, the child was later removed from the teacher's home to foster care pending the investigation of allegations of sexual abuse. This emotionally affected the teacher who was placed on paid leave by his school district during the investigation. Ultimately, a jury found that the abuse charges were unwarranted and the teacher was rehired for the 1991-92 school year. However, during the preceding summer, the teacher's conduct was the subject of discussion in the community and several parents requested that their children be assigned to a different teacher. The teacher attempted to counteract the negative publicity by writing letters to the newspaper and by appearing on radio shows. Soon after, however, the superintendent recommended that the teacher be dismissed based on the facts above and their cumulative effect on his fitness to teach. A hearing officer made extensive findings and concluded that the teacher started with good intentions to assist the boy but ended up exploiting the teacher/student relationship, and the consequences of that relationship constituted "good and just cause" for termination. The relationship affected the teacher's performance and was detrimental to other students. The school board agreed and dismissed the teacher. Do you think the teacher went too far, or was the school board simply being hard-hearted? How would you resolve the teacher's appeal to overturn his dismissal?

Case No. 3: Going on the attack

A classroom teacher physically attacked his principal after meeting in the principal's office about an alleged hazing incident. The teacher struck the first blow, and, after the principal fell, the teacher straddled him and continued his assault. As a result, the teacher was suspended and ultimately terminated from his job. Following an investigation and hearing, the state education agency determined that the teacher's conduct made him unfit to instruct the youth in the state and revoked his teaching certificate. After a district court upheld the agency's decision, the teacher appealed while arguing that the administrative hearing record had not been properly considered by the court, that there was no evidence of his unworthiness to instruct youth, that revocation was too harsh a penalty, that there was not enough evidence to demonstrate that he was unfit to teach, and that the agency's description of the attack represented "arbitrary and capricious" decision-making. Given these facts, do you agree the teacher should lose both his job and his teaching certificate? Or do you think the penalty in this case was too harsh?

Case No. 4: Stressed out

An elementary music teacher had taught for thirteen years and was well thought of in his school and the community. One day in April 1989, the teacher left a taped telephone message that he would be absent from his job due to illness. He returned four days later and signed a form stating his absence had been due to illness. Later, it was discovered that he had not been ill but instead had been with his family in Florida. The school board notified him that they were considering termination and the teacher requested a hearing. A referee recommended suspension rather than termination on the basis of the teacher's excellent past record, the fact that the teacher was under emotional distress from the deterioration of his marriage and his thinking that the trip to Florida would help maintain family stability. However, the school board chose to terminate the teacher due to his falsification of the sick leave statement. The teacher appealed, asking that the termination decision be reversed and that the referee's recommendation be adopted. What do you think was the result? Is an excuse of stress sufficient to avoid termination in this situation?

Case No. 5: Pretext or not?

A non-tenured African-American teacher taught one year and her contract was not renewed for the following school year. Her principal (who was also an African-American) had evaluated her and recommended that since her performance was unacceptable, her contract should not be renewed. He based his recommendation on numerous specific incidents wherein he felt that the teacher had been uncooperative, hostile, and insubordinate toward other school personnel and administrators and that she was unable to work harmoniously with them. The principal's recommendation was reviewed by the personnel director who confirmed the conflict involving the teacher. The superintendent and assistant superintendent also reviewed the teacher's file. When the school board met to consider recommendations on non-tenured teachers, this teacher was one of four being considered. (The other three teachers were white.) Each case was discussed, and none of the four teachers were renewed. The African-American teacher filed suit alleging that there was racial discrimination in the school board's hiring practices since a white teacher was ultimately hired to fill her vacated position. The plaintiff stated that she had tried to be the best teacher she could be and that she had tried to work in harmony with other educators. She did not present any evidence to refute or explain the specific incidents demonstrating uncooperativeness, hostility and insubordination, which had been presented to the school board for consideration. Do you think racial discrimination might have been a factor in the school board's decision? Or is it likely that any person who is described as "uncooperative, hostile and insubordinate" will not be rehired?

Case No. 6: On the other hand

An African-American math teacher was hired as a bilingual elementary instructor in 1983. Later she was reprimanded in an incident for "indiscriminate grabbing/jerking" of a student. She transferred to a new elementary school in 1986 after claiming that the "grabbing" incident was a misunderstanding. Throughout, she was the only African-American teacher employed in the school district. When the principal introduced her to the students at the new school, he referred to her as "the lady with the best suntan" and referred to other teachers by their hair color or dress to help students remember them. Subsequently, however, complaints ensued about the African-American teacher's teaching abilities. An alleged dispute with a special education teacher over a student who was later moved to another school and other occurrences (i.e., a missed deadline, an art project turned in late, a missed PTO meeting, being "huffy and rude" at a parent-teacher meeting, parents' comments noting changes in the teacher's behavior, and her abuse of her teenage daughter) led to the school board's decision to terminate the teacher's employment. The teacher had explanations for all of the incidents (she had responded before the deadline, the art project was optional, she was ill at the time of the PTO meeting, her principal never informed her that her behavior was inadequate, and she was undergoing counseling after admitting that her daughter was in need of supervision). Indeed, her performance evaluation received prior to the time for contract renewal was complimentary of her teaching and the principal spoke of her improvement and described her as "an outstanding conscientious teacher." It was only after this time that the principal made racially objectionable remarks in front of the teacher and, in addition, he claimed some parents thought the teacher gave too much homework and unfairly restricted their children's recess time.

The teacher's relationship with her principal had continued to deteriorate and there were numerous additional incidents which occurred between them. Eventually the principal had relieved her of her duties and had presented her with a seven-page "plan of assistance" for completion during the next school year. Issuance of a "plan of assistance" is usually the first step toward the nonrenewal of a tenured teacher. Although the teacher attempted to comply with the plan, the principal continued to rate her as not living up to minimum expectations and exhibiting unprofessional behavior. One final point—when the school board voted not to renew the teacher, twenty-seven of her students signed a petition asking the school board to reconsider. Does it sound like the teacher was treated unfairly and do you think she was a victim of discriminatory conduct?

Case No. 7: Sex discrimination and job vacancy notices

A special education teacher was just completing an advanced graduate degree when she applied for a new administrative position in her school district. The school superintendent chose to post the vacancy notice for the "Director of Special Education" position both within the school district and at the state's universities. During the search process, the superintendent allegedly stated that he did not want a female to fill the position. Of note, it was undisputed that this particular teacher was the only qualified in-district applicant for the job. A screening committee interviewed five applicants and presented three names to the superintendent—including this teacher's name. However, the superintendent eventually recommended to the school board that a male from outside the school district be hired as the most qualified candidate. The school board voted unanimously to hire the male candidate recommended by the superintendent. Although she acknowledged that the successful male candidate was "best qualified" for the position, the teacher nonetheless filed a Title VII sex discrimination complaint against her school district claiming that the position vacancy notice was only posted outside the district in order to avoid hiring her. What do you think—was this an example of sex discrimination?

Certification

What is a teaching certificate?

A teaching certificate or credential is a state-issued license to teach. It certifies that certain minimum requirements have been fulfilled. It does not guarantee you a job; rather it is the equivalent of a "job hunting license" in the state(s) in which you hold a valid certificate.

What is the purpose of a teaching certificate?

It may have many purposes. The primary one is to prevent injury to the public—and particularly children—by ensuring that those people engaged in the teaching profession will be competent and worthy. Another purpose is to protect the public treasury since a school district usually may not legally expend public funds for teaching services to anyone who is not the holder of a valid certificate. Over time, certification standards tend to upgrade the teaching profession as well as to contribute to the improvement of individual teachers. Teachers are compelled to maintain professional standards or risk certificate revocation and the corresponding loss of employment.

Is a teaching certificate limited in scope?

Yes. Since the certificate is merely a license, it only proves that the holder was qualified at the time of issuance. States usually incorporate time lines or durational limitations, subject or endorsement area restrictions, and other qualifications that limit the certificate. The state may revoke the certificate under particular conditions. The continuing validity of the certificate usually depends upon a certain number of months of teaching and/or the successful completion of recertification coursework. In most cases when a certificate lapses, it is annulled completely and is subject to renewal only upon full compliance with certification standards in effect at the time of renewal. In other words, if a teacher fails to obtain *re*-certification status, then she may be faced with getting *certified* all over again.

May a state require a minimum score on a statewide or national teacher competency examination as a prerequisite for certification?

Yes. For example, in *State of Texas v. Project Principle, Inc.*, 724 S.W.2d 387 (Tex. 1987), the Texas Supreme Court upheld the constitutionality of legislation requiring all current teachers and administrators in the state to pass a competency test in order to retain certification. The court ruled that teachers' due process rights were adequately protected since they could take the test more than once if they failed. Further, the state's legitimate interest in maintaining competent teachers in the public schools outweighed any inherent unfairness with the testing requirement. Despite a "disparate racial impact," the practice of requiring teacher competency testing was neither a violation of the Equal Protection Clause of the Fourteenth Amendment nor a violation of the Title VII (of the Civil Rights Act of 1964) prohibition against racial discrimination. Lower court findings showed that the state had not intentionally discriminated against minority teachers in issuing certificates and setting teacher pay scales based on National Teachers Examination scores. In addition, the state had shown that the process was a more efficient system for determining teacher competency than the plaintiffs' suggested alternative—mere graduation from an approved teacher education program.

When must a teacher have a teaching certificate: When she signs a contract, when she begins teaching, or before she gets paid?

State statutory requirements vary as to when it is necessary to hold certification status in order to complete the contractual relationship. For example, in Colorado it is sufficient that a teacher possesses a valid certificate before she receives pay for teaching. A teacher in New York must have the certificate at the time she signs her teaching contract, while in Arkansas and Tennessee she needs to be fully certified before beginning to teach.

You should become familiar with your own state's requirements as to how and when to obtain certification so as to not risk missing a deadline. In some states it may take up to several months or longer for a state to process an application for a teaching certificate (in other words, you usually will not receive a teaching certificate as quickly as you might obtain a driver's license).

What is the legal status of one who teaches without having a valid teaching credential?

With few exceptions, such an individual is a volunteer and cannot be paid for teaching services performed without valid certification. Today, however, many states provide for temporary certification which conditions continued employment on satisfactory progress toward obtaining the necessary full certification. Temporary certification (not to be confused with "alternative certification" for those entering the teaching profession with something other than the traditional background of teacher preparation coursework and/or student teaching experiences) may be available for up to several years and is one solution that has been used to combat a teacher shortage problem in some geographical locations and particularly in certain subject areas like mathematics and the sciences.

What are the possible consequences of allowing a teaching certificate to lapse?

A teacher in Oregon renewed her certificate and paid the renewal fee with a personal check sent to the appropriate state agency. Subsequently, she was informed that her certificate was invalid because *her check had bounced*! When the local school board learned that the teacher did not have a valid certificate, she was dismissed. Although the teacher contested the dismissal through the courts, she lost because without a valid certificate, she was not a legally protected "teacher" under the state's statutory definition. *Wagenblast v. Cook County School District*, 707 P.2d 69 (Or. 1985).

How does certification differ from accreditation?

Certification is the legal device by which the state licenses those individuals who are qualified to teach in the state. Certification applies to a person, and a certificate is not transferable. On the other hand, accreditation is a control exercised by the state or a voluntary organization for the overall improvement of an institution. Thus, a teacher is "certified" (or has a credential) to teach, while a school district, college or university is "accredited" by a regional or national accrediting agency or organization, such as the North Central Association.

Have states stopped issuing "life" certificates?

Most of them have done so. The "life certificate," which was popular some years ago, entitled a teacher to continue teaching without having to renew the certificate for practically as long as the teacher lived. However, due to rapid changes in methodology and substantive attempts at educational reform, most states have now gone to a system whereby each teacher must periodically take a certain number and/or type of graduate courses or have certain in-service experiences in order to retain certification status.

May a state change certification requirements?

Although this question has not been fully litigated in every state, the rule of thumb seems to be that a state can change certification requirements as it reasonably sees fit. For the most part, courts have recognized that a teaching certificate is a license rather than a contract; thus, it is within the state's prerogative to impose reasonable modifications and adjustments in certification requirements.

May the state revoke a teacher's certificate?

Yes. Most states provide for revocation or suspension of the teaching certificate on the grounds that the power to issue the certificate implies a corresponding right to revoke. The revocation must occur, however, only for just cause. It is limited to the state board of education or the state credentialing board's discretion and is subject to appropriate standards for due process. Pursuant to state statutes, such grounds as immorality, conduct unbecoming a teacher, conviction of a felony, or other similar grounds are reasons for which most revocations take place. Since a certified teacher is considered competent, the state bears the burden of proving the grounds for removing certification in a revocation proceeding. An example of a case in which a teacher's certificate was properly revoked is *Everett v. Texas Education Agency*, 860 S.W.2d 700 (Tex.Ct.App. 1991), described in this chapter's Case No. 3. Everett physically attacked his principal and knocked him to the ground.

If a teacher is certified in one state, can he readily obtain certification in other states as well?

Although some states recognize a system of reciprocity for certification purposes, the practice is by no means automatic or universal. Therefore, in order to verify what you need to do to get certified in another state, you should write to the state education agency or state department of education (sometimes called the state board of public instruction) in the state in which you wish to teach and obtain all necessary information and application forms. Getting certified for the first time is usually the biggest hurdle a teacher will face. However, since each of the fifty states has the option of establishing its own certification standards independently of what other states have done, you may find that obtaining supplemental certification in a second state is just as—if not more—difficult than it was to get certified initially.

Contracting and Tenure

What are the elements of a valid contract?

Even though a teacher's employment contract is probably fairly standard in the sense that it resembles most of the other employment contracts used in a particular school district, it still must satisfy the basic elements of contract law in order to be valid and enforceable. The five essential elements of a valid teaching contract are: (1) the contract must be between parties who have the legal capacity to contract; (2) there must be a meeting of the minds (sometimes called mutual assent) or "offer and acceptance" as to the terms of the contract; (3) it must be supported by valid consideration (for example, the teacher's promise to serve as a teacher in exchange for salary and benefits paid by the school district; (4) it must be in the proper written form and be sufficiently specific as to the duration, rights and obligations of the parties (e.g., length of contract, provisions for personal and professional leave, extracurricular assignments); and (5) it must not be illegal or against public policy (in other words, it is not possible to enforce a contract which promotes an illegal act).

As mentioned, most teaching contracts are fairly standard and the employment process usually allows little flexibility for negotiation. However, if you are unsure as to the language or implications of your contract or if you question whether the contract is valid and enforceable in every way, then you should have your contract examined by a competent attorney *before* you sign your name and commit yourself to the terms and conditions of employment.

When does a contract to teach actually become binding?

Although a teacher may have signed a contract to teach, it is generally not binding until the local school board acts officially to accept or ratify the contract. In effect, what the teacher signed amounts to an offer to teach; for there to be a valid contract it must be accepted by the school board as the other contracting party.

Can a teacher be required to sign a loyalty oath as a condition of employment in a public school?

It depends. The loyalty oaths now in use in many states and school districts have changed considerably from those used in the 1950s and 1960s. At that time many oaths required that teachers not belong to or support the beliefs of subversive organizations which had as their objective the violent overthrow of the United States government. In a series of cases the United States Supreme Court and several lower federal courts declared most of these statutory loyalty oath requirements unconstitutional on the grounds they were too vague—a teacher could not tell if she was within the requirements or not. Consequently, most states have revised their loyalty oath statutes to fall within the constraints of the Constitution. Although the scope of loyalty oaths used today varies from state to state, the general rule is that most such oaths simply affirm a teacher's support for and agreement to abide by the federal and state constitutions and laws. (Loyalty oaths are discussed in greater detail in the next chapter.)

Can a school board require prospective teachers to submit to a physical examination or meet certain job-related physical criteria before being hired?

Yes, but only if there is a reasonable and non-arbitrary relationship between the examination or physical criteria and the work to be performed. Further, such requirements cannot violate federal or state laws which protect disabled persons. An example of a permissible pre-employment condition would be a requirement that all school employees obtain a chest X-ray to ensure that students are not exposed to tuberculosis.

May a teacher be discharged for deliberately falsifying an employment application?

Yes. Falsification of an employment application is not only fraudulent but also "a continuing deception." *Negrich v. Dade County Board of Education*, 143 So.2d 498 (Fla. 1962). In one case, a court found that a teacher who wrote on his application that he was not a homosexual but who later "came out of the closet" was properly discharged by the school board—not because of his homosexuality but rather because of fraud. *Acanfora v. Board of Education of Montgomery County*, 491 F.2d 498 (4th Cir. 1974), *cert. denied*, 419 U.S. 836 (1974). Today, some states require that an employing school district obtain a criminal history record for all new employees. For example, if a mandatory background check in Texas reveals that the employee's completed job application failed to mention a prior felony conviction or offenses involving moral turpitude, then the employee may be discharged.

Is a teacher bound by school board resolutions and policies that are adopted after the teacher has been on the job?

Yes. The original employment relationship may undergo many changes as the school board adopts and modifies policies and procedures to meet the school district's changing needs. In a sense, this is no different than Congress or a state legislature passing new legislation to better serve society's needs. Changes in school board policies do not constitute a breach of the employment contract so long as the changes are reasonable and not arbitrarily implemented or enforced.

Does a teacher's employment contract contain provisions describing all of the teacher's obligations?

Generally not. Most school districts prefer to use standardized teaching contracts that are usually rather short and don't go into great detail. An ordinary school district employment contract will show only the parties' names, the length of time the contract is to run, the salary, the general teaching area (such as high school English or an elementary grade level), and whatever state requirements which must be included. The teaching contract may also include coaching or other specific extra-duty assignments or those duties may be covered by means of a supplemental contract. Usually the contract includes by implication all subsequent policies or by-laws adopted by the school board as well as all state laws governing teaching contracts.

Does the employment contract imply that a teacher may be assigned to extracurricular duties or other general responsibilities not specifically listed in the contract?

Yes. It is likely that you may be assigned to certain extracurricular duties such as a club sponsorship or supervisory duties at an activity or event. In most cases, however, courts have said that there must be a reasonable relationship between the extra duties and the teacher's normal teaching assignment. For example, where a teacher was assigned sponsorship of a noncompetitive bowling club that was not directly associated with the school and which practiced after school and on Saturdays, a New York court ruled that such an assignment was not sufficiently or reasonably related to the academic program. Therefore, the teacher could refuse to accept a sponsorship which, in effect, amounted only to "baby-sitting a bowling ball." *Parrish v. Moss*, 106 N.Y.S.2d 577 (N.Y.App.Div. 1951), *aff'd*, 107 N.Y.S.2d 580 (N.Y. 1951). Conversely, supervisory hall duty before and after school and during between-class passing periods has been found to fall within the normal scope of the educational process—and a classroom teacher can reasonably be expected to perform such duties. *Lockhart v. Board of Education of Arapahoe County School District No. 6*, 735 P.2d 913 (Colo.Ct.App. 1986).

What is tenure and what legal rights accrue to a teacher with tenure?

Tenure is defined as a statutory right to continued employment which requires proof of "good cause" prior to its removal. Generally, tenure granted by the state means at least two things for a teacher: (1) continuing employment without the necessity of annual notification; and (2) if employment is to be terminated, the school board must provide the teacher with adequate reasons for termination and opportunity for an impartial hearing ensuring the attributes of fundamental fairness. (As is discussed in greater detail in the next several questions, this principle of "fundamental fairness" is the underlying feature behind procedural due process.) Some states that do not provide a statutory basis for tenure use "continuing contracts" or other comparable employment protections to accomplish a similar purpose. The decision of whether to recognize "tenure status" in a particular state is left to the discretion of the state legislature. Although there are numerous exceptions and variations, tenure usually attaches after a teacher has taught successfully in a particular school district for three years. A teacher is considered to have probationary status prior to achieving tenure. Commonly, a *probationary* teacher is not entitled to know the reasons a school board has in deciding to terminate the employment relationship at the end of the contract period; therefore, in most cases a probationary teacher is not given an opportunity for a hearing. Even though the school board is not compelled to inform the probationary teacher of the reasons for nonrenewal, it is important to recognize that those reasons cannot violate the teacher's constitutionally or statutorily protected rights. In other words, the school board cannot use such things as the teacher's race, religion, gender or protected speech as the basis for nonrenewal.

What is the distinction between dismissal and nonrenewal of a teaching contract?

Although the terms may be used slightly differently in different states, *dismissal* generally refers to the termination of employment *prior* to the end of a probationary contract. It also refers to the termination of a tenured teacher's contract at *any* time. Because a teacher being dismissed is considered to have a constitutionally protected "property" interest in staying employed throughout the contract term, he is entitled to (1) notification of the reasons for dismissal; (2) an opportunity for a hearing and a chance to respond to or rebut all stated reasons; and (3) a fair and impartial hearing panel. These are the essential elements of due process as it is protected under federal and state constitutions. By comparison, contract *nonrenewal* usually requires that a school board simply give a probationary teacher timely notice that his contract is not being renewed. In most states, the school board does not have to give reasons for the nonrenewal of a probationary teacher.

What due process procedures are normally guaranteed under statutory tenure?

States differ in how a local school district must proceed in terminating a tenured teacher or dismissing a probationary teacher in mid-contract. Regardless of the specific statutory language in a given state, all applicable tenure protections must be closely followed in order for a school board to successfully dismiss a teacher and withstand a subsequent legal challenge. As a general rule, there must be a written notice specifying grounds on which the school board is considering its action. Usually this notice is issued after school administrators have decided to recommend to the school board that a particular teacher not be retained as an employee in the school district. In most states, the teacher being considered for dismissal is entitled to a due process hearing before the school board sitting as a fair and impartial tribunal. The school board must base its ultimate decision on the facts found at the

hearing and not on any individual or collective biases or prej-
udices held by the school board members. If the school board
reaches a conclusion adverse to the teacher, then the decision
may be appealed through the judicial system. In some states,
however, it may first be necessary to exhaust all available administrative remedies (by appealing to the state's commissioner of education, for example) prior to seeking the
assistance of the courts.

Are tenure protections *only* conferred by statute?

No, in some cases it may be possible to make the argument
that a particular teacher is entitled to "tenure-like" protections
despite the fact that he is not "tenured" by statute. For example, in *Perry v. Sindermann*, 408 U.S. 593 (1972), the United
States Supreme Court considered the circumstances under
which a public employee might gain procedural rights to due
process despite not being accorded tenure by the legislature.
In *Perry*, a community college professor claimed that although
he was not tenured in the traditional statutory sense, his "ex-
pectancy of reemployment" gave rise to a constitutionally-
protected property interest sufficient to compel his employer
to provide him with notice and an impartial hearing prior to
dismissal. The professor had taught for a number of years in
the state's college system and had been at his latest institution
for four years. He argued that the school had a *de facto* ("in
fact") or implied tenure policy that entitled instructors to go
through the hearing process prior to dismissal. In asserting his
claims, the professor was able to point to a provision in the
faculty guide prepared by the college which stated that "[t]he
Administration of the College wishes the faculty member to
feel that he has permanent tenure as long as his teaching services are satisfactory . . . " *Id*. at 600. Since the teacher's "ex-
pectancy" of reemployment was based on something greater
than a mere subjective "desire" or "hope" for reemployment,
the Court held that a due process hearing was in order.

When must a school board notify nontenured or probationary teachers that their contracts will not be renewed?

States vary on this requirement. Usually the school board must notify a teacher of nonrenewal sometime in the spring and before the end of the school year; for example, by March 15 or April 1. Failure to notify the teacher in the manner specified (e.g., by registered mail if required to do so by statute or collective bargaining agreement) and by the specified date will most likely result in the teacher's being re-employed for the next school year.

What are some of the grounds that justify dismissal?

The most common grounds for the dismissal of teachers are incompetency, immorality, insubordination, unfitness to teach, the inadequate performance of duties, the teacher's services are no longer needed due to declining enrollment or financial exigency, conviction of a felony or a crime involving moral turpitude, and any cause that constitutes grounds for the state's revocation of a teaching certificate. There is normally an "elastic" clause added to this list—something to the effect of "other good and just cause." The school district has the burden of proving any of these charges and, to do so, must be able to show persuasive evidence that the teacher being dismissed either failed to do something which he should have done or did something which he should not have done.

What are the general categories into which cases involving teacher dismissal will ordinarily fall?

The four general types of teacher dismissals are: (1) where the charge is incompetency but where the teacher's performance may be "remediable"; (2) where the teacher is incompetent and no amount of help will cure the defect ("irremediable"); (3) where the teacher is competent in the classroom but is considered deficient in some other aspect of his non-teaching performance (for example, by doing things outside the classroom which are considered "counterproductive" to the school's mission); and (4) where the teacher is competent and what he is doing is protected by constitutional or statutory provision.

What rights does the teacher have who is incompetent yet remediable?

Teachers whose performance is deemed unsatisfactory are usually entitled to timely notification of their deficiencies. Such notification must be made early enough so that remediation has an opportunity to take place. Further, teachers are entitled to assistance from school districts in the form of supervisory help, conferences, visitations, and all the other in-service aids that the district can muster before a declaration of incompetency is made. Since first-year teachers sometimes run into difficulty making adjustments, most probationary teachers are entitled to assistance along the way according to the particular district's policies. Each teacher has the right to succeed, and a school district should notify all teachers of any remediable defects before dismissing any such teachers for incompetency.

What rights does a teacher have whose performance in the classroom is both incompetent and irremediable?

Such teachers are generally entitled to all the assistance mentioned above. If a teacher has tenure status, she will also be entitled to a hearing on the merits of her situation prior to dismissal. The school board must prove that the teacher is indeed incompetent and, in doing so, it must cite facts rather than mere opinions to support its case.

What rights does a teacher have who is competent but whose conduct outside the classroom is counterproductive?

Again, the burden of proof rests with the board of education. The school board must prove that although the teacher is competent to teach, his behavior, lifestyle, activity, or pronouncements outside the classroom detract so much from his effectiveness as a teacher as to render him unfit to continue teaching.

What rights does a competent teacher have who exercises a constitutionally protected right?

As is illustrated by a number of cases discussed in this book, it is now well-settled law that a teacher who is competent and who exercises a constitutional right may not be punished for doing so. For example, the nonrenewal of even a probationary teacher may not be predicated on the protected exercise of a First Amendment right. *Gray v. Union County Intermediate Education District*, 520 F.2d 803 (9th Cir. 1973). In Wyoming, a competent non-continuing contract teacher was denied reemployment after she encouraged students to start their own underground newspaper. A federal district court ruled that her right to procedural due process had been violated by the school board. The Tenth Circuit Court of Appeals affirmed the trial court and remanded the case with directions to reinstate the teacher. *Bertot v. School District No. 1*, 522 F.2d 1171 (10th Cir. 1975), *appeal after remand,* 613 F.2d 245 (10th Cir. 1979).

May a school district dismiss a teacher due to such factors as declining enrollments or fiscal shortfalls?

In most instances, yes. School districts (particularly those in certain parts of the country hardest hit by population shifts and an aging citizenry) are often faced with a variety of factors that require the district to cut its teaching staff—either temporarily or permanently. This practice, which is commonly referred to as "reduction in force" (RIF), is usually authorized by statutes that are unique to each state and make it difficult to generalize across state boundaries. It is, however, possible to make a few statements that are applicable to RIF in most states.

First, a school district has the burden of establishing the necessity for abolishing positions and reducing its workforce on the basis of one or more of the legislated reasons (e.g., declining enrollment, fiscal exigency, school district reorganization, and "other good and just cause").

Assuming that the school district is able to justify its need to effectuate a RIF, the next determination involves the order in which teachers will be released. For the most part, nontenured teachers are released prior to the dismissal of tenured teachers. As among tenured teachers, seniority (years of service in the school district or within a particular field of teaching) is most frequently used to evaluate teachers for RIF. Some states provide for more senior teachers to "bump" those with less seniority from a particular teaching assignment while a few other states require that the school district "realign" staff to accommodate those with greatest seniority.

If a RIF is temporary (i.e., "laid off" or "suspended" rather than "terminated") and the school district is subsequently faced with restaffing certain positions, many states provide a statutory basis for recall for those RIFfed teachers with the greatest seniority. Keep in mind that RIF may be further complicated by collective bargaining agreements and/or local school board policies that may serve to supplement and perhaps even preempt certain aspects of a given state's statutory RIF guidelines. In the event of a RIF, several states exempt school districts from providing teachers with due process rights to a hearing.

One final point: An employer may not use RIF as a pretext to dismiss a teacher for unauthorized reasons. For example, a school district would not prevail simply by *claiming* that a particular teacher was RIFfed due to a "valid" reason if it is later shown that the *real* reason the school district acted was because the teacher had exercised constitutionally protected rights to speak out by becoming involved in a school board member recall election. *Claiborne County Board of Education v. Martin*, 500 So.2d 981 (Miss. 1986). Similarly, three tenured teachers who were allegedly RIFfed due to "economic necessity" were reinstated with back pay after an Illinois court found that the school district was unable to present convincing evidence of financial need and, instead, that the school district had acted in retaliation for union organizational activities undertaken by the teachers just two months earlier. *Temple v. Board of Education of School District No. 94, Cook County*, 548 N.E.2d 640 (Ill.App.Ct. 1989).

What damages may be sought if a teacher is improperly dismissed?

An improperly dismissed teacher is entitled to damages equal to the amount of his actual loss (i.e., compensatory damages). Calculation of the amount of "actual" loss may go well beyond a simple determination of lost salary and benefits; given the right set of circumstances it may include such things as compensation for harm done to one's reputation and the negligent or intentional infliction of emotional distress. Other types of commonly sought relief include reinstatement to a former position and, on occasion, punitive damages.

What does it mean to "mitigate" damages?

Within the context of a teacher seeking damages for improper dismissal, *mitigation* means to seek and, if reasonable, accept comparable employment elsewhere pending the outcome of litigation. If a school board's action in dismissing a teacher has been wrongful and deprived her of a protected right, then her recovery will normally be reduced by the amount of income she made (or could have made had she accepted an employment offer) during the period of time that litigation was pending. Since litigation in an employment case may take several years to resolve, the consequence of "mitigating" one's damages may amount to a substantial sum of money.

What is meant by breach of contract?

Breach of contract is the failure of one or both parties to a contract to live up to the conditions in the contract. For example, teachers in the Hortonville school district discussed in the previous chapter (Case Description No. 5) who went out on strike in violation of state law were considered to have breached their teaching contracts. A teacher who signs a contract to teach school in one district, but who leaves prior to the end of his contract to teach elsewhere breaches his contract unless a release is obtained from the first school district exonerating the teacher from his contractual obligations. A school board may also breach an employment contract if it summarily dismisses a teacher without legal justification.

Who determines whether a contract has been breached?

In many cases, a court. A party to a contract who feels that the other party has broken the contract may ask a court of law to uphold all contractual interests. Note, however, that in many states teachers and school districts are required to seek and exhaust administrative remedies prior to petitioning a court for redress. This administrative prerequisite step helps alleviate some of the backlog of cases in the judicial system and, at least in theory, is intended to speed up the process in reaching a satisfactory and just solution.

Does being convicted of a felony constitute a teacher's breach of contract?

Ordinarily, yes. A teacher who is convicted (i.e., found guilty) of a felony will be considered to be in breach of his employment contract. This answer is not as clearly defined for teachers convicted of a misdemeanor (which, in most situations, is not considered to be as serious as a felony) or for anyone who has merely been arrested for, but not yet convicted of, a criminal offense of either type. This kind of breach of contract is usually premised on the notion that teachers are expected to be positive role models for their students. Felony convictions are not congruent with this expectation and are obviously deleterious to the teacher's effectiveness. Principles of "double jeopardy" do not apply in this context. Courts have held on numerous occasions that a civil sanction (i.e., the loss of employment) following a criminal conviction is not in violation of the Double Jeopardy provision in the Fifth Amendment (see appendix A).

What penalties may be levied against a teacher who breaches an employment contract?

The penalties may range all the way from loss of employment or suspension of a teaching certificate to having to pay a penalty in order to compensate the school district for its time and costs in finding a replacement teacher. For example, when a teacher whose husband was being transferred asked to be released from her contract just six days before the beginning of a new school year, the North Dakota Supreme Court found that she was properly required to pay damages to the school district amounting to four percent of her salary for the coming year. Even though the school district was promptly able to find a replacement teacher, the district was still entitled to enforce the fixed-damages provision in the contract. The court took into account a number of factors in developing the rationale for its decision: the difficulty in ascertaining the exact amount of damages incurred by a school district in this type of situation (thus the need to impose a "set" amount by contract—in this case, four percent); the debilitating effect that such an interruption may have upon the learning process in a school system; and the possibility that the replacement teacher might be a less effective instructor than the teacher who was in breach of her contract. *Bowbells Public School District No. 14 v. Walker*, 231 N.W.2d 173 (N.D. 1975).

Has a school district ever breached its contract with a teacher?

In *James v. Hitchcock Independent School District*, 742 S.W.2d 701 (Tex.Ct.App. 1987), a tenured teacher had a continuing contract with her school district which provided for an extra 20 days of employment each year. When the local funding which paid for the extra days was no longer available, the school district decided unilaterally to cut the teacher's extra days and, in effect, modify her contract. When the teacher sued the school district for breach of contract, the court held that the district's actions were improper since it could not modify the employment contract without at least giving the teacher the benefit of a hearing to discuss the ramifications of the funding situation.

Discrimination and Sexual Harassment

What are some different kinds of discrimination that may affect a teacher's employment?

Beginning with the proposition that it would take a multi-volume treatise to fully explore *all* of the legal intricacies governing discrimination and a teacher's entitlement to equal employment opportunities, the discussion in this section is, by necessity, primarily intended to provide an overview of the topic. The most common anti-discrimination measures are intended to protect individuals from adverse employment consequences due to their race, gender, age, religion, national origin, and certain disabilities. To varying degrees, each of these classifications are governed by statutory and constitutional provisions and each is subject to its own "standard" for application and judicial interpretation.

What laws serve to protect individuals from employment discrimination?

Essentially, two standards guard against discriminatory employment practices. The first of these standards encompasses federal and state legislation designed to rectify past discrimination against those in specific minority groups or populations and to prevent discriminatory acts against the same individuals in the future. An example of this type of statutory protection would be most of the civil rights legislation enacted by Congress since the 1960s. The various federal acts (which are discussed at greater length in the following questions and answers) usually provide specific remedies for discriminatory governmental actions. Some federal anti-discrimination legislation even extends to private sector employers as well. Federal—and, in most cases, comparable state—constitutional protections guaranteeing equal protection rights comprise the second type of anti-discrimination protections. The Equal Protection Clause found in the Fourteenth Amendment to the United States Constitution is the primary source of this type of anti-discriminatory protection. As a general rule, it is necessary for a plaintiff seeking redress under an equal protection claim to demonstrate either intentional or purposeful discrimination on the government's part in order to prevail.

What is Title VII of the Civil Rights Act of 1964 and how is it used to challenge discriminatory employment practices in public schools?

Title VII is the statute used most frequently to seek redress from alleged discriminatory employment practices. In a nutshell, it prevents both public and private employers (with fifteen or more employees) from discriminating against current or prospective employees on the basis of their race, color, religion, gender or national origin. Although Title VII allows certain exceptions in areas other than race and color for *bona fide occupational qualifications,* it comprehensively governs most employment circumstances including hiring, promotion, compensation, and benefits.

What are *bona fide occupational qualifications*?

Title VII provides for *bona fide occupational qualifications*, or "*BFOQs*," which exempt an employer from strict adherence to the sex, religion and national origin provisions in the Civil Rights Act of 1964 *if* an employer is able to demonstrate why a certain trait is necessary for an employee to hold and satisfactorily perform a particular job. For example, a school district could make a viable argument that it needs to hire a female teacher to coach the high school girls' swimming or basketball teams if locker room supervision and in-the-locker room coaching duties are requisite attributes for the position. Similarly, a parochial school may be able to use religious affiliation as a *BFOQ* when hiring a teacher for certain positions in the school.

What is an example of a case in which Title VII was used to assert a claim of racial discrimination?

In *Richardson v. Alabama State Board of Education*, 935 F.2d 1240 (11th Cir. 1991), a school district nonrenewed an African-American teacher's contract. In defending against a Title VII civil rights claim premised on racial discrimination, the school district claimed in its defense that its nonrenewal decision was ostensibly due to the fact that the teacher did not hold a valid teaching certificate. The Eleventh Circuit Court of Appeals rejected the school district's defense after recognizing that the state's certification procedure had been invalidated and was under appeal as part of a class action suit at the time this particular teacher was facing nonrenewal. Further, the school board had successfully petitioned the state for temporary certificates for three other teachers—but not for the plaintiff.

By contrast, in a case argued to the United States Supreme Court, a school board was found to have met its obligation under Title VII to offer reasonable accommodation for a teacher's religious beliefs. *Ansonia Board of Education v. Philbrook*, 479 U.S. 60 (1986). At issue in *Ansonia* was whether a teacher could be required by school board policy to take unpaid leave for holy day observances that exceeded the number of days allowed in a collective bargaining agreement. The Court held that the school board's allowance for each teacher's use of up to three days of accumulated leave during each school year for "necessary personal business" was a reasonable accommodation to all employees and it thus did not need to make a separate exception for Mr. Philbrook.

What is an example of sex or gender discrimination?

An excellent example of a sex discrimination claim brought under Title VII is *Cesaro v. Lakeville Community School District*, 953 F.2d 252 (6th Cir. 1992), *cert. denied*, 113 S.Ct. 195 (1992), discussed in Case No. 7 at the beginning of this chapter. In contrast to the *Cesaro* case, female job applicants have found success where they were able to prove that they were better qualified than other male applicants for a particular position but were "passed over" because of stereotypic attitudes about their capabilities. *Farber v. Massillon Board of Education*, 917 F.2d 1391 (6th Cir. 1990); *cert. denied*, 111 S.Ct. 952 (1991). In addition, courts have viewed with disfavor job vacancy notices which are designed to exclude those of a particular gender (i.e., "prefer male"). *Coble v. Hot Springs School District No. 6*, 682 F.2d 721 (8th Cir. 1982).

How does Title VII protect against sexual harassment?

Federal law defines sexual harassment as a form of prohibited sex discrimination. Guidelines that have been adopted to supplement Title VII define sexual harassment as "unwelcome sexual advances, requests for sexual favors, and other verbal or physical conduct of a sexual nature." 29 C.F.R. 1604.II(a). Harassment exists if this type of conduct "has the purpose or effect of unreasonably interfering with an individual's work performance or creating an intimidating, hostile, or defensive working environment." *Id.* Sexual harassment cases usually fall into one or both of two categories: *quid pro quo* harassment (in which there is a tradeoff between sexual advances and employment conditions) and "hostile environment" harassment (in which unwelcome comments, sexual advances or other verbal or physical conduct create an offensive working environment). In addition to federal restrictions on sexually harassing conduct, several states have corresponding legislation which criminalizes such behavior under state law.

What is affirmative action?

Although affirmative action is probably most frequently thought of in terms of racial discrimination, it may also be used to promote greater balance when considering factors of gender, creed and age. Two types of affirmative action may occur in a school setting, and they are designed to remedy discriminatory practices. In the first, if a court determines that a school district had previously engaged in discriminatory practices, then it can impose prescriptive requirements to remedy the past discrimination through affirmative measures. In the second type, a school district voluntarily and without court supervision or mandate adopts a preferential staffing plan to rectify its own perceived past hiring inequities and prevent future discrimination. In effect, both types of affirmative action attempt to ensure that persons or populations previously excluded from employment are given notice of job vacancies and assistance in applying for openings. However, neither court-ordered nor voluntary affirmative action efforts *necessarily* impose preferential treatment requirements for hiring minority applicants; rather, this feature is decided on a case-by-case and "as needed" basis. The United States Supreme Court has usually upheld only narrowly drawn affirmative action programs that have been carefully designed to avoid discriminating against majority group members while at the same time seeking to overcome the negative effects of past discrimination.

What is the difference between affirmative action and reverse discrimination?

By definition, reverse discrimination occurs when bias is exercised against a particular person or group of people in order to correct a pattern of discrimination against another person or group. Affirmative action plans that are not neutral and are either intentionally or more indirectly discriminatory are subject to a reverse discrimination challenge. The most highly publicized United States Supreme Court case in this area was *Regents, University of California v. Bakke*, 438 U.S. 265 (1978). In *Bakke*, the Court held that a quota fixing the number of minority applicants admitted to a state medical school was prohibited under federal law. In reexamining the question of quotas in several subsequent cases, the Court further refined the "quota question" by allowing the use of quotas as one of several factors in hiring and promotion decisions—but never as the single determining factor. In the most recent school-related United States Supreme Court case in this area, the Court rejected a collectively bargained affirmative action plan which required the dismissal of Caucasian teachers with greater seniority before laying off African-American teachers with less seniority. *Wygant v. Jackson Board of Education*, 476 U.S. 267 (1986), *rehearing denied*, 478 U.S. 1014 (1986). The Court distinguished between affirmative action *hiring* plans which may be permissible and similarly structured *layoff* plans which may violate a person's constitutionally protected rights to equal protection. The Court's rationale in *Wygant* focused on the different burdens that an unsuccessful *applicant* for a job will incur as opposed to those of an "innocent" employee with a seniority-based expectation of employment stability and security who is laid off in favor of a less-senior minority coworker.

What are some of the other significant civil rights protections against discriminatory employment practices?

Although Title VII is the most prominent federal statute protecting individual citizens from various types of discriminatory conduct, a variety of other federal provisions extend additional protections to others faced with certain types of discrimination. For example, the Equal Pay Act of 1963 prohibits gender-based wage discrimination. The Age Discrimination in Employment Act (ADEA) of 1973 prohibits employment discrimination against those forty or older. Employees with certain types of disabilities are protected under § 504 of the Rehabilitation Act of 1973 as well as under the more recent Americans With Disabilities Act (ADA) of 1990. Although enacted two years earlier, the ADA only became effective with regard to schools in 1992. Title IX of the Education Amendments of 1972 was originally enacted to prohibit gender-based discrimination in educational programs or activities receiving federal funds. The United States Supreme Court's decision in *North Haven Board of Education v. Bell*, 456 U.S. 512 (1982), clarified that Title IX was intended to prohibit *all* gender-based discrimination in federally funded educational programs and thus it extends to employees as well as to students. Finally, many states have enacted their own anti-discrimination legislation to supplement federal legislation. For example, Illinois' Human Rights Act prohibits discrimination on the basis of marital status. Minnesota's statutes provide for honorably discharged veterans of military service to be given a preference when being considered for civil service employment.

How does the Equal Pay Act work?

In prohibiting gender-based wage discrimination, the Equal Pay Act of 1963 is designed to insure that male and female employees are paid equally for doing the same type and amount of work. As stated more directly by the Sixth Circuit Court of Appeals in *Odomes v. Nucare, Inc.*, 653 F.2d 246, 250 (6th Cir. 1981), the plaintiff in an "equal pay" case must prove that her employer "pays different wages to employees of opposite sexes for equal work on jobs the performance of which requires equal skill, effort, and responsibility, and which are performed under similar working conditions." Thus, a school district was found in violation of the Equal Pay Act when it paid its female coaches of girls' teams less than it paid its male coaches of boys' teams. *Equal Employment Opportunity Commission v. Madison Community Unit School District No. 12,* 818 F.2d 577 (7th Cir. 1987).

How does the Age Discrimination in Employment Act of 1973 (ADEA) help protect public school teachers?

The ADEA was enacted (and later amended in 1991) "to promote employment of older persons based on their ability rather than age; to prohibit arbitrary age discrimination in employment; to help employers and workers find ways of meeting problems arising from the impact of age on employment." 29 U.S.C. § 621. Similar to most of the other anti-discrimination legislation in this area, the ADEA is not intended to protect employees whose performance or skills are inadequate for a certain job; rather, it simply requires that employment decisions must generally be made due to conditions other than an employee's age. Among its protections, the ADEA prohibits age-based mandatory retirement and applies to employees age forty or older.

What is an example of a recent case involving the ADEA?

In *Wooden v. Board of Education of Jefferson County, Kentucky,* 931 F.2d 376 (6th Cir. 1991), a school district successfully defended an age discrimination lawsuit brought by a fifty-four-year-old unsuccessful applicant for one of several teaching position vacancies in the district. In its defense, the school district was able to produce evidence that the plaintiff's employment interview with school administrators was "unimpressive," the applicant's teaching performance while employed by the district in a previous part-time position was "unfavorable," more than forty percent of the jobs in the school district were presently filled by persons over forty, and that there were more than 2,000 applicants for each of the vacant positions.

How are teachers with disabilities protected from employment discrimination?

Public school teachers who are disabled are protected under both §504 of the Rehabilitation Act of 1973 and the Americans With Disabilities Act (ADA) of 1990. In simplest terms, both of these laws protect teachers and other government employees who are "otherwise qualified" for a particular position from disability-based discrimination. These protections extend from pre-employment stages (recruiting and interviewing), through the hiring and promotion processes, and finally to termination. For the most part, both of these acts define a disabling condition as a physical or mental impairment which "substantially limits" a major life activity. Although the exact coverage of the disability protections governed by these legislative provisions is beyond the scope of this book, the bottom line comes down to whether an employer can provide "reasonable accommodations" with which the disabled employee (or prospective employee) will be able to perform the job in question. By necessity, each determination of whether an employee is "otherwise qualified" and competent to perform the demands of a particular position and whether the employer has "reasonably" attempted to accommodate the employee's disability is made on a case-by-case basis.

When is the first time in an employment relationship that problems with discrimination will usually arise?

As mentioned in previous questions, employers are prohibited from taking such things as a person's race, gender, religion, national origin or disabilities into account when making hiring decisions. Consequently, a school district must be cautious in determining how pre-employment questions will be asked of a prospective employee as well as how other information will be sought about the person's background and abilities. Complaints arising during the employee selection process are most frequently brought to the attention of the Equal Employment Opportunity Commission (EEOC) which then investigates how and why certain information was sought. As a rule of thumb, all questions that a school district asks of a job applicant should relate fairly directly to the projected job performance requirements. With the advent of greater site-based decision making in many school districts around the country, more and more teachers are becoming actively involved in making personnel decisions in their schools. It is essential that *everyone* involved with the process understand and "internalize" the importance of avoiding discriminatory action.

What are some fertile areas for discriminatory interview questions?

Unless a prospective employer can show substantial justification for "needing to know," questions about pregnancy (or plans for raising a family), personal faith, personal appearance (including asking about height and weight), arrest record (as opposed to a person's record of criminal convictions), and personal finances are almost always off limits.

If a teacher is convinced that his school district is doing something which deprives him of his civil rights, what should he do?

Several avenues are open to the teacher. One is to contact the teacher's association or union that represents the teachers in a given school district. This organization may support the teacher in filing a grievance against the school district. Another option is to seek the assistance of the state's civil rights commission (it should be listed in the telephone directory). The commission will usually make an investigation of the charge; then, if grounds are found which demonstrate the denial of a civil right, the commission will attempt to mediate between the teacher and the school district to rectify the problem.

What is probably best considered to be a last resort is the possibility of a teacher filing a lawsuit against his school district. Prior to taking this significant step, it is usually better to try some of the other less-drastic options before full-blown litigation. Do not forget that there are almost always disadvantages to engaging an employer in costly and time-consuming litigation. As a rule, it is always wise to carefully consider the potential personal and professional implications of filing a lawsuit.

Case Resolutions

Case No. 1: Avoid impulsive decisions (see page 34)

Although the teacher had attained tenure status, he voluntarily chose to resign. Subsequently, he agreed to re-employment conditions based on the understanding that he had resigned and would be rehired as a probationary teacher. Thus, his resignation lawfully terminated his employment as a teacher and eliminated his tenure and "property" rights to that job. The court found that the teacher was not entitled to a nonrenewal hearing under these circumstances. *Kilgore v. Jasper City Board of Education,* 624 So.2d 603 (Ala.Civ.App. 1993), *cert. denied,* (Ala. 1993)[citation unavailable].

Case No. 2: How involved should a teacher get with a student? (see page 35)

Under Colorado law, a teacher may be dismissed for physical or mental disability, incompetence, neglect of duty, immorality, unsatisfactory performance, insubordination, certain criminal convictions, and "other good and just cause." A school board is required to review a hearing officer's recommendation and make its own decision which cannot be "arbitrary, capricious or legally impermissible." On appeal in this case, the court concluded that the hearing officer's findings were supported by substantial and competent evidence. The school board's decision was not arbitrary, capricious, or legally impermissible. Although the teacher argued that the alleged effect of his relationship with the student did not cause significant disruption in the school district or impair his teaching performance, the hearing officer and the school board found otherwise— and the court agreed. The teacher had repeatedly questioned other students and school personnel about the boy. Many parents expressed concern about the situation and did not want their children around this particular teacher. The power to dismiss a teacher is justified by the state's legitimate interest in protecting the school community—and particularly its students—from harm, and it can only be justified by showing that harm has or is likely to occur. Applying the "good and just cause" standard to review the teacher's termination, the court agreed that the teacher's conduct *outside* the classroom constituted a valid justification for dismissal. The teacher's conduct affected his fitness to discharge his duties, his performance was detrimental to students, it clouded his professional judgment, and it caused disruption in the school district. Further, the teacher's exercise of free speech in his own defense was not a motivating factor in his dismissal. The dismissal was affirmed. *Kerin v. Board of Education, Lamar School*

District, 860 P.2d 574 (Colo.Ct.App. 1993), *cert. denied,* (Colo. 1993) [citation unavailable].

Case No. 3: Going on the attack (see page 36)

Because the record of the administrative hearing was not properly admitted into evidence as required by law, the appeals court could not consider it in reviewing the case. Without this record to show there was any error, the agency's order of certification revocation is presumed to be valid and legal, and it was the teacher's burden to prove otherwise. Addressing the teacher's other points without the benefit of considering the record, the district court's decision upholding revocation was affirmed. *Everett v. Texas Education Agency*, 860 S.W.2d 700 (Tex.Ct.App. 1993).

Case No. 4: Stressed out (see page 37)

The school board's decision was reversed as an abuse of discretion. An appellate court concluded that the referee's recommendation should have been given due deference because he was in the best position to observe the demeanor of witnesses and weigh their credibility. Although the school board gave a reason for termination, its resolution was deficient because it did not explain why it rejected the referee's recommendation for suspension. Moreover, the superintendent did not even consider the teacher's excellent record or past performance when he recommended termination—even though the superintendent was required to do so according to both Ohio law and by contract. Similarly, the school board must also consider a teacher's past employment record when making this type of employment decision and it too had failed to do so. The court found that a most severe sanction (termination) was imposed when a more appropriate sanction commensurate with the offense and the particular circumstances surrounding the situation was in order. *Katz v. Maple Heights Board of Education*, 622 N.E.2d 1 (Ohio Ct.App. 1993).

Case No. 5: Pretext or not? (see page 38)

The school board gave legitimate, nondiscriminatory reasons for not renewing the African-American teacher's contract. The school board chairman and the principal (who were also African-American) and the superintendent and personnel director (who were both white) all stated that the fact that the teacher was black did not influence any action with regard to nonrenewal of the contract. The teacher completely failed to present any evidence that would show discrimination on the basis of race in nonrenewing her contract. In addition, the teacher was unsuccessful in convincing the court that the school board's hiring practices in filling her former position with a white teacher constituted racial discrimination. Consequently, her nonrenewal was affirmed. *Sommerville v. Tuscaloosa City Board of Education*, 579 So.2d 628 (Ala.Civ.App. 1991).

Case No. 6: On the other hand (see page 38)

A federal trial court found that there appeared to be no legitimate reason for the teacher's termination. She had not made any mistakes that were not also made by white instructors. In the court's view, the principal clearly exhibited racial animus against the teacher from the first day of school when she was introduced to the students. She did not appear to violate school policies, she was supported by her students, she was not rude or insubordinate, and no negative incidents were found in the principal's evaluation which, instead, indicated that she was doing very well as a teacher. White teachers who were accused of deeds similar to the African-American teacher's received no comparable disciplinary action. Further, there was direct evidence of a pretext motive on the principal's part in that the plan of assistance was created to help the teacher with her alleged child abuse problem (a domestic rather than a school problem in this case) instead of assisting her with perceived teaching difficulties. The court concluded that the teacher had a viable claim for discriminatory treatment, harassment, retaliatory discharge and the violation of her rights to equal protection; consequently, the extent of her injuries should properly be decided by a jury. *Ginwright v. Unified School District No. 457*, 756 F.Supp. 1458 (D.Kan. 1991).

Case No. 7: Sex discrimination and job vacancy notices (see page 40)

Among other things (i.e., race, color, religion and national origin), Title VII of the Civil Rights Act of 1964 forbids discrimination on the basis of an individual's sex or gender. The teacher in this case claimed that hers was a "mixed motive" case—in other words, discrimination occurred as a result of a mixture of legitimate and illegitimate circumstances. However, the teacher could not show that the school board acted with any discriminatory intent when it made the ultimate decision to hire the male candidate recommended by the superintendent. Apparently, the school board members were unaware of the superintendent's alleged motivation for posting the position vacancy notices at the universities and outside the school district. Thus, the teacher's gender played no part in the school board's decision. Under Title VII, the United States Supreme Court has said that the critical inquiry is "whether gender was a factor in the employment decision *at the moment it was made. . . . Price Waterhouse v. Hopkins*, 490 U.S. 228, 240 (1989). "In saying that gender played a motivating part in an employment decision, we mean that, if we asked the employer *at the moment of the decision* what its reasons were and if we received a truthful response, one of those reasons would be that the applicant or employee was a woman." *Id.* at 250. In this case, the teacher claimed that the superintendent's involvement in the selection process was the discriminatory conduct. However, this theory could produce an anomalous result which would allow the teacher to recover even if another female applicant from outside the school district had been hired. Title VII was not meant to extend to a decision in the process *preliminary* to the hiring decision; rather, Title VII focuses on job qualifications—and that is what the school board did in deciding to hire the male candidate. *Cesaro v. Lakeville*

Community School District, 953 F.2d 252 (6th Cir. 1992), *cert. denied,* 113 S.Ct. 195 (1992).

One additional point needs to be made—following the United States Supreme Court's decisions in *Price Waterhouse* and several other cases, Congress enacted legislation to reverse a trend in the way the Court was narrowly interpreting various civil rights provisions. By enacting the Civil Rights Act of 1991 (42 U.S.C. § 2000(e)), Congress amended Title VII to allow courts to award both compensatory and punitive damages (although school districts are specifically exempt from punitive damage remedies). Previously, Title VII has been interpreted to only provide for intentionally discriminatory employment actions, but the Civil Rights Act of 1991 expanded a plaintiff's protection in a "mixed motive" case—the Act provides that even if an employer demonstrates that it would have made the same decision regardless of the discriminatory factor, then there is a Title VII violation but the plaintiff is limited to injunctive relief, attorney's fees and costs but not monetary damages.

Chapter Three

Freedom of Expression

Under the United States Constitution, teachers are entitled to a variety of "freedoms" shared by others living in this country. These protected rights include activities governed by the First Amendment which can be classified as being "expressive"— particularly freedom of speech, and, to a lesser degree, freedom of the press, freedom of association, and the right to petition the government. In this sense, expression may assume different forms including written and spoken words or symbolic acts and gestures. In analyzing the extent of a teacher's freedom of expression, this chapter is loosely divided into two parts. Following the case descriptions which provide an introductory taste of the scope of a teacher's expressive opportunities, the chapter focuses on in-school or in-the-classroom types of teaching activities. These activities are generally characterized by a concept commonly known as "academic freedom." The latter portion of the chapter focuses on activities which are less directly connected to a teacher's assigned duties in the classroom. Such activities include a teacher's right as a citizen to speak out on matters of public concern or to engage in political activities outside the classroom setting.

Case Descriptions

Case No. 1: The hemlock drink

His motto was "Know Thyself," and his students were Athenian youths of the fourth century B.C. Although not a religious man, Socrates frequently spoke of an "inner voice" that guided his course. The virtue that he sought among men through questioning them was "the good life" for everyone—but his questions often created doubt and uncertainty in the minds of his listeners. Anytus, a former pupil and politician, secretly brought criminal charges against Socrates under an Athenian law which prohibited "impiety." Although the evidence against Socrates was weak and despite the fact that Anytus himself would be heavily penalized if one-fifth or more of the jury did not vote for conviction, he was depending on a jury of hundreds to be swayed by his argument that "Socrates has corrupted the youth of Athens." In turn, Socrates gave a moving speech in his own defense. What was the outcome of this early trial involving elements of academic freedom?

Case No. 2: Teaching human reproduction

A tenured teacher and one of his students initiated a lawsuit alleging that the teacher's liberty and property rights under the Fourteenth Amendment had been violated and that the school board, the school district, individual board members, former and present superintendents, the principal and two parents of students in the school conspired to violate both the teacher's and the student's First Amendment rights. The case began when one of the parents brought to the school board's attention her own and other parents' complaints about the methods the teacher was using to teach about human reproduction in a life science class. The textbook that the teacher used for the class had been approved by the school board and the accompanying films obtained from the county health department had been shown at school in previous years without incident. The films were shown separately to the boys and girls in the class.

In addition, the teacher also showed pictures of his wife taken during her pregnancy. The parents' protests were vehement and continual although based primarily on unfounded rumors about the allegedly explicit nature of the photos and films. Eventually the teacher was discharged from his teaching position. The teacher was not given an opportunity to present his side and, from the time of the incident until the trial, he and his family endured three years of harassment and abuse. At trial, the jury found for the defendants in the claims raised by the student, but found in the teacher's favor in his claims against most of the defendants. Compensatory damages of $275,000 and punitive damages of $46,000 were awarded to the teacher against the school board, the individual school board members and the school officials. A separate $18,250 judgment (of which $10,000 was for punitive damages) for the teacher was awarded against one of the parent defendants. Following the jury trial, the trial judge set aside the judgment against the parent (in other words, granted judgment notwithstanding the verdict) on the basis that the parent had immunity for her right to petition under the First Amendment. Several appeals resulted. Do you think the school board, its members, and the school administrators violated the teacher's constitutional rights and that judgment against them should be sustained on appeal? Do you think the private citizen/parent should be immune from suit even though, as the court said, "[her] role in these events is not a pretty one?"

Case No. 3: When does a "teaching technique" reach the level of "immoral conduct?"

A tenured English and media teacher edited student assignments submitted for placement in a media class publication. The eventual publication (which was only intended to be an in-class exercise) included articles and advertisements which involved explicit, crude and tasteless sexual references, articles which promoted or condoned the use of drugs, and accusations that the local police were substance abusers. The teacher critiqued the material for the class and indicated that some of it was unacceptable; however, he did not retrieve all copies of the publication and some were subsequently circulated in the community. Upon learning of this matter, the superintendent suspended the teacher and gave him notice of the charges against him. After a hearing, the school board decided to terminate the teacher based on evidence that he had engaged in immoral conduct. Do you think this was immoral conduct? Was termination warranted in this case?

Case No. 4: Academic freedom in assigning homework

Insubordination and conduct unbecoming a teacher were the charges against a teacher who assigned her students to write essays expressing their opinions about the recent firing of a television sports commentator. In the materials for the assignment, the teacher included her own "letter to the editor" which expressed her opinion about the subject. When the teacher refused to rescind the assignment and refused to turn over her lesson plan and grade books to the superintendent, her actions were alleged to constitute insubordination and conduct unbecoming a teacher. The school district sought to discipline the teacher and, at a subsequent hearing, she claimed that the district's actions interfered with her academic freedom. A hearing panel declined to decide that issue but did recommend a semester-long suspension without pay for refusing to rescind the assignment and turn over her books at the request of the superintendent. The teacher appealed to the state commissioner of education who concluded that the teacher's academic freedom had been infringed by the school district's actions but that the other charges were substantiated. The commissioner reduced the suspension to three months without pay. The teacher then went to court to appeal the commissioner's decision. What should be the result?

Case No. 5: Showing objectionable films in class

A high school social studies teacher had taught with an unblemished record for fourteen years. During that period he also served as head of the social studies department for eight years. In 1987 he decided to show two R-rated films to high school students (ages 15-17) in his World Geography and World History classes. One film depicted prehistoric man's quest for fire and contained nudity, violence, and procreative encounters. The other film illustrated terrible experiences that happened to a novice ouija board player who attempted to communicate with "spirits." It had profanity, violence and female frontal nudity. The teacher felt that both films were pertinent to the topics being discussed in his classes—ancient Chinese culture and the origins of Halloween, respectively. After the films were shown, several people in the community complained. Upon investigation, the principal concluded that the films were not relevant to the subject matter of the classes. Further, the principal found that the teacher had not complied with school rules about the use of classroom media. The teacher was dismissed by the school board for incompetency and he appealed his dismissal. Do you think the teacher was incompetent and that dismissal was warranted, or should he get his job back?

Case No. 6: Speaking of pay

A school district was facing budgetary problems and decided to pay its teachers biweekly over the summer months rather than with a lump sum payment at the beginning of the summer as had previously been the custom. A teacher with ten years of teaching experience wrote a letter to his fellow teachers in which he objected to the new pay policy, criticized the school administration for its inability to balance the school district's budget, accused them of mismanagement and being top-heavy, and encouraged other teachers to participate in a "sick-out" during exam week. Upon learning of the letter, the superintendent met with the teacher and the building principal. The teacher admitted writing the letter and complained about being mistreated with respect to his pay. Hearing this, the superintendent summarily terminated the teacher on the grounds that he was a disruptive influence and that proposing to abandon his duties and encouraging other teachers to do the same made him unfit to continue teaching. Following a hearing, the school board affirmed the teacher's termination. The teacher filed suit claiming that he had been terminated for exercising his right to speak on issues of public importance. Was this teacher properly terminated, or do First Amendment free speech rights protect this teacher from termination?

Case No. 7: Troublemaker or victim of retaliation?

A tenured teacher with a good performance record had taught for ten years in one school district. In 1975, she moved to a different school in another district to set up a new high school reading program. Unfortunately, she had conflicts with the superintendent and principal at the second school. In 1978, she filed her first grievance, and then filed a second grievance in 1979. Also in 1979, the teacher was criticized for counseling two students who wanted to appeal disciplinary sanctions. In 1980 the teacher learned that her reading program would be cut back and she would be reassigned to teach high school English. The teacher publicly objected to the changes at school meetings and in a letter to the local newspaper. The teacher also protested by becoming "decertified" to teach English (i.e., she dropped the English teaching endorsement from her certificate). Despite her objections, the changes were implemented and she eventually filed two more grievances.

Allegedly, the school administrators retaliated against her in 1981 by sending her a termination letter based on an incident in which she asked another teacher to excuse a student in order to take a required test, but instead the student wanted to discuss personal problems and then left the school without permission. In finalizing the termination, the administrators did not follow their usual procedures and, in actuality, did not even have authority to effectuate the termination. The school board tacitly acknowledged this when they reinstated the teacher and treated the time she missed from work as a suspension with pay.

After that, the teacher claimed retaliation continued in specific instances—following a death in her family she was harshly questioned about her "unauthorized absence" despite the fact that she reported her absence in the manner expected by the school district; her reassignment to teach elementary grades when a reading specialty position was open in the junior high; and when she applied for a vacant reading specialist position and her application was rejected despite her experience and in favor of a teacher with very little experience in that area. In this last situation, the teacher filed another grievance and an arbitrator ruled there was a violation of a collective bargaining agreement—the teacher was then assigned to the reading specialist job.

As a result of all of the actions taken by the administrators, the teacher brought suit seeking compensatory and punitive damages for the school administrators retaliatory actions to her exercise of First Amendment rights. In defense, the school administrators claimed that they were reacting to the teacher's improper conduct and that they would not have done anything different regardless of her constitutionally protected activities. They pointed out that there was an eight-month gap between the teacher's activities and the second termination. Do you think the teacher was too outspoken and a "troublemaker" or could she prove there was retaliation against her?

What is Academic Freedom?

The concept of academic freedom in the American classroom was influenced in part by the doctrine of *die akademische Freiheit*. This doctrine served as the underlying basis for German higher education and consisted of two components: *Lernfreiheit* (freedom to learn) and *Lehrfreiheit* (freedom to teach). Although nineteenth-century Germany was autocratic, the university campus environment was decidedly open for both students and professors. In a figurative sense, students were encouraged to roam from place to place sampling academic wares and they were not accountable for regular attendance. Professors were free to experiment and could try to persuade students as to the merits or strengths of a particular ideology.

Two major changes took place when this system was transplanted to the public schools in this country. First, students were required to attend classes and study certain specified curricula adopted by state or local boards of education. Compulsory attendance not only mandated school attendance but, to some extent, it also limited student freedom to choose what material would be studied—and when it would be covered. Second, teachers were prohibited from using the classroom as a forum to proselytize students in a particular way of thinking.

Since public school teachers work for the government, they are expected to teach from specified curricula and to present controversial issues in such a way that each student can make informed and individualized decisions concerning what conclusions should be drawn. Moreover, a teacher is usually limited to teaching in certain specified areas of expertise; in other words, a teacher is expected to take advantage of academic preparation which is generally evidenced by certification or endorsement status in a given field or specialty area. Despite these restrictions, students still retain an underlying interest in accessing ideas and knowledge which will help prepare them for assuming productive roles as citizens in contemporary society.

Directly connected to a student's right to access information is a teacher's right within the classroom to select appropriate and viable instructional methodologies. The law recognizes that a teacher must enjoy certain rights to freedom of expression in order to best accomplish educational objectives. Some common issues that face a teacher as an employee in a school district are: May a teacher assign books or articles that offend parents or school authorities? May a teacher use teaching methods that are somewhat unorthodox or not approved by the majority of citizens in that community? Should a classroom teacher be permitted to express controversial personal views to students?

New and important scientific and sociological discoveries are constantly being made with a corresponding impact on what is and what needs to be taught in today's public schools. For example, in *An American Renaissance in the Year 2000*, Martin Cetron suggests that all of the technological knowledge presently available will represent only about one percent of the knowledge that will be available to mankind in the year 2050. It is important that teachers remain free to evaluate and criticize the values, styles and truths of the past and the present. This is the purpose of academic freedom—to open the door to the new and the different.

In 1969, the United State Supreme Court said that "in our system, students may not be regarded as closed-circuit recipients of only that which the State chooses to communicate. They may not be confined to the expression of those sentiments that are officially approved." *Tinker v. Des Moines Independent School District*, 393 U.S. 503, 511 (1969). Thus, although state and/or local boards of education adopt general policies and guidelines for curricula, teachers have an independent interest in selecting instructional methodologies to provide students with access to ideas and knowledge. A teacher is generally given some degree of discretion in using teaching strategies which he feels will "fit" his students' needs and abilities, the school district's curricula and course content, and his own teaching style. Often added to the mix of state, teacher and student interests is a fourth component comprised of parental involvement in controlling or influencing educational directions. While these groups share a fundamental interest in the education and ultimate well-being of young people, the discussion which follows points out that the sphere of academic freedom is best characterized as being "in transition" or "subject to change" depending on the circumstances.

What do teachers have in common with monkeys and the concept of academic freedom?

On an extremely hot and humid day in Dayton, Tennessee, approximately 900 people attempted to jam into a small courtroom to attend the trial of John Thomas Scopes. Scopes, a first-year science teacher, was accused in 1925 of violating a Tennessee statute which made expounding the theory of evolution in Tennessee's schools a criminal offense. Prior to his arrest, Scopes had substituted for a biology teacher who was ill. Although it was never actually proven that Scopes taught that man had descended from a strain of monkeys—or, for that matter, any other "lower order" of animal life—he was nonetheless convicted by a jury and was fined $100 by the judge. The courtroom pyrotechnics of the prosecuting attorney, William Jennings Bryan, and Scopes' defense counsel, Clarence Darrow, enthralled those in attendance and captured the attention of the nation. Upon appeal, Scopes' attorneys argued that the state had deprived Scopes of his constitutional rights. However, although Scopes' conviction was overturned on the basis of the Tennessee Supreme Court's holding that the jury—and not the judge—should have set the fine, the court's disposition of the constitutional issues is illustrative:

> We think there is little merit in this contention. [Scopes] was a teacher in the public schools of Rhea county. He was an employee of the state of Tennessee . . . He was under contract with the state to work in an institution of the state. He had no right or privilege to serve the state except upon such terms as the state prescribed. His liberty, his privilege, his immunity to teach and to proclaim the theory of evolution, elsewhere than in the service of the state, was in no wise touched by this law. *Scopes v. State*, 289 S.W. 363 (Tenn. 1927), *superceded by statute as stated in State v. Durso*, 645 S.W.2d 753 (Tenn. 1983).

In passing, it is interesting to note that Scopes' defense was partially funded by the newly formed American Civil Liberties Union (ACLU). After his ordeal, Scopes studied geology at the University of Chicago and then got a job as a geologist in Venezuela. In 1960 he returned to Dayton to attend the premiere of *Inherit the Wind*, a movie depicting his trial. In his own account of his experiences entitled *Center of the Storm*, Scopes disclosed that one reason he did not take the witness stand to testify during his trial was that he knew very little about evolution.

Where is "academic freedom" mentioned in the United States Constitution?

It isn't; rather, the concept of academic freedom is derived from the freedom of speech provision in the First Amendment and a long history of court cases which considered the importance of free expression in the classroom. In essence, the First Amendment's restriction on laws abridging freedom of speech says that "free speech is the rule and not the exception." Only where the state can show that free speech should be limited for the greater good can this right be restricted.

What is an example of a situation illustrating the point that academic freedom is not an "absolute" right?

A classic and often-cited example borrowed from Justice Oliver Holmes' opinion in *Schenck v. United States*, 249 U.S. 47 (1919) is the situation where someone shouts "FIRE!" in a crowded theater. Common sense and the public welfare dictate that when there is no fire and the potential for unwarranted panic is great, then a person's right to shout "FIRE!" should not go unchecked. From a teacher's perspective, academic freedom is grounded on being able to fully and reasonably communicate with students so as to carry out the educational objectives that the teacher was hired to perform. In this sense, the scope of the teacher's "freedom" to teach is constrained by a sense of "appropriateness" entirely dependent upon such characteristics as student age and maturity as well as the nature of the subject matter being taught.

How has the United States Supreme Court traditionally viewed the concept of academic freedom in public school classrooms?

Although the United States Supreme Court has expressed support for the idea that professors enjoy a certain amount of academic freedom in their college or university classrooms, the Court has never spoken as clearly with regard to elementary and secondary public school teachers. Thus, the Court's attitude toward academic freedom and the nature of the relationship between teaching and learning can best be deduced by looking at a sampling of the Court's decisions over the years. For example, in 1923 the Court struck down a Nebraska statute which made it a criminal offense to teach a foreign language to any student not yet in the eighth grade. *Meyer v. Nebraska*, 262 U.S. 390 (1923). In effect, the *Meyer* Court concluded that the statutory restriction on foreign language instruction was an arbitrary and unreasonable attempt by the state to constrict the amount of knowledge to which students might be exposed.

Forty-five years later in *Epperson v. State of Arkansas*, 393 U.S. 97 (1968), the Court held that an Arkansas statute which made it illegal to teach about evolution in the state's public schools and universities was unconstitutional. The Arkansas anti-evolution statute had been adopted in 1928 following the *Scopes* "monkey trial" in Tennessee. The statute created a misdemeanor criminal offense which was punishable by dismissal for a teacher "to teach the theory or doctrine that mankind ascended or descended from a lower order of animals." When the Little Rock, Arkansas, school system adopted a new biology textbook containing a chapter on "the theory about the origin . . . of man from a lower form of animal," a young biology teacher in the school district faced a dilemma—she was expected to use the new textbook for classroom instruction but doing so would subject her to a criminal sanction as well as dismissal from employment. In holding that the statute violated the Establishment and Free Exercise Clauses of the First Amendment (which serve to ensure the separation of church and state), the *Epperson* Court concluded:

> By and large, public education in our Nation is committed to the control of state and local authorities. Courts do not and cannot intervene in the resolution of conflicts which arise in the daily operation of school systems and which do not directly and sharply implicate basic constitutional values. On the other hand, "[t]he vigilant protection of constitutional freedoms is nowhere more vital than in the community of American schools," *Shelton v. Tucker*, 364 U.S. 479, 487 (1960). As this Court said in *Keyishian*

v. Board of Regents [*of the University of the State of New York*, 385 U.S. 589, 603 (1967)], the First Amendment "does not tolerate laws that cast a pall of orthodoxy over the classroom." *Epperson v. State of Arkansas*, 393 U.S. 97, 104-105 (1968).

As can be seen from the results in these and other related cases, the United States Supreme Court has recognized at least a nominal right of teachers and students to engage in an open exchange of ideas. Laws or regulations which tend to contract rather than expand knowledge within a public school setting have traditionally met with disfavor. Although a teacher's right of academic freedom is balanced against other competing interests and is far from absolute, it nonetheless has often played a prominent role in American public education.

Do today's public school teachers have the same amount of academic freedom that they have enjoyed in the past?

Although it is still too early to answer this question with certainty, it appears that the scope and extent of a public school teacher's right to academic freedom is coming under fire and may be on the decline. In 1988 the United States Supreme Court decided *Hazelwood School District v. Kuhlmeier*, 484 U.S. 260 (1988). As previously noted, *Hazelwood* involved a high school principal's authority to delete several articles dealing with teenage pregnancy and divorce which had been written and submitted by students for publication in the school newspaper. (The facts in this case are covered in greater detail in Chapter 4.) In holding that the principal's actions in *Hazelwood* did not violate students' First Amendment rights to free speech, the Court articulated a new standard for school control over student expression. The Court stated:

> [W]e hold that educators do not offend the First Amendment by exercising editorial control over the style and content of student speech in school-sponsored expressive activities so long as their actions are reasonably related to legitimate pedagogical concerns. *Id.* at 273.

As the result of the decision in *Hazelwood*, various lower courts have picked up on the new standard and have applied it in a broader range of circumstances than just those dealing with students and student newspapers. The trend since *Hazelwood* appears to be that school authorities may exercise much greater control over activities involving both students and teachers if the school authorities are able to establish a connection between their actions (particularly "in class" or "in school" actions) and a "legitimate pedagogical concern." Moreover, the Court appears to have left the determination of what constitutes a "legitimate pedagogical concern" solely in the hands of school authorities.

Has the *Hazelwood* standard been applied in a case after a teacher claimed a right to academic freedom?

Take a moment and look back to the very first case in Chapter 1, which was used to introduce this book. In *Miles v. Denver Public Schools*, 944 F.2d 773 (10th Cir. 1991), the teacher not only claimed that the school district violated his free speech rights but he also claimed that his right to academic freedom under the First Amendment had been infringed. After recognizing the school district's legitimate pedagogical interests in preventing teachers from discussing unsubstantiated rumors, ensuring that teachers exhibit professionalism and sound judgment, and providing an educational atmosphere in which teachers do not make statements about students that embarrass those students among their peers, the court rejected the teacher's free speech claim. Further, the court found that the mild four-day paid suspension imposed on the teacher did not threaten to cast "a pall of orthodoxy" over the teacher's classroom. The *Miles* court concluded its opinion in no uncertain terms by stating, "We find no merit in the argument that Miles has a constitutional right—based on academic freedom or something else—that protects his substantiation of a rumor in a classroom setting." *Id.* at 779.

Are there other recent cases in which public school teachers have been unsuccessful in claiming a right to academic freedom?

Unfortunately (from a teacher's perspective), the answer is yes. In a Louisiana case, a high school history teacher was transferred to a middle school position. The teacher had divided her history class into groups and assigned each group a project dealing with a different aspect of the First Amendment. One group of students decided to focus on freedom of the press by publishing a newspaper entitled "Your Side." Although intended as a parody, the newspaper included articles which advocated cheating in class, mentioned erotic sexual dreams, and recommended that students who are bored should drop out of school. The school board objected to the teacher's methods and issued a written letter of reprimand in addition to transferring her to another building. After the teacher challenged her reprimand and transfer on the basis of an alleged First Amendment right to academic freedom, both a federal trial court and a federal appellate court found that the teacher had failed to rebut the school district's evidence that it had three legitimate reasons to transfer the teacher: inadequate supervision, violations of the school district's financial policies, and willful neglect. Thus, neither federal court ever actually considered the merits of the teacher's claim that her alleged First Amendment right to academic freedom had been violated. In addition, several other circumstances in the case served to work against the teacher's claim: she never sought the school administration's approval for the class project and she recognized that the newspaper content would create problems for the administration. *Moody v. Jefferson Parish School Board*, 2 F.3d 604 (5th Cir. 1993).

Do teachers *always* lose in court when they have claimed a right to academic freedom?

No, although teachers have been unsuccessful in claiming a right to academic freedom far more often than they have been successful. In some instances, though, teachers have pre-vailed. For example, in a 1980 Texas case involving an American history teacher, the teacher used a role-playing simulation exercise to introduce her students to the concept of life during the Reconstruction Era following the Civil War. After the class-room exercise resulted in controversy within the community, the teacher was told by her principal and other school district administrators not to discuss African-Americans and, for that matter, to avoid discussing anything in class that might generate controversy. However, since the teacher was not told to discontinue the role-playing exercise, she completed the activity with her class. Although she was subsequently recommended for re-employment at the end of the school year by her principal and the superintendent, the school board voted not to issue a contract. The Fifth Circuit Court of Appeals held that the teacher's classroom discussions involved constitutionally protected activity. The court declared that since the school board could not demonstrate that the controversy or disruption that resulted from the classroom activity impaired the teacher's instructional effectiveness, the teacher was entitled to be reemployed. The court ordered that the teacher be reinstated in addition to being given back pay and her attorney's fees. *Kingsville Independent School District v. Cooper*, 611 F.2d 1109 (5th Cir. 1980).

Similarly, in an earlier case involving a senior English class, the First Circuit Court of Appeals found that a high school teacher was protected by the principle of academic freedom when he assigned the students to read an article in the September 1969 *Atlantic Monthly* magazine. Prior to making the assignment, the teacher discussed with his class that the article contained a particularly offensive word which, in the court's words, "is a vulgar term for an incestuous son." The teacher made it clear to his students that anyone who found the assignment to be personally distasteful could have an alternate assignment. When the teacher was called to appear before the local school board on the following evening and defend his use of the offending article, the majority of the school board members asked the teacher if he would agree not to use the offensive word in class again. After the teacher stated that his conscience would not allow him to agree with this restriction, the school board voted to suspend and then discharge the teacher from further employment. The First Circuit Court of Appeals reviewed the article in question and found that the school board's rigorous attempt at censoring what the court concluded was a "scholarly, thoughtful and thought-provoking" article was improper under these particular circumstances. In addition to recognizing that the "sensibilities" of some parents who had been offended by the teacher's assignment did not constitute the proper measure for the appropriateness of this particular assignment, the court also noted the school board's "inconsistency" in sanctioning this teacher when there were at least five different books in the high school library which contained the same offensive word and which were readily available to all students. The court stated that, "It is hard to think that any student could walk into the library and receive a book, but that his teacher could not subject the content to serious discussion in class." *Keefe v. Geanakos*, 418 F.2d 359 (1st Cir. 1969).

What reasonable limits are normally placed on a teacher's academic freedom in the classroom?

Several generally well-settled principles govern a teacher's academic freedom: (1) a teacher may not use her classroom as a forum for imposing her own ideas or personal beliefs on a captive audience—the students; (2) the age and maturity of the students usually determine the limits as to what should or should not be discussed in class (since younger or less mature students are usually more impressionable, their teachers are provided correspondingly less leeway than are teachers of older and more mature students); (3) a school board may set reasonable limits within the curriculum which control excursions outside those limits; (4) a teacher is restricted to teaching within her own area(s) of expertise; and (5) a school board may impose other prohibitions by resolution or prescribe the way, if any, that controversial subjects will be handled in the classroom.

What kinds of topics may a school board place off limits for discussion in the classroom?

In addition to the kinds of topics which are "automatically" beyond the scope of the general limitations suggested in the previous question, unique circumstances may exist from time to time within a school district wherein the school board or school administration acts preemptorily to avoid an anticipated problem. This point is illustrated in a case that developed following a long and bitter teachers' strike in Michigan. After the strike ended and classes resumed, the school board enacted a resolution prohibiting teachers from mentioning or discussing the strike with their students. One teacher knowingly disobeyed the prohibition because of his strong and very personal feelings about the proper time and place to conduct a student discussion. As a result, the teacher was terminated for insubordination. A court upheld his dismissal on the grounds that the school board had a viable reason for prohibiting any discussion of the strike—to prevent further hard feelings and to get on with the school's educational purpose which had temporarily been neglected during the duration of the strike. The court felt that it was a reasonable exercise of school board authority to adopt a "no classroom discussion" policy promoting harmony and preventing further disharmony in the school and community. *Nigosian v. Weiss*, 343 F.Supp. 757 (E.D. Mich. 1971).

What if a school board has not adopted a specific policy guiding or prohibiting the use of certain instructional materials in the classroom?

This is where common sense and good judgment must prevail. For example, a tenured English teacher with thirty-two years of experience showed part of an R-rated movie to her seventh-grade reading class. The school board suspended the teacher without pay for a semester and put her on probation for the remainder of the school year. The teacher argued that the school board had no policy about showing films. Contrary to the teacher's claim, a court found substantial evidence to support the disciplinary action taken by the school board.

> The lack of an official policy, however, does not relieve the teacher of a general obligation to screen the content of materials prior to exposing students to them. We conclude that a teacher need not have violated a specific School Board policy in order to be found guilty of willful neglect of duty. *Roberts v. Rapides Parish School Board*, 617 So.2d 187, 191 (La.Ct.App. 1993), *cert. denied,* 619 So.2d 1068 (La. 1993).

Thus, in many cases it is presumed that teachers will anticipate the existence of certain standards regardless of whether the school board has adopted specific regulations to guide teacher conduct.

What is the difference, if any, between academic freedom in public elementary and secondary schools and academic freedom at the university level?

Simply put, the difference is in the way society views the function of the public schools in contrast with higher education. The latter encourages scholars to conduct research and discover truth wherever it may be found and to expand the knowledge base of usable and productive information. By contrast, elementary and secondary school teachers have a primary function of transmitting knowledge within the constraints and expectations of the school district curriculum.

Is a teacher's right to teach a derivative of his students' right to know?

Yes. A long line of court cases from across the country illustrate that a student's right to learn and be informed *(Lernfreiheit)* far exceeds a teacher's right to teach *(Lehrfreiheit)*. A teacher who contends that he has a right to academic freedom in the classroom should present such a right as a derivative of his students' right to know and learn. Thus, a teacher is arguing for freedom in the classroom not necessarily for himself but rather for his students. The teacher's role in this regard is that of the child advocate and it is this status which has long been recognized and given the greatest protection. Students should not be compelled to go outside the school to find materials or information that are germane to their educational interests. They should not be placed in the position of Charlie Brown, the character in Charles Schultz's comic strip "Peanuts," who once complained that going to school "interferes with my education." In a more serious—but not necessarily more accurate—vein, academic freedom thus becomes a question of whether or not the information or message that the teacher is trying to convey is something that these particular students in this particular school should be exposed to at this particular time. By extension, timing considerations and community values assume major roles in resolving this question. Similarly, another critical feature is whether or not the school board has adopted policies or implemented regulations governing certain types of classroom expression. In this regard, the question that needs to be asked is whether the teacher has been forewarned or placed "on notice" as to what will be tolerated by the school board.

How does a teacher keep from using her classroom as a forum for presenting her own ideas to students?

The answer to this question is easier said than done. If a teacher presents one side of an issue she is obligated in most cases to present the other side in such a way that her students can draw their own conclusions. For example, following World War II, there was a tendency by most teachers to avoid making classroom references to the Communist form of government found in the Soviet Union. That meant that students either had *no* access to accurate information about the governmental structure of an emerging world power or, perhaps worse, they only received *biased* information. Consequently, many state boards of education established requirements that schools must teach the merits and disadvantages of the Communist form of government as compared with other forms of government. These requirements imposed upon teachers (and schools) an obligation to present objective, well-researched information on various economic and governmental systems thus providing students a chance to draw their own conclusions as to the relative merits of each. Taken from a slightly different angle, this point was clearly emphasized by the United States Supreme Court's opinion in *Ambach v. Norwick*, 441 U.S. 68, 78-79 (1978):

> Within the public school system, teachers play a critical part in developing students' attitude toward government and understanding of the role of citizens in our society. . . . Further, a teacher serves as a role model for his students, exerting a subtle but important influence over their perceptions and values.

What limits may a school board place on the curriculum?

Local school boards generally require that certain materials be covered each year at each grade level. They can reasonably expect that these materials will be covered and that by limiting extraneous materials or "diversions," teachers will zero in on completion of what is contained in the school district's prescribed course of study.

Why is a teacher's area of expertise the only area in which he can "safely" teach?

One of the important factors a court will examine in deciding a question premised on academic freedom is the relationship between the teacher's assigned course of instruction and the inclusion of objectionable material or comments. For example, a teacher who talked about his own personal sexual exploits when he was supposed to be teaching speech was properly dismissed for failure to teach what he was paid to teach. *State ex rel. Wasilewski v. Board of Education, Milwaukee,* 111 N.W.2d 198 (Wis. 1961), *cert. denied,* 370 U.S. 720 (1962). The court concluded that if he had been teaching biology, then the teacher's conduct *might* have been protected. However, in this case, the court found that the teacher exceeded the bounds of his teaching area.

> [W]e deem that it constituted bad conduct which would warrant a discharge even though there was no express rule prohibiting it and he had received no warning to desist therefrom. As an intelligent person trained to teach at the high school level, [the teacher] should have realized that such conduct was improper. *Id.* at 206-207.

Classroom Activities

In making classroom assignments, what are some good "rule of thumb" limitations which a teacher should observe?

A teacher should consider three factors before making a potentially controversial classroom assignment. First, does the proposed assignment have a valid educational purpose; is it a viable part of the lesson plan; is it appropriate within the course of study? Second, is the potentially objectionable material suited to the age, maturity and general development of the students with whom it is being used? And, third, has the material in question (or other similar material or activities) been barred by prior school board action? In the absence of any previously implemented restrictions by the school board, a teacher is relatively free to assign materials in the classroom so long as they satisfy the first and second requirements. It does not matter that the materials are experimental, or that some "expert" testifies that the materials are suitable or unsuitable for students of that age. What counts is that the teacher uses the materials to teach a valuable lesson that is suited to the general maturation level of the children and had not previously been prohibited by the board of education. Of course, it always helps to seek and secure the approval of the school board or school administrators prior to venturing into "uncharted waters."

What is meant by having a "valid educational objective" for materials introduced into the classroom?

An Illinois case illustrates the use of materials that fail to have an educational objective and for which three non-tenured teachers lost their jobs. The three "team teachers" attended a showing of the movie "Woodstock" and obtained promotional material on the movie in the lobby. They took the material to their classrooms and handed it out without comment to elementary school children. The incident came to the attention of the school board, which terminated the teachers after charging that the materials met no valid educational purpose, that they were obscene, and that they induced students to sample marijuana and LSD. In this case, the teachers were unsuccessful in their attempts to show sound educational connections between their classroom activities and the Woodstock materials. *Brubacker v. Board of Education, District 149, Cook County, Illinois*, 502 F.2d 973 (7th Cir. 1974), *cert. denied*, 421 U.S. 965 (1975), *and clarified*, 527 F2d 611 (7th Cir. 1975).

Is abortion automatically an improper topic of discussion for a seventh-grade class?

A negotiated contract between a school district and its teachers' association provided that controversial issues could be studied in an unprejudiced and dispassionate manner whenever appropriate for the maturation level of a particular group of students. Thus, by contract, teachers were delegated authority to determine what controversial subjects should be covered in a given class. However, after a seventh-grade teacher was directed by the superintendent not to conduct a "debate" on the subject of abortion, the teacher filed a grievance. Upon review, the court concluded that the negotiated clause giving teachers the right to decide what topics to discuss in which classes was *ultra vires* (outside the power of the school board to delegate decision-making authority) and therefore was unenforceable as a grievance since the negotiated agreement was null and void on its face. *Board of Education of Rockaway Township, Morries County v. Rockaway Township Education Association*, 295 A.2d 380 (N.J.Super. Ct.App.Div. 1972).

Is birth control a proper subject for discussion?

Although the United States Supreme Court affirmed a lower court ruling that a state may statutorily prohibit the discussion of birth control in its public schools, the Court's 1974 ruling in *Mercer v. Michigan State Board of Education*, 379 F.Supp. 580 (E.D.Mich. 1974), *aff'd mem.*, 419 U.S. 1081 (1974) appears to have diminished in significance over the last two decades. From a legal perspective, the fact that the Court did not write an opinion in *Mercer* has left the scope and impact of the decision somewhat up in the air. Perhaps more importantly from a pragmatic point of view, the present-day focus on sexually transmitted diseases (especially AIDS) and teenage pregnancy has resulted in many states and local school districts going the opposite direction and mandating that sex education classes *do* teach students about effective birth control measures.

May a teacher be required to lead her students in the Pledge of Allegiance?

At least one court has held in the negative. A teacher's employment in New York was terminated because she refused to carry out a school board regulation requiring her to lead her class in pledging allegiance to the United States flag. Taking her case to court, she objected to the regulation on the grounds that Americans had not yet achieved "liberty and justice for all." Her attitude toward the flag was respectful and there was no indication that she tried to influence students to follow her example or that any classroom disruption resulted from her action.

Both at trial and in a subsequent appeal, the courts recognized that importance of balancing state and personal interests and noted that this teacher's students were not children but young men and women who should be forming their own judgments about a wide range of conflicting values. A critical feature in the case was the absence of any proselytizing efforts on the part of the teacher. *Russo v. Central School District No. 4*, 469 F.2d 623 (2nd Cir. 1972), *cert. denied*, 411 U.S. 932 (1973).

However, in a more recent case, the Seventh Circuit Court of Appeals upheld the dismissal of a probationary kindergarten teacher who refused to lead her students in the Pledge of Allegiance. The teacher, a Jehovah's Witness, also refused to teach her students patriotic songs. The court found that the school district had made a reasonable attempt at accommodating the teacher's religious beliefs and ultimately concluded that the school's compelling interest in adopting and controlling the curriculum justified the teacher's dismissal. In this sense, the school district had adopted a neutral stance with regard to this particular teacher's religious beliefs and was simply trying to provide a consistent and uniform educational program for all its students. *Palmer v. Board of Education of Chicago*, 603 F.2d 1271 (7th Cir. 1979), *cert. denied*, 444 U.S. 1026 (1980).

By comparison, may students refuse to recite the Pledge of Allegiance?

Yes. The United States Supreme Court held in 1943 that a student's attendance in a public school may not be conditioned upon saluting the flag if the student's refusal is premised on religious grounds. Similarly, a student may not be required to stand at attention nor may the student be banished from the classroom during the Pledge of Allegiance simply for refusing to recite it. *West Virginia State Board of Education v. Barnett*, 319 U.S. 624 (1943).

Should teachers be careful when selecting instructional materials for the classroom?

Absolutely. There must always be a certain amount of self-censorship, common sense, and good judgment. Frequently teachers have a tendency to try to grab students' attention by using startling or suggestive materials because this generation of youngsters is accustomed to being entertained by television and other types of media. However, it is a grave mistake if we assume that today's best-seller or video release is automatically a valid teaching tool in the classroom. As a precaution, it is almost always wise to confer with your building administrators or senior faculty for their seasoned advice as to the appropriateness of unorthodox instructional materials *prior* to exposing students to them.

Is there a First Amendment protection for teachers or students to use obscenities in the classroom?

No, although this issue is slightly more complicated since there is not a clearcut or precise definition as to what constitutes an obscene expression. In a non-school case, the United States Supreme Court held that contemporary community standards for obscenity should be interpreted on the local rather than a national level. The Court adopted the following test for identifying obscene material which is not worthy of free speech protection:

(a) whether "the average person, applying contemporary community standards" would find that the work, taken as a whole, appeals to the prurient interests; . . . (b) whether the work depicts or describes, in a particularly offensive way, sexual conduct specifically defined by the applicable state law; and (c) whether the work, taken as a whole, lacks serious literary, artistic, political or scientific value. *Miller v. California*, 413 U.S. 15, 24 (1973), *reh'g. denied*, 414 U.S. 881 (1973).

No wonder there have been so many court cases on the subject of obscenity: the definition is so vague that the justices on the Court as well as the judges in many lower courts cannot agree on a consistent basis as to precisely how the test should be applied. One problem with this approach is defining what the "community" consists of—a city, a county or a whole state. Connected with this is the inherent uncertainty for teachers as to how they are supposed to learn what people in "the community" think is objectionable or obscene, since there is such a wide divergence of opinion from house to house, between neighborhoods and from region to region.

In 1986, the United States Supreme Court did help clarify the issue of a student's use of vulgar or offensive speech in a school setting. In *Bethel School District No. 403 v. Fraser*, 478 U.S. 675, 677 (1986) (a case discussed at greater length in Chapter 4), the Court held that school administrators have broad authority to punish students for using "offensively lewd and indecent speech" in classrooms, assemblies and other school-sponsored educational activities—even if the speech does not "qualify" as being legally obscene.

Along these same lines, the use of profanity by a teacher in a classroom has also been denied constitutional protection. In 1986, the Fifth Circuit Court of Appeals held that a college instructor's use of words like "hell," "damn" and "bullshit" for the ostensible purpose of motivating students did not constitute protected speech and this justified termination. The teacher had ignored a warning to discontinue his use of such words. Further, he was unable to show how his profanity related to the subject matter of this course. *Martin v. Parrish*, 805 F.2d 583 (5th Cir. 1986). If this is the applicable standard at the college level (at least in some circuit courts), then surely the same or even a stricter standard would apply at the elementary and secondary school levels.

How free is a teacher to experiment with different teaching methods to "reach" a particularly difficult student (i.e., the "unteachable")?

Within reason, teachers have the professional freedom to try to teach "difficult" and/or learning disabled students according to the teacher's best judgment. For example, a teacher in California who had a class of non-readers asked the students to write about their own personal experiences in the hope they might develop an interest in better English. Because their writing was illegible, the teacher had the sentences typed and then distributed them to the class. Some of the sentences contained references to male and female genitalia as well as to sexual intercourse. Although the teacher intended to collect all the papers at the end of the period, one copy turned up in the principal's mailbox about two weeks later. After the principal asked the teacher to explain her methodology, the teacher was given a hearing and ultimately terminated. Upon appeal, a court concluded that under the circumstances the teacher's conduct did not make her unfit to teach; therefore, she should not have been dismissed. *Oakland School District v. Olicker*, 102 Cal.Rptr. 421 (Cal. 1972).

How far may a teacher go in urging students to follow a particular course of action?

The three levels of an individual's freedom of expression are: (1) the right to believe; (2) the right of advocacy; and (3) the right to urge action. Although the first two of these rights are commonly recognized as being broad in scope and depth, an individual's right to urge others to act is not as limitless—particularly where the action becomes non-peaceable, disruptive, or results in a riot. For example, teachers who urged students to resist the draft during the Vietnam war frequently faced dismissal for their actions. In one case, a teacher who urged his students to drive off military recruiters was terminated for his speech despite the fact that he was speaking on a matter of great public interest. Although a teacher may believe almost anything (e.g., that the world is flat), and can advocate that a certain course of action be taken in solving a problem, he oversteps the bounds of any First Amendment protections when his words produce disruption, riots, the destruction of property or the invasion of others' rights. *Birdwell v. Hazelwood School District*, 491 F.2d 490 (8th Cir. 1974).

May teachers use instructional techniques which emphasize a need for change in the school?

Yes, such techniques are not uncommon. For example, an Arkansas teacher's classroom water fountain had broken. Several weeks after the break occurred and during which time the fountain had not been repaired, the teacher asked her students during art class to draw pictures of classmates to express how each one felt. Some of the students drew pictures showing fellow students lying on the floor asking for water, and others drew wilted flowers. The teacher showed some of the drawings to the principal but did not go further. However, some of the pictures came to the attention of the superintendent, as did complaints about an incinerator outside the teacher's window which she said sent choking fumes into her classroom. At the end of the school year the teacher's contract was not renewed. After finding that the teacher was being punished for something she had to do—namely, protect the health of her students—a federal district court ordered the teacher's reinstatement with full rights and she received compensation for lost wages. *Downs v. Conway School District*, 328 F.Supp. 338 (E.D.Ark. 1971).

Are religious subjects and symbols barred from a public school classroom?

No, not directly. What is prohibited is the establishment of a religion by the state. Numerous legal challenges have been instituted against schools using Christmas carols, displaying creches depicting the nativity, and posting copies of the Ten

Commandments or other religious symbols on the grounds that such practices amount to the establishment of religion in violation of the First Amendment. For example, in *Stone v. Graham*, 449 U.S. 39 (1980), *reh'g denied*, 449 U.S. 1104 (1981), the United States Supreme Court held that a Kentucky statute requiring the posting of the Ten Commandments in every public school classroom in the state was unconstitutional even though the documents were procured with private contributions and despite each bearing a statement that the Commandments form the "secular" basis of the system of laws in the United States.

In resolving the case, the *Stone* Court concluded that the statute lacked a secular purpose. "The pre-eminent purpose for posting the Ten Commandments on schoolroom walls is plainly religious in nature. The Ten Commandments are undeniably a sacred text in the Jewish and Christian faiths and no legislative recitation of a supposed secular purpose can blind us to that fact." *Id.* at 41.

It should be noted that there is no constitutional prohibition against studying all religions on a comparative basis. Similarly, a teacher can use the Bible to study literature or history. The key factor is this: in matters of religion, the United States Supreme Court has directed that the state must remain "neutral" with regard to the establishment of any one religion or religion in general. While it is important to teach students moral and spiritual values, this must be done in such a way that no preference is shown for one religion over another; nor may any religion be hindered to the advantage of another.

May a state legislature compose a prayer and require that it be recited at a specified time in the classroom?

Not at the present time, despite a ground swell of resurgent national sentiment to the contrary. In *Engel v. Vitale*, 370 U.S. 421 (1962), the United States Supreme Court held that a New York state board of regents' ruling requiring the recitation of a daily prayer in all public schools violated the Establishment Clause of the First Amendment and was therefore unconstitutional. The next year, the Court also declared prayer and Bible reading resolutions in Baltimore, Maryland, and a state statute in Pennsylvania to be similarly offensive to the Establishment Clause. *Murray v. Curlett*, 374 U.S. 203 (1963) decided with *School District of Abington Township v. Schempp*, 374 U.S. 203 (1963). The classroom prayer issue resurfaced yet again when the Court decided in 1985 that an Alabama statute encouraging "silent prayer" during a period for silent meditation violated the Establishment Clause. *Wallace v. Jaffree*, 472 U.S. 38 (1984). However, because of the manner in which the *Wallace* case was litigated, the end result was that the "moment of silence" alone was not unconstitutional so long as there was no mention of or direct intent to encourage prayer. Thus, a student or a teacher may silently pray, just so long as a state or school district does not designate or require such a religious observance.

What about prayers at high school graduation ceremonies?

The issue of prayers being said at public high school graduation ceremonies has been one of the most hotly debated school law issues in recent years. In its 1992 decision in *Lee v. Weisman*, 112 S.Ct. 2649 (1992), the United States Supreme Court held by a 5-4 margin that school-sponsored sectarian or nonsectarian invocations and benedictions at graduation ceremonies violate the Establishment Clause of the First Amendment if the school selects the clergy and advises them as to what kind of prayer to give.

Shortly after *Lee* was decided, the Fifth Circuit Court of Appeals reconsidered an earlier ruling in *Jones v. Clear Creek Independent School District*, 977 F.2d 963 (5th Cir. 1993), *cert. denied*, 113 S.Ct. 2950 (1993). The court in *Jones* distinguished the facts and circumstances in that case from those in *Lee* and concluded that a graduation prayer *could* be said *if* the message was nonsectarian, nonproselytizing, and given by a student volunteer. Since the United States Supreme Court subsequently refused to grant *certiorari* to review the *Jones* decision, there is little certainty at this time as to how this issue will ultimately be resolved. Other federal circuit courts have reached conclusions contrary to the result in *Jones* (for example, in *American Civil Liberties Union v. Black Horse Pike Regional School District*, Dkt. No. 93-5368 (3rd Cir. 1993), *appeal dismissed per stipulation*; the Third Circuit Court of Appeals barred *any* form of prayer at graduation ceremonies). The only safe assumption is that continued litigation in this area is inevitable.

May a parent or teacher challenge teaching the theory of evolution in the public schools?

Yes, but probably not successfully. For example, a lawsuit filed in Texas sought to enjoin the teaching of evolution in the public schools on the grounds that putting it into the curriculum constituted the establishment of a sectarian, atheistic religion and inhibited the free exercise of religion in violation of the First Amendment. The court held that it could not by judicial decree do that which the United States Supreme Court had previously declared that state legislatures are powerless to do—prevent the teaching of the theory of evolution in public schools for religious reasons. The court found that "to require the teaching of every theory of human origin, as alternatively suggested by plaintiffs, would be an unwarranted intrusion into the authority of public school systems to control the academic curriculum." *Wright v. Houston Independent School District*, 486 F.2d 137, 138 (5th Cir. 1973), *cert. denied*, 417 U.S. 969 (1974).

Teacher Expression Outside the Classroom

May a school board control or limit a teacher's expression outside the classroom?

It all depends. For the most part, a teacher does not forfeit or forego his First Amendment free speech right to comment on matters of public concern simply because he is a teacher. The First Amendment also protects a teacher's right to circulate petitions on school premises during his free time unless such activity poses a serious and imminent threat to the order or efficiency of the school. Generally, the only limitations on this rule are when it can be demonstrated that the teacher's comments violate confidentiality or seriously impair the working relationship of the teacher with the administration and operation of the school. Another possible although less common exception might be when a teacher makes statements which he knows are baseless and primarily intended to injure someone's reputation.

What is the legal threshold for applying constitutional free speech standards to teachers?

In 1968, the United States Supreme Court established that since teachers enjoy a constitutionally protected right to speak on matters of public importance, the only way a school district could overcome this right would be to show that a "compelling state interest" necessitated imposing limits on the teacher's speech. As a direct result of the Court's decision in *Pickering v. Board of Education*, 391 U.S. 563 (1968), a teacher's personal interests in speaking out are balanced against the public's interest in effectively and efficiently operating its schools. Through subsequent litigation, the "*Pickering* balance" has evolved into a three-pronged "test" to determine whether a teacher's (or, for that matter, most any public employee's) comments are protected under the First Amendment.

Who was Pickering of *Pickering v. Board of Education* and what was he talking about?

Pickering was a public school teacher whose employment was terminated after he sent a letter criticizing the school board to a local newspaper. The letter concerned a tax increase being proposed by the school board as well as the way in which the superintendent of schools had previously handled proposals for generating new revenues for the school district. Because the letter contained some false statements and was determined to be detrimental to the interests of the school district, the teacher was dismissed. A unanimous United States Supreme Court overruled the termination after concluding that: the false statements contained in the letter had not been made carelessly; the statements were not aimed at any particular person with whom the teacher might come in contact during the normal school day; and, most importantly, the comments would not impede normal school operations. Again, in reaching its decision, the Court "balanced" the teacher's outside-the-classroom rights of expression on matters of public concern with the legitimate interests of the school board in assuring a safe and efficient learning environment. This "balance" clearly recognizes an individual teacher's protected right to speak freely outside of school; however, at the same time, it also restricts the right in light of the employer's interests.

What other cases have helped define the "test" for public employee free speech?

Following *Pickering*, the United States Supreme Court was asked to decide several additional public employee/free speech cases. In *Connick v. Myers*, 461 U.S. 138 (1983) (a case involving an assistant district attorney's use of a questionnaire to solicit her co-workers comments about working conditions and office morale), the Court distinguished between speech, which deals with "a matter of public concern," and that which is basically of a personal nature and thus not a matter of public concern. Another significant free speech case involving a teacher was *Mt. Healthy City School District Board of Education v. Doyle*, 429 U.S. 274 (1977). *Mt. Healthy* involved a nontenured teacher who made comments critical of the school district over a local radio station. When he was not given a continuing contract, the teacher claimed that his nonrenewal was in retaliation for his constitutionally protected speech. Although the Court agreed that the teacher's speech was entitled to protection, it also wanted to avoid the possibility of a marginally qualified teacher "ensuring" himself of future employment under a cloak of protected speech. Thus, the Court established another "prong" of its "test"—if a public employee is successful in sustaining his burden and showing evidence that an adverse employment decision was substantially based on the exercise of his protected right to free speech, then the employer must prove that it would have taken the same employment action *regardless* of the employee's comments. In other words, in the *Mt. Healthy* case, the school district needed to show that it would have nonrenewed Mr. Doyle regardless of his comments over the radio and that the no renewal decision was justified on the basis of other performance problems—in essence, that the teacher's speech was not the "motivating factor" behind the school board's decision not to rehire. Since the trial court had failed to make a determination along these lines, the case was remanded in order to determine whether the teacher's teaching performance had been substandard (e.g., arguments with fellow teachers, the use of obscene gestures directed at students, referring to students as "sons of bitches").

So, in a nutshell, what is the "test" that governs a teacher's freedom of expression outside the school?

Pickering and its progeny of cases established a "test" governing public employee free speech employment cases. Perhaps the best example of a case illustrating this test is found in *Roberts v. Van Buren Public Schools*, 773 F.2d 949 (8th Cir. 1985). In *Roberts*, the court stated:

Pickering v. Board of Education held that "[p]ublic employee[s do] not relinquish First Amendment rights to comment on matters of public interest by virtue of government employment." Consideration of such claims involves a three-step analysis. First, plaintiffs must demonstrate that their conduct was protected; second, plaintiffs must demonstrate that such protected conduct was a substantial or motivating factor in the adverse employment decision; and third, the employer may show that the employment action would have been taken even in the absence of the protected conduct.

Since *Connick*, identification of protected activity is a two-step process in itself. As a threshold matter, the speech must have addressed a "matter of public concern," then the interest of the employee in so speaking must be balanced against "the interest of the State, as an employer, in promoting the efficiency of the public services it performs through its employees." This "*Pickering* balance," as it has come to be known, looks to the following factors: 1) the need for harmony in the office or workplace; 2) whether the government's responsibilities require a close working relationship to exist between the plaintiff and co-workers when the speech in question has caused or could cause the relationship to deteriorate; 3) the time, manner, and place of the speech; 4) the context in which the dispute arose; 5) the degree of public interest in the speech; and 6) whether the speech impeded the employee's ability to perform his or her duties. (Citations omitted.)

What is a recent example of a case involving a teacher in which this test was used?

In *Vukadinovich v. Board of School Trustees of Michigan City Area Schools*, 978 F.2d 403 (7th Cir. 1992), *aff'd*, 978 F.2d 403 (7th Cir. 1992), *cert. denied*, 114 S.Ct. 133 (1993), a teacher and part-time volunteer basketball coach criticized the school board's hiring of its new superintendent. The comments were made at a school board meeting. Shortly after the meeting, the superintendent suggested to the teacher that it was not "appropriate" for the teacher to appear at school board meetings to say things that he "shouldn't be saying in public." *Id.* at 406.

More than two years later and following two separate incidents in which the teacher was convicted of a variety of criminal offenses (driving while intoxicated, public intoxication, resisting arrest, and operating a motor vehicle without a valid license), the school district terminated the teacher for immorality, neglect of duty, and other good and just cause. The teacher then sued the school board and several school administrators claiming that his termination had been in retaliation for his criticism of the school board's superintendent hiring decision. In a short but forceful opinion, the Seventh Circuit Court of Appeals applied the *Pickering* test and rejected the teacher's First Amendment argument. The court concluded that even if the teacher's public comments were constitutionally protected speech, his speech was not a substantial or motivating factor in the school board's employment action. What is perhaps most remarkable about this particular case is that it falls on the heels of a prior Seventh Circuit case decided four years earlier which involved the same teacher suing another school district for violating his First Amendment rights to free speech. In *Vukadinovich v. Bartels*, 853 F.2d 1387 (7th Cir. 1988), the teacher was nonrenewed after he was quoted in a newspaper article concerning his removal as an assistant high school basketball coach despite a winning season. In this case, the court ruled that the teacher's newspaper comments were not constitutionally protected since they did not involve a matter of public concern. In effect, even though the teacher's comments were published in the local newspaper, the focal point of the case was that he was articulating his own personal and private dissatisfaction with the termination of his coaching duties—and this was not a matter of public concern.

Are teachers entitled to speak at meetings of the local board of education?

Yes, if they ask for and are granted a place on the meeting agenda. They may also be given an opportunity to speak if the school board invites comments from the "general public" as part of its meeting agenda. Note, however, that school boards frequently impose time limitations (i.e., five minutes or so) on this latter type of "public input." Some school boards encourage teachers to attend and participate in their meetings. Such a stance on the part of the school board would serve to show teachers that they will not face employment retaliation simply because of remarks made by the teachers in open meetings—and even though some of the remarks might be critical of the school board. For example, a school board in Wisconsin was negotiating with the teachers' union which was seeking an "agency shop" agreement. An "agency shop" requires an employee to pay dues for union representation but it does not require union membership (as would be the case in a "union shop"). A non-union teacher was permitted to address the school board in opposition to the union's position. In response, the union claimed an unfair labor practice since it had exclusive bargaining rights with the school board. The United States Supreme Court held that a teacher may not be compelled to give up his right to speak to the board of education as a private citizen and non-union member. *City of Madison v. Wisconsin Employment Relations Commission*, 429 U.S. 167 (1976).

May a teacher engage in civil rights activities and still keep her job?

It all depends. As a general rule, so long as the outside activities do not interfere with her teaching competency in the classroom and the teacher does not use her classroom as a forum, such outside-the-classroom activity is protected. In *Johnson v. Branch*, 364 F.2d 177 (4th Cir. 1966), *cert. denied*, 385 U.S. 1003 (1967), an African-American teacher was dismissed because of her civil rights activities. The school board argued that the teacher was slighting her regular duties in supervising students, arriving late at extracurricular activities and checking in late at school and only shortly before classes were scheduled to begin. The court found that in the "emotional background" of a small southern town that was 51 percent African-American, the school board should give the teacher "the benefit of the doubt." It concluded that the grounds on which the school board based its termination decision were trivial in light of the teacher's twelve successful years in the same teaching position. The court held that the school board's actions in the case clearly showed that the board was biased in its judgment and actions in dismissing the teacher.

Loyalty Oaths

What is the history behind a teacher being required to take a loyalty oath as a condition of employment?

It goes without saying that anyone who could gain control of a nation's school system (as Hitler did in Germany) could wield a heavy club over its government. As early as 1925, the United States Supreme Court suggested that a state could require its teachers to "be of good moral character and patriotic disposition." *Pierce v. Society of Sisters of the Holy Names of Jesus and Mary*, 268 U.S. 510, 534 (1925). During both the First and Second World Wars, loyalty was important as evidenced by the popular slogan "the slip of a lip can sink a ship." During the McCarthy era in the 1950s, citizens and government were suspicious of any teacher who might have been a communist or socialist sympathizer. Part of the purpose of a loyalty oath was to see that a teacher did not use the classroom as a forum to downgrade our democratic system of government. This sentiment was an extension of a primary reason that schools exist—to provide continuity to the American way of life through preparing students to take their places as worthy, law-abiding citizens of the republic.

Why have teachers historically been singled out for special treatment under the freedom of speech and freedom of association guarantees?

In *Adler v. Board of Education of City of New York*, 432 U.S. 485 (1952), *overruled in part by Keyishian v. Board of Regents of the University of the State of New York*, 385 U.S. 589 (1967), a teacher challenged his discharge for belonging to an organization that advocated the overthrow of the government by force. This "guilt by association" principle was upheld by the United States Supreme Court on the basis of a teacher's potential influence in shaping the attitudes of young minds towards the society in which they live. The Court concluded that the state has a vital role in preserving the integrity of the schools. Following *Adler*, teachers with "unacceptable" beliefs or associations were free to live according to their principles—they just did not have a constitutionally protected right to maintain employment in a public school district. The "*Adler* rule" of guilt by association for governmental employees persisted until 1967 when it was overturned in *Keyeshian v. Board of Regents of the University of the State of New York*, 385 U.S. 589 (1967). In *Keyeshian,* the Court rejected the *Adler* rationale when it concluded that three teachers had been improperly dismissed for refusing to sign disavowal certificates stating that they had never been members of the Communist Party. The Court eliminated "guilt by association" as an employment condition for teachers because it distinguished between *membership* in a controversial organization and *participation* in unlawful activities. This relationship is analogous to the differentiation noted earlier in this chapter between belief and action.

May a teacher refuse to answer questions concerning his loyalty?

It all depends on who is asking the questions. In 1956, a teacher was called before a Congressional committee investigating Communist activities in the schools. During his testimony, the teacher claimed a right under the Fifth Amendment to remain silent. A section of the city charter in which he worked provided that if any teacher "took the Fifth," his employment would be automatically terminated. The United States Supreme Court held that the teacher had the right to remain silent and that the city charter was unconstitutional since the privilege against self-incrimination bears no presumption of an unfitness to teach. *Slochower v. Board of Higher Education*, 350 U.S. 551 (1956), *and overruled as stated in Caloric Corp. v. Commonwealth Unemployment Compensation Board of Review*, 452 A.2d 907 (Pa. 1982). However, the opposite result was found two years later in a Philadelphia case when the superintendent of schools questioned a teacher concerning his loyalty. The teacher refused to answer and was subsequently fired by the school board. The United States Supreme Court held that the termination was properly based on the teacher's insubordination and lack of candor—and not on his loyalty, per se. *Beilan v. Board of Philadelphia*, 357 U.S. 399 (1958), *reh'g denied*, 358 U.S. 858 (1958). The majority opinion in *Beilan* stated that a teacher's classroom conduct is not the sole basis for determining his fitness to teach.

May a teacher be required to annually list every organization to which she belonged or regularly contributed during the past five years?

No. In 1960, the United States Supreme Court overturned such a state requirement in *Shelton v. Tucker*, 364 U.S. 479 (1960). Such a requirement is "overly broad" and required Arkansas employees to be sanctioned where state officials did not share certain organizations' goals and objectives. Nor may teachers be required to swear that they are not "subversive persons." *Baggett v. Bullitt*, 377 U.S. 360 (1964). Another state's loyalty oath that was declared unconstitutional by the United States Supreme Court required all state employees to swear that they had never lent their "aid, support, advice, counsel or influence to the Communist Party." *Cramp v. Board of Public Instruction*, 368 U.S. 278 (1961).

Is the controversy over loyalty oaths still ongoing in the 1990s?

Not really, although the issue still comes up occasionally. Since the United States Supreme Court acted in the 1960s to invalidate a number of oaths which were essentially negative (e.g., "I am not a member of . . ."), states and school districts have been left with the option of using "positive" or "affirmative" oaths. Positive oaths (e.g., "I will support the Constitution and laws of . . .") tend to avoid the vagueness and overly broad characterizations common to most negative oaths. Thus, today a significant number of public school teachers in this country still are expected to swear or affirm their loyalty before beginning their employment. However, since positive oaths do not really add anything to the traditional expectations for good citizenship (i.e., agreeing to abide by the laws of the state and nation are, in a sense, a given part of life in the United States), it is arguable whether such oaths accomplish any useful purpose. After all, as the late Justice Black said in his concurring opinion written in *Speiser v. Randall*, 357 U.S. 513, 532 (1958), *reh'g denied*, 358 U.S. 860 (1958):

> I am certain that loyalty to the United States can never be secured by the endless proliferation of "loyalty" oaths; loyalty must arise spontaneously from the hearts of people who love their country and respect their government.

Case Resolutions

Case No. 1: The hemlock drink (see page 77)

Socrates was arguably the first in a long line of teachers who have refused to compromise a personal sense of truth and a strong belief in doing what was right. By a vote of 281 to 220, the jury found Socrates guilty of corrupting the youth of Athens. Next, the jury voted the death penalty by eight more votes than had been cast for the conviction. Although he could easily have escaped or bought his freedom, Socrates chose death rather than dishonor. "The hour of departure has arrived," he said, "and we go our ways—I to die, and you to live. Which is better God only knows." Socrates was put to death (by drinking hemlock) on a religious charge for what was essentially a political crime.

Case No. 2: Teaching human reproduction (see page 77)

The appeals court agreed with the trial judge that the private citizen/parent had immunity because her petition to the school board about the teacher's life science class was addressed to the proper authority having responsibility for the educational system within the community. Thus, setting aside the judgment against the private citizen/parent was affirmed.

However, as to the other defendants, the jury award on behalf of the teacher was upheld. The teacher had consulted with and obtained approval from the principal as to the methods and instructions used. Despite this approval, neither the school board nor school officials had been willing to defend the teacher when protests arose. In effect, the school board and the school administration caved in when the parents showed up at a school board meeting in an uproar, threatening to "tar and feather" the teacher. The teacher was subsequently suspended pending evaluation. Despite the teacher's protests to the contrary, the school board appointed a committee of parents to investigate their own complaints. When the teacher and his attorney raised questions about the lack of due process, the school board did not respond but the superintendent did issue a letter of reprimand to the teacher. The teacher sought reinstatement and removal of the reprimand letter from his file. The school board informed him that his rights under his contract would not be restored unless he accepted the letter.

After the jury found that the teacher's reputation and his professional career were damaged, the court held that the teacher's First Amendment rights were infringed and that his exercise of "academic freedom" had, in fact, consisted of following his superior's instructions. The discharge also affected the teacher's property interests and imposed a stigma on his reputation. He was never given a fair opportunity to present his defense and the school board did not act in good faith. The damages awarded were just compensation for the lifetime career damages that the teacher had suffered. *Stachura v. Truzkowski*, 763 F.2d 211 (6th Cir. 1985), *cert. granted in part*, 474 U.S. 918 (1985), *and reversed and remanded* [on issue of damages], 477 U.S. 299 (1986).

One final point: as noted in the citation to this case, the United States Supreme Court reversed the Sixth Circuit Court of Appeals' decision as to the issue of damages to which the plaintiff/teacher was entitled. The jury instruction on damages requested by the teacher erroneously asked for two types of compensatory damages—one for the teacher's actual injury, and another for the value of the violation to his constitutional rights. This second type of damages for the "value" or "importance" of a person's constitutional rights is not a permissible element of compensatory damages in a federal civil rights (§1983) case. Thus the jury award of a lump sum for compensatory damages makes it impossible to determine how much of the amount was impermissibly awarded for the second type of injury. A new trial on the issue of compensatory damages was ordered.

Case No. 3: When does a "teaching technique" reach the level of "immoral conduct"? (see page 78)

The teacher lost in this case. Missouri law defines "immoral conduct" as "conduct rendering the teacher unfit to teach," and it was one of six reasons under which a tenured teacher in that state can be terminated. The teacher was responsible for the publication; he edited and approved all the material. Students would view the publication as the teacher's tacit approval of the contents regardless of the teacher's contention that it was a "teaching technique" and thus was not immoral conduct as defined by the law. Noting that a school district has a right to disassociate itself from offensive speech and that teachers serve as role models, the court deferred to the school board's expertise in determining that the teacher's conduct constituted immoral conduct which rendered him unfit for his duties. The conduct was not just an exercise in bad judgment but "it violated even the most relaxed standards of acceptable human behavior." *Gerig v. Board of Education*, 841 S.W.2d 731, 735 (Mo.Ct.App. 1992).

Case No. 4: Academic freedom in assigning homework (see page 79)

The three-month suspension without pay was upheld by the court. The state commissioner of education is not bound by the same legal restrictions as are courts when deciding the scope of a teacher's right to academic freedom. Thus, the commissioner's determination can properly include consideration of educational policy. The commissioner found that the homework assignment was appropriate for students of that age and maturity and student opinions were not adversely affected by the teacher's "editorial." The assignment was consistent with a teacher's role in eliciting student opinion and providing assignments to strengthen analytical skills. The school district's attempt to interfere with the homework assignment was an unreasonable intrusion into the teacher's academic freedom. However, the commissioner agreed that the school district had final authority to review and assign grades and the superintendent's request for the teacher's lesson plan and grade books did not intrude on her academic freedom. The teacher's refusal to turn over her books was sufficient justification for the three-month suspension without pay. *Malverne Union Free School District v. Sobol*, 586 N.Y.S.2d 673 (N.Y.App.Div. 1992).

Case No. 5: Showing objectionable films in class (see page 80)

In this case, the teacher prevailed. Louisiana law does not allow removal of a "permanent" teacher except for "willful neglect of duty, or incompetency or dishonesty [or being a member of a prohibited group]." This law is designed to protect the job security of teachers and has been liberally interpreted in their favor as the intended beneficiaries of the teacher tenure act. While the facts indicate that this teacher may have been incompetent at selecting appropriate films for student viewing, there was no evidence that his performance as a teacher was deficient in other substantive ways. The teacher's past record was excellent. Although some discipline was proper, the court found that dismissal in these circumstances was an abuse of the school board's discretion and too harsh a remedy. The case was remanded to the school board to determine other disciplinary action consistent with the court's views. In effect, the court concluded that the teacher's offense in this case was remediable. *West v. Tangipahoa Parish School Board*, 615 So.2d 979 (La.Ct.App. 1993), *cert. denied*, 618 So.2d 414 (La. 1993).

Case No. 6: Speaking of pay (see page 80)

The teacher in this case was found to have been outside the bounds of protected free speech. For the most part, his letter was a personal grievance responding to a change in school district payment procedures which the Fourth Circuit Court of Appeals concluded was not protected by the First Amendment. However, the part of the teacher's letter that alleged school district mismanagement was a matter of public concern and must thus be weighed against the state's interest in providing a sound and efficient public education. By advocating a "sick-out," the teacher encouraged violation of employment policies and professional standards. A person does not give up his First Amendment rights to free speech and to comment on public issues simply by being a teacher; however, when doing so conflicts with the state's interest in providing public education, the teacher's and the state's interests must be balanced to see which prevails. A teacher's speech is protected when (1) he speaks as a citizen about a matter of public concern, and (2) when his interest in exercising free speech is not outweighed by the state's countervailing interest in providing the public service the teacher was hired to help perform.

In this case, the court found that the personal complaints about employment matters did not constitute speech about matters of public concern but, instead, were more concerned with the speaker's self-interest. The court also held that any comments in the letter which deserved First Amendment protection (i.e., mismanagement of funds) were outweighed by the state's interest in providing public education and the school's interest in having its employees follow sick leave policies. Consequently, the court held that the school district's actions were proper and the teacher's termination was affirmed. *Stroman v. Colleton County School District*, 981 F.2d 152 (4th Cir. 1992), *amended and corrected,* (4th Cir. 1993)[citation unavailable].

Case No. 7: Troublemaker or victim of retaliation? (see page 81)

The court agreed that the teacher's termination eight months after public controversy over the reading program was not sufficient to show a violation of free speech rights—however, there was more. The evidence showed the teacher was outspoken, made herself ineligible for a new position and lied about the student who left the school. But it also showed that a jury could reasonably believe that the teacher was improperly terminated and that she had been deprived of a job to which she was entitled by the administrators' retaliatory course of conduct following her landing on the superintendent and principal's "hit list." The jury returned a verdict against the superintendent for $5,036.42 in compensatory and $39,000 in punitive damages. The verdict against the principal was for $5,036.42 in compensatory and $26,000 in punitive damages. Attorney fees of $17,958.50 (out of $21,701 requested) were also awarded to the teacher.

As noted in an appellate court opinion following an appeal after the trial, the superintendent and the principal were described as having been "not particularly good [n]or as particularly forthcoming witnesses." Further, the teacher demonstrated that the administrators "acted with reckless or callous indifference to the plaintiff's constitutional rights, or with evil motive or intent." This factor allowed the jury to consider punitive damages for the administrators' campaign of harassment. As the court noted, punitive damages "are designed by the law to punish extraordinary misconduct." The administrators attempted to show that punitive damages were not justified because their conduct was not "that bad" in comparison to other situations. In other words, they argued that a retaliatory dismissal for the teacher's exercise of her First Amendment rights is not enough to warrant punitive damages. The court dismissed this argument stating that it belittled the First Amendment. Consequently, the punitive damage awards, though high, were not excessive, and the superintendent and principal did not present any evidence to show that this "would send [them] to the poorhouse." *Fishman v. Clancy*, 763 F.2d 485 (1st Cir. 1985).

Chapter Four
Student Issues

For nearly 200 years after our country declared its independence, it was generally assumed that the United States Constitution stopped short of according public school students with a substantial number of protected rights. For most of our nation's history, courts—and most noticeably the United States Supreme Court—had usually been reluctant to interfere with the ways in which schools handled students. In a sense, public school teachers, administrators and local school board governing bodies had relatively free rein to impose discipline, restrict student conduct, dictate how schools would be organized, and, in a broader sense, to "manage" students and the educational mission with only nominal regard for the kinds of constitutionally protected rights enjoyed by adults in our society. This traditional way of "doing business" began to change with the landmark desegregation case decided by the United States Supreme Court in 1954—*Brown v. Board of Education of Topeka*, 347 U.S. 483 (1954).

In *Brown*, the Court held that public school students could not be discriminated against in their admittance to schools on the basis of race. The Court rejected the "separate-but-equal" doctrine announced by the Court nearly 60 years earlier in *Plessy v. Ferguson*, 163 U.S. 537 (1896). *Plessy* had established the concept that although the Constitution required racial equality, it did not mandate racial commingling or the abolition of social distinctions based on skin color. In overruling *Plessy*, the Court held that the segregation of public school students due to their race violated the Equal Protection Clause of the Fourteenth Amendment because minority students were being deprived of equal educational opportunities.

Until recently, the overall trend toward an ever-expanding recognition of constitutionally-protected student rights and freedoms seemed to be moving fairly inexorably in one direction. For example, in terms of student freedom of expression the Court's 1969 decision in *Tinker v. Des Moines Independent Community School District*, 393 U.S. 503, 506 (1969) included the frequently-cited principle that students do not "shed their Constitutional rights to freedom of speech or expression at the schoolhouse gate." Since students are "persons" under the Constitution, the Court held that school officials may properly infringe on students' First Amendment rights *only* when it is likely that the expression of opinion would materially and substantially interfere with the school's operation and the rights of other students to learn. As a result of the *Tinker* decision, students protesting the United States' involvement in the Vietnam War were allowed to wear black armbands to their public schools so long as their doing so did not create a disruption or disorder.

For the most part, the upswing in students' rights beginning with *Brown* and reinforced by *Tinker* (and several other landmark cases discussed elsewhere in this chapter) continued throughout the 1970s and well into the 1980s. It wasn't until the Court decided two important student expression cases in 1986 and 1988 that any significant change in this long-developing trend became apparent.

In the first of these cases, a student delivered a lewd speech while nominating a friend for a student council office during a high school assembly. *Bethel School District No. 403 v. Fraser*, 478 U.S. 675 (1986). The Court depicted the student's speech as using "an elaborate, graphic, and explicit sexual metaphor" and concluded that school officials have broad authority to discipline students for using "offensively lewd and indecent speech" during school activities even if the speech did not cause a disruption. *Id.* at 677. In *Bethel*, the Court essentially balanced the student's freedom of expression against the school's interest in teaching students the boundaries of socially appropriate conduct. The Court concluded that protecting minors from exposure to vulgar language created a viable basis upon which to approve the sanctions that the school imposed on the student. In doing so, the Court upheld the student's three-day suspension and the school's removal of his name from a list of student candidates being considered for giving a speech during the school's graduation ceremony.

In the other recent landmark case, the Court in *Hazelwood School District v. Kuhlmeier*, 484 U.S. 260 (1988), was faced with a principal who unilaterally deleted two pages from the high school newspaper prior to its publication by the journalism class. The two newspaper pages contained student-written articles dealing with the effect of divorce and teenage pregnancy. In deciding in favor of the school authorities who were sued by students objecting that their First Amendment rights to freedom of the press had been violated, the Court distinguished the right of individual students under *Tinker* to express personal and controversial views on school grounds from the school's right in *Hazelwood* to exercise broad discretion over school newspaper articles which may be unsuitable for immature audiences. The Court held that the school newspaper—as part of the school curriculum—was not a "public forum" and therefore school officials were entitled to regulate the contents of the newspaper in a reasonable manner so long as doing so was related to a "legitimate pedagogical concern." *Id.* at 273.

You may recall from reading about the *Miles* case in the introductory chapter to this book that other courts have applied the *Hazelwood* rationale to circumstances extending far beyond school newspapers and, in doing so, have empowered school administrators with greater control over school operations—including certain aspects of a teacher's claim to academic freedom.

The "case descriptions" and "questions and answers" which follow provide an overview of the wide variety of student issues which teachers encounter in schools on a regular basis. As is the case in the other chapters in this book, it is impossible to discuss *every* student issue that may arise; therefore, the primary objective for selecting cases for this chapter is to provide the reader with a sampling of student-related legal issues that are fairly common and perhaps more likely to raise concerns of particular interest to teachers. Attention has also been given to the student-related cases decided by the United States Supreme Court.

Case Descriptions

Case No.1: More than just muffins
or
Due process never takes a holiday!

A senior high school student in New York was a member of the varsity wrestling team. He had an outstanding academic record in addition to his state championship and Olympic caliber athletic potential. While the student was a spectator at a junior varsity wrestling match at his school in 1992, he and other students entered the cafeteria and stole eight packages of muffins which they later gave to the junior varsity team in the locker room. When the incident was discovered, the student freely admitted his participation and he was disciplined for his misconduct. His principal imposed academic suspension for two days, social probation for the remainder of the school year, and notified the student's parents of the punishment by a letter confirming a conversation with the student's mother. Later, the athletic director stated that he had also suspended the student from further participation in the wrestling program because his conduct was contrary to the athletic code of conduct in the Interscholastic Athletic Guide. Although the athletic director contended that the principal and coach concurred in this decision, it was not mentioned in the letter notifying the student's parents of the disciplinary actions. Following the school district's internal procedures, the student's parents quickly sought to protest their son's suspension from the wrestling program and immediately upcoming tournaments. They argued that the disciplinary measures were arbitrary and capricious, grossly disproportionate to the offense and would destroy the student's chances to obtain a college athletic scholarship. When the parents approached the school board, the athletic director and superintendent were both out of town over a holiday break. Consequently, the school board refused to address the situation until the superintendent reviewed the matter. The assistant superintendent (who was in attendance at the school board meeting) also refused to take any action after concluding that the matter was out of his hands. The frustrated parents then sought a court order to annul the student's suspension from the wrestling team. Was the punishment in this case disproportionate to the crime or was it deserved? Should the student be allowed to participate in the upcoming wrestling events? Were academic suspension and social probation appropriate?

Case No. 2: Classroom management as an aspect of teaching performance

A tenured teacher with fourteen years experience was employed as a library media specialist. She was also assigned to teach two seventh-grade geography classes. In order to evaluate the teacher's performance, her principal observed her two all-boys classes where he saw students talk without raising their hands, become disruptive, and make inappropriate remarks. The teacher subsequently received written evaluations which were generally favorable but which included a recommendation to improve student discipline. The teacher was also given a "plan of improvement" to address the lack of student discipline, and she received a letter of admonishment setting out areas of concern, none of which covered her performance in library management. The principal counseled the teacher but felt that her classes remained "out of control." After a series of meetings, the teacher was told that the principal would recommend she not be renewed. The superintendent and school board concurred and did not renew the teacher's contract for "willful neglect of duty and incompetency." Following a hearing, however, a hearing panel ordered reinstatement since there was insufficient evidence that the teacher had failed to perform essential job duties. The school district went to court and the trial court reversed the hearing panel's reinstatement order. On appeal, the teacher argued that she did not purposefully violate a rule or duty owed to the school, she was only given thirteen instructional days to resolve alleged teaching deficiencies, and there was no proof that she was incompetent as defined by law. Do you think the teacher was treated unfairly? Is classroom management a tough issue to deal with in the context of teaching performance?

Case No. 3: Procedure to object to discipline of a handicapped child

Two siblings were tested and evaluated for placement in their school's Personal/Social Adjustment Program (PSA program). Their mother met with school personnel, agreed to the placement, and signed a consent form which allowed her to ask for a hearing or request a reevaluation of the students at any time. Subsequently, both children were placed in the program. During the school year both were disruptive and violated school rules. As a result, they were often required to stay in a three-by-five foot room for "time-out" periods and in-school suspensions. Although aware of these disciplinary techniques, neither of the children's parents requested a change in placement or objected to use of the "time-out" room; neither did they avail themselves of hearing or administrative procedures which were available. Instead, the parents filed a court action alleging constitutional violations resulting from use of the "time-out" discipline. The school district argued that the case should be dismissed because the parents did not first pursue their remedies under the Education for All Handicapped Children Act (EAHCA and now known as the Individuals with Disabilities Education Act or IDEA). This act imposes extensive procedural requirements on states that receive federal funds for educational purposes. It provides procedures to resolve complaints by parents about student evaluation or placement. Do you think that the disciplinary measures giving rise to the parents' court action are included in the provision of a "free appropriate public education" which is guaranteed under the IDEA? Do you agree with the parents that the disciplinary measures which they are protesting constitute an improper "change in placement" under the IDEA?

Case No. 4: Search and seizure

A teacher with fifteen years of teaching experience reported to the principal that a student had reported another student (Snyder) offering to sell marijuana. As reported to the teacher, Snyder revealed three bags of marijuana in a video cassette case which he then placed in his bookbag. After the teacher repeated the information to the assistant principal, the school administrators decided to search Snyder's locker without first confronting him. The search produced the bags of marijuana which were then taken to the principal's office. Snyder was brought to the office and asked if he had offered to sell marijuana. He admitted that he had but that he had never done such a thing before and that he was trying to "back out" of his participation in the deal and get the person who provided him with the marijuana to come and pick it up.

After the police were called, they gave Snyder his Miranda warnings (i.e., that he has the right to remain silent; that any statements he makes may be used as evidence against him; that he has the right to the presence of an attorney; and that if he cannot afford an attorney one will be appointed for him prior to any questioning if he so desires), and took him to the police station. The person who Snyder had called to come and get the marijuana (a former graduate of the school) was also picked up in the school.

At his criminal trial, Snyder tried to get the evidence of the marijuana and his admissions suppressed by arguing that he should have been advised of his rights before talking to the school administrators. What rights did Snyder have in this situation? Should his locker have been searched on the basis of the information provided to the teacher? Was Snyder tricked into admitting his intent to sell marijuana?

Case No. 5: Student-to-student sexual harassment under Title IX

A junior high student (Jane Doe) claimed that school officials did nothing to stop or curtail sexual harassment inflicted on her by fellow students at school during her seventh- and eighth-grade school years. The harassment, which began in 1990, was mostly verbal (e.g., references and rumors spread about her activities with hot dogs). Jane reported the comments to her counselor and asked him to help put a stop to the harassment. The counselor did nothing even though Jane went to him approximately every other week. He said all he could do was warn the other students; he did not advise Jane of the school's Title IX Student/Parent Grievance Policy or direct her to see the Title IX compliance officer for the school. (Title IX is a provision in the education amendments passed by Congress in 1972 that prohibits gender discrimination against participants in or beneficiaries of federally funded educational programs.) He also did not tell Jane's parents about possible recourse under Title IX when they spoke to him; instead, he told them that "things would be all right" and the "kids just needed time to adjust."

The harassment continued. On one occasion in 1991, the counselor did call two male students into his office and gave them a warning about sexual harassment; however, he said he could not do anything about harassment by female students except to ask them to "work it out" with Jane. The comments continued through the summer of 1991 and into Jane's eighth-grade year. She again made frequent reports to the counselor as he had requested her to do, and got the reputation as a tattle-tale. Increasingly, it became emotionally difficult for Jane to go to school. Jane's parents continued to speak with the counselor who assured them that he would talk to the students and that eventually the kids would "mature."

The incidents escalated, some became physical, and eventually the situation came to the attention of the Title IX officer and vice-principal who had not been informed by the counselor about Jane's harassment because "he didn't feel it was important." Finally, Jane's parents transferred her to a private school in March 1992. Along with having to pay tuition to attend the private school, Jane suffered physical and mental injuries as a result of the harassment. She filed suit against the counselor, principal and school district. How do you think Jane Doe's suit under Title IX was decided? Did Jane have a remedy under Title IX? Should the counselor have been more attentive to Jane's problem, and is he liable for damages she suffered as a result of his failure to provide appropriate assistance? Should the school district be liable for Jane's damages?

Case No. 6: Sexual harassment by a teacher under Title IX

In a case with a unique twist, a mother had been romantically involved with a teacher at her daughters' school in 1987 and 1988. Sometime later, one of the daughters alleged that the teacher molested her when he accompanied the family on a trip in 1988. The mother reported this to the police who investigated and reported the allegations to the school administration. Although the teacher admitted abusing cocaine and alcohol, he denied that anything improper had happened with the daughter. Subsequently, criminal charges were filed, the teacher was placed on compulsory leave of absence without pay, and his teaching credential was suspended. The charges were later dismissed on the condition that the teacher participate in counseling. His credential was reinstated in 1989 pending possible disciplinary action. Also, in 1989, a second daughter told her mother that the same teacher had molested her in 1987. This matter was investigated but charges were never filed against the teacher. In the following years, this second daughter went through counseling and did very poorly while attending several different schools. In the meantime, the teacher continued teaching music at the school where the first daughter had previously attended and where the second daughter might have attended had the teacher not been there. The mother claimed that the continuing presence of the teacher created such a hostile environment that the daughters were deprived of full enjoyment of their education at that school and that the school district was liable for sex discrimination under Title IX. Did this mother have a viable Title IX claim on behalf of her daughters?

Case No. 7: Play ball?

A high school junior played basketball during the 1990-1991 season. At the end of the regular season and before the play-offs, the student withdrew from school suffering from a serious sinus infection. Although the student had passed physicals, he apparently had the sinus infection throughout the school year and it may have adversely affected his grades during the fall semester. By withdrawing, he did not receive grades for the spring semester. Because all of the student's classes were year-long, it was felt to be in his best interest to repeat his entire junior year in the 1991-1992 school year. When he returned to school in the fall of 1991, the Indiana High School Athletic Association's (IHSAA) eligibility rules counted the previous year against his player eligibility. Due to the fact that he withdrew from school as a result of a serious illness, the student sought a waiver of the eligibility rule. The request was denied. When the matter went to hearing before the IHSAA executive committee, the commissioner learned that the student had not received any academic credit for the 1990-1991 year which affected his current eligibility to play regardless of whether a medical waiver was granted. Although the executive committee denied his appeal for a waiver with respect to his player eligibility, it did not rule on his eligibility to play beginning in the fall of 1991. However, the commissioner later made a unilateral ruling that the student was not eligible to play during the fall of 1991 because the student's enrollment in subjects which he was repeating did not meet eligibility requirements. After another hearing, the executive committee upheld the commissioner's decision. Prior to the latest hearing, the student filed a court action challenging the ruling making him ineligible to play. After various legal maneuverings, a state court ruled that the purpose of the IHSAA eligibility rule was to prevent students from obtaining longer eligibility for athletic participation; with that as the primary objective, the rule was arbitrary and capricious as applied to this student who was denied an opportunity to participate due to his illness and through no fault of his own. Thus, the court held that the rule violated the student's rights to equal protection and due process. The court declared the student eligible to play and ordered that the school and IHSAA allow him to participate beginning in the spring of 1992. Naturally, there was another appeal to a higher court. What do you think that court decided? Should the eligibility rule be applied differently depending on the unique circumstances in a given situation?

Student Discipline and Control

What is meant by the term *in loco parentis*?

The Latin term *in loco parentis* means "in the place of a parent." In a school setting, the term has historically meant that teachers and administrators have the same rights and obligations to regulate student behavior as would a typical parent acting in a child's best interest under similar circumstances. In other words, under the doctrine of *in loco parentis*, a teacher or administrator exercising the same kind of authority and discretion that an "average" parent would have been likely to use in a given situation will enjoy legal protection when disciplining a student.

Where did the doctrine of *in loco parentis* originate?

Greek slaves were often used by Roman parents to serve as teachers and instruct the Roman children. Because the "master" (or teacher) must outrank his students, the legal fiction of *in loco parentis* was invented and has been passed down to our contemporary culture through the English system of education. The British historian Sir William Blackstone noted that "a parent may delegate part of his parental authority, during his life, to the tutor or schoolmaster of his child; who is then *in loco parentis*, and has . . . a portion of the power of the parent, viz., . . . restraint and correction as may be necessary to answer the purposes for which he is employed." (*Blackstone's Commentaries*, 453.) As is evident in the latter portion of this quote, a teacher does not have absolute control over students, but only over students' educational needs while attending school.

Is the doctrine of *in loco parentis* still viable?

Although the scope of teacher authority under the *in loco parentis* doctrine in contemporary education has been limited in such areas as student expression and the right to assemble, the concept of having professional educators assume the "role" of a parent when dealing with routine classroom management and discipline is still viable. However, even though the doctrine vests educators with certain "rights" (i.e., to direct student learning experiences and maintain discipline), it also imposes "responsibilities" to ensure that children under a teacher's care and supervision be given a safe place in which to study and learn. Thus, it is the "responsibility" aspect of the doctrine that relates to many negligence and civil rights deprivations, covered more fully in Chapter 5.

Of the major problems confronting the public schools, which are mentioned most frequently by the general public?

The 26th Annual Phi Delta Kappa/Gallup Poll of the Public's Attitudes Toward the Public Schools published in the September

1994 issue of *Kappan* reports that the growth of "fighting, violence and gangs" and the "lack of discipline" in schools are perceived as the two most serious problems in the United States' public schools. Both of these problems were mentioned by eighteen percent of the poll respondents. "Lack of proper financial support" for schools and "drug abuse" trailed with thirteen percent and eleven percent of the survey responses, respectively. When compared with the survey results and responses generated ten years earlier, it is interesting to note that while "lack of discipline" was the top-ranked category with twenty-five percent of the responses in 1985, "fighting" (as a category) was mentioned as the most significant problem only one percent of the time. From all of this, it is easy to see that at the present time the American public appears to place an extremely high priority on the importance of controlling and disciplining students within the school setting.

How has the use of corporal punishment in the schools developed over time?

Historically, public school teachers could administer corporal punishment to unruly students. When asked in 1975 to examine the propriety of corporal punishment in a public school setting, the United States Supreme Court affirmed (without a formal opinion) a lower court's ruling that a statute allowing reasonable corporal punishment for the purpose of maintaining order was constitutional if it met three criteria: (1) a student had to be warned in advance that certain conduct was punishable by paddling (with an exception given for particularly disruptive or antisocial misconduct); (2) a second teacher or school official who is knowledgeable about the reason for the punishment must be present when the punishment is inflicted; and (3) parents are entitled upon request to a written account of the punishment and the name of the observer who was present. *Baker v. Owen*, 395 F.Supp. 294 (M.D.N.C. 1975), *aff'd*, 423 U.S. 907 (1975). In addition, the *Baker* Court acknowledged that parents do not necessarily have a right to veto the use of corporal punishment with a child. Two years later, the Court held that the use of corporal punishment or "spanking" in the public schools did not violate the Eighth Amendment's bar of cruel and unusual punishment so long as the punishment was reasonable under the circumstances. *Ingraham v. Wright*, 430 U.S. 651 (1977). The Court ruled that in the event that punishment is "degrading or unduly severe," the threat of a civil suit and/or the possibility of criminal sanctions provides a student with sufficient remedies to protect against unreasonable punishment. In addition, the Court found that the administration of corporal punishment in a school setting did not violate the Due Process Clause of the Fourteenth Amendment. Although some states and individual school districts have subsequently prohibited or significantly restricted the use of corporal punishment in their schools, *Baker* and *Ingraham* still establish the parameters for its use in those public schools where such disciplinary actions are employed. It is also worth remembering that teachers who violate state corporal punishment statutes or local school board policies governing the same may be subject to employment termination or other sanctions for their actions.

Is detention or other short term in-school suspension a legally acceptable means of controlling student behavior?

Yes. Courts have routinely upheld the right of teachers and school administrators to impose detention on unruly and nonattending students. For example, students in a Nebraska school district objected to a school rule specifying periods for after-school detention in the event of unexcused absenteeism and tardiness. The students challenged the enforceability of the rule on the basis that it was unconstitutionally vague. A federal district court disagreed with the students' contention and held that requiring students to make up lost instructional time did not give rise to a constitutional violation. *Fielder v. Board of Education*, 346 F.Supp. 722 (D.Neb. 1972).

What rules apply when students are being suspended from school?

Two landmark cases decided by the United States Supreme Court in the mid-1970s first established and then added "clout" to the essential elements which must be followed when suspending a student from school. In *Goss v. Lopez*, 419 U.S. 565 (1975), the Court held that students who are suspended for up to ten days must be accorded minimal constitutional protections. These protections involve: (1) giving the student oral or written notice of the charges; (2) providing an explanation of the evidence against the student if she denies the charges; and (3) giving the student an opportunity to present her view of the alleged incident. These required procedures are expected to precede the student's suspension unless her continued presence creates a threat to other persons, property, or the academic program. If immediate removal is necessary for reasons of safety or to ensure a return to normal school operations, then the student is entitled to notice and her hearing within a reasonable time. Since the Court found that students have both a constitutionally protected "property" interest in receiving a public education as well as a "liberty" interest in their reputation and "good name," a pre-suspension "notice and informal hearing" is what is required under the Due Process Clause of the Fourteenth Amendment. Further, the Court also noted that suspensions from school for longer periods of time (i.e., suspensions of more than ten days or expulsions) will generally require more formal procedures. These steps include allowing the student to be represented by legal counsel and the right to present and confront (and, in some cases, cross-examine) witnesses at a hearing.

In 1978, the Court gave added weight to the procedural due process protections first recognized in *Goss* when it held that school officials were *not* entitled to qualified immunity from damages under a civil rights lawsuit when they suspended two students from school for twenty days without the benefit of any type of adjudicative hearing. *Carey v. Piphus*, 435 U.S. 247 (1978). In *Carey*, the Court said that the school officials *should have known* that a lengthy suspension without the benefit of a hearing would clearly violate the procedural due process requirements addressed in *Goss*. The Court ruled that regardless of whether the students incurred and could prove that they were actually injured as a result of their suspensions, they were still entitled to recover *nominal* damages (i.e., amounting to no more than $1.00 but representing an absolute right to procedural due process—and ensuring the additional recovery of their attorneys' fees and costs associated with their litigation). As an aside, it is interesting to note the reasons why the two students in *Carey* were suspended—one for smoking marijuana on school property during school hours and the other for wearing an earring in violation of a school policy designed to discourage gang activities in school.

What about when students are expelled from school?

As suggested in the previous question and response, students facing expulsion or long term suspension from school are entitled to a more formalized procedure which will ensure fairness but which usually will not amount to a full blown judicial hearing. As a general rule, a student facing expulsion or suspension for longer than ten days is entitled to be represented by legal counsel or an adult advisor. It should be noted, however, that even though students subject to an expulsion proceeding may have a right to confront and cross-examine their accusers, the scope of this right is not as broad as it might be in a criminal proceeding. Depending on the circumstances, it may not be proper to allow a student (or representative legal counsel) the right to confront and cross-examine *all* witnesses relied upon by school authorities—especially if such witnesses are fellow students. Also, some states have statutorily shortened the ten-day requirement in *Goss*; for example, students facing suspension for more than six days within any one semester in Texas are entitled to all of the federal due process protections necessary to guarantee a full and fair hearing that are normally accorded students looking at ten-day suspensions in most other states.

Do the same rules apply when disabled or handicapped students face expulsion from school?

No. In 1988 the United States Supreme Court held that, for the most part, disabled or handicapped students may not be excluded from school for more than ten days without all of the due process procedures being provided as required under the Education for All Handicapped Children Act (EAHCA and now referred to as the Individuals with Disabilities Education Act or IDEA). *Honig v. Doe*, 484 U.S. 305 (1988). With this ruling, the Court recognized the "stay put" provision contained in the EAHCA/IDEA and the underlying Congressional intent requiring parents and school officials to negotiate a bilateral modification in a particular disabled student's Individualized Educational Program (IEP). This decision rejected the school district's contention that it should be allowed to unilaterally exclude "special education" students for their disruptive or dangerous conduct.

What kinds of due process requirements exist when students face such "penalties" as academic sanctions, the suspension from extracurricular activities, or corporal punishment?

As a general rule, it can be said that the same type of procedural due process discussed above with regard to student suspensions and expulsions is not usually required of teachers and school officials when imposing academic sanctions, suspending students from extracurricular activities, or prior to administering corporal punishment. However, that is not to say that *some* due process is not appropriate. For example, if academic sanctions are being imposed for non-academic reasons, then school authorities probably need to ensure that a timely notice of charges and an opportunity for a hearing have been provided in advance of imposing the sanction. With regard to corporal punishment, the United States Supreme Court noted in *Ingraham v. Wright*, 430 U.S. 651 (1977), that although such measures in a public school implicate a constitutionally protected liberty interest, the traditional common law remedies of civil and criminal sanctions are "fully adequate" to afford due process. Again, because "fairness" is the underlying precept upon which procedural due process is based, and since professional educators (and most other people as well) don't like to find out after the fact that they may have made a mistake, providing students who face any of these disciplinary measures with a simple notice and an informal hearing is probably the most educationally sound course of action. Put another way, practicing the "Golden Rule" and "doing unto others . . ." comes highly recommended.

In light of the safety and drug-related issues presently facing the public schools, what is the standard for searching students suspected of misconduct?

The standard which teachers and school administrators must satisfy when considering whether to search a student was established by the United States Supreme Court in *New Jersey v. T.L.O.*, 469 U.S. 325 (1985). *T.L.O.* involved a high school principal's search of a female student's purse after she was accused by a teacher of smoking in a school lavatory. The search ultimately revealed that the student's purse contained a small quantity of marijuana and other drug-related paraphernalia. When delinquency charges were filed against the student by the police, she sought to have the evidence of the search suppressed as a violation of her rights under the Fourth Amendment. The Court disagreed and held that the "probable cause" requirement for law enforcement searches under the Fourth Amendment does not apply to public school officials. Instead, the Court held that such searches must meet two criteria in order to be constitutionally sound: (1) the search must be justified at its inception (in other words, the school authority must have a "reasonable suspicion" that the search will uncover evidence of the violation of a school rule or law); and (2) the scope of the search must be reasonably related to the circumstances supporting the search in the first place (the search cannot be excessively intrusive in light of the age and sex of the student and the nature of the probable infraction). Although the school-based "search and seizure" issue may extend to lockers, cars, personal possessions, the use of drug-detecting dogs, drug testing, strip searches, metal detectors and numerous other areas, the *T.L.O.* standard provides the essential ingredients for evaluating the constitutionality of most student-related searches.

How protected are student records?

Congress passed the Family Educational Rights and Privacy Act (known as FERPA or the Buckley Amendment) in 1972. This legislation applies to all public and nonpublic schools and colleges which receive federal financial assistance. Essentially, FERPA dictates who may have access to student records and how materials contained within a student's record may be challenged. The law requires that parents be provided with annual notification of their rights under the Act. Such rights include a parental right to inspect and request the modification or "correction" of a child's record. Further, the Act limits the number of school district employees who are allowed access to student records. It also requires that on-going lists be kept of every person (other than a school employee) who requests or obtains access to a particular student's record.

Student Expression

What characterizes the rights of students to express themselves in school?

You will recall that three significant United States Supreme Court cases dealing in various ways with student expression were discussed at some length in the introduction to this chapter: *Tinker v. Des Moines Independent Community School Dis-*

trict, 393 U.S. 503 (1969); *Bethel School District No. 403 v. Fraser,* 478 U.S. 675 (1986); and *Hazelwood School District v. Kuhlmeier,* 484 U.S. 260 (1988). Without going into great detail, it is reasonably safe to posit a generalization about student expression in the public schools. *Tinker* supports the proposition that the First Amendment provides substantial protection to students expressing their personal views. Under *Hazelwood* and *Bethel,* the protection narrows significantly when the expression comes in areas that are considered part of the school curriculum or other school-related activities. Thus, the time, place and manner in which students choose to express themselves often determines the propriety of their actions and whether teachers and other school officials can (or should) attempt to restrict or limit such expression.

What is meant by "symbolic speech" and is it protected by the First Amendment?

Symbolic speech is defined as the conveyance of a message (i.e., opinions or thoughts) without the use of words. Such conduct may or may not be protected by the First Amendment. The black armbands worn by students to protest our country's involvement in the Vietnam War in *Tinker* were protected as a form of "pure speech" because very little conduct was actually involved. By contrast, in *United States v. O'Brien,* 391 U.S. 367 (1968), *reh'g denied,* 393 U.S. 900 (1969), the United States Supreme Court held that the burning of a draft card was not protected speech because of the government's substantial interest in regulating the non-speech elements of the conduct. Similarly, in another case from the *Tinker* era, the Sixth Circuit Court of Appeals voiced its approval of school district actions in banning the wearing of *all* buttons, emblems and insignia in a school setting where administrators feared the potential of racial strife and the threat of violent disruption. *Guzick v. Drebus,* 431 F.2d 594 (6th Cir. 1970). The district court in the *Guzick* case characterized free speech as "the single most important element upon which this nation has thrived. Wherever reasonably possible, it must be upheld, cherished, and nurtured." *Guzick v. Drebus*, 305 F.Supp. 472, 481 (N.D.Ill 1969) However, the court went on to say that in certain situations "free speech, or manifestations which are 'closely akin' to free speech, must be exercised with care and restraint; and there are situations in which the manifestations of speech may even be prohibited altogether." *Id.* Finally, applying some of these same principles in a more recent case, a federal district court in Oklahoma held that twenty-six high school students were improperly suspended for wearing and refusing to change T-shirts bearing the slogan, "The best of the night's adventures are reserved for people with nothing planned." *McIntire v. Bethel School, Independent School District 3,* 804 F.Supp. 1415 (W.D. Okla. 1992). The school district superintendent had banned the shirts after he concluded that the slogan violated a school policy against wearing clothing which promoted al-coholic beverages. The court concluded that the shirts con-veyed an idea rather than a product endorsement and, as such, entitled the students to First Amendment protection.

Where does the Pledge of Allegiance and a salute to our nation's flag fall with regard to student expression?

In 1940, an 8-1 majority of the United States Supreme Court held that the First Amendment's protection of freedom of reli-gion was not violated by a requirement that public school stu-dents salute the flag and recite the Pledge of Allegiance. *Minersville School District v. Gobitis,* 310 U.S. 586 (1940). Stu-dents who refused to comply with this requirement were de-nied access to a public education. In its reasoning, the Court balanced an individual's First Amendment guarantees to free-dom of speech and religious belief against what the Court viewed as the stronger right of the state to legislate measures which were designed to promote good citizenship and a sense of national pride.

Just three years later and by a 6-3 margin, the same Court emphatically reversed the *Minersville* decision in *West Virginia State Board of Education v. Barnette,* 319 U.S. 624 (1943). This case held that public school officials may not require students to salute and pledge allegiance to the flag since doing so violates the First Amendment. The Court found that the mere passive refusal to salute the flag—by itself—does not create a danger to the state which would allow the state the right to punish or expel students from school. Thus, the students successfully challenged the unconstitutionality of a school board policy which conditioned public school attendance on compliance with the flag-salute requirement. The same principle exemplified in *Barnette* appears to still hold true today. For example, in *Sherman v. Community Consolidated School District 21 of Wheeling Township,* 758 F.Supp. 1244 (N.D.Ill. 1991), *aff'd,* 980 F.2d 437 (7th Cir. 1992), *cert. denied,* 113 S.Ct. 2439 (1993), both the trial and appellate courts held that a "voluntary" Pledge of Allegiance requirement did not represent the endorsement of religion, its recitation was patriotic rather than religious, and it did not violate any aspects of the First Amendment's Establishment Clause since the statute did not require all students to recite the pledge nor did it penalize those who chose not to participate.

How have the courts dealt with student dress codes and student appearance requirements?

The prospect of courts being asked to get involved when school districts attempt to control student attire and appearance is certainly not a recent development. For example, in 1923 the Arkansas Supreme Court held that a school board acted properly when it adopted and enforced a rule which prohibited female students from wearing "immodest" clothing or cosmetics. *Pugsley v. Sellmeyer,* 250 S.W. 538 (Ark. 1923).

By declaring in *Tinker* that students cannot be disciplined for their symbolic speech unless it can be shown that there is the likelihood of substantial disruption to school operations and student learning, the United States Supreme Court set the stage for more recent and on-going debates over dress codes and student appearance requirements (i.e., hair length and grooming standards).

To date, the Court has never shown any inclination to help resolve the disparities between the way different state and federal courts around the country have handled such regulations. Consequently, a rather wide gap exists between those parts of the country that view dress and appearance codes somewhat permissively and those that are far less tolerant. A sampling of several of the more interesting cases along these lines reveals some of these differences. For example, in *King v. Saddleback Junior College District,* 445 F.2d 932 (9th Cir. 1971), *cert. denied,* 404 U.S. 979 (1971), the court upheld the right of school officials to impose grooming regulations on students. However, in *Massie v. Henry,* 455 F.2d 779 (4th Cir. 1972), an appellate court reviewing several male students' claims that their high school's hair length requirements were unconstitutional agreed with the students. The court concluded that rather than focusing on the "symbolic speech" aspects of hair length, it was instead inclined to view the issue in light of personal freedoms and liberties under the Due Process and Equal Protection Clauses in the Fourteenth Amendment. In weighing the respective arguments favoring the students and the school authorities, the court held that the hair length regulation lacked sufficient justification to overcome the individual rights of a minor student to choose the length of his hair.

How has the United States Supreme Court dealt with the issue of censorship activities as they relate to students' First Amendment rights?

In its only decision thus far on the school-related censorship issue, the United States Supreme Court held in 1982 that a local school board may not remove books from the school library simply on the basis that board members dislike some of the ideas contained in those books. *Board of Education, Island Trees Union Free School District No. 26 v. Pico,* 457 U.S. 853 (1982). The Court found that in addition to the school board's motivation in removing controversial books from the school district's junior high and high school libraries, there were also some procedural irregularities in how the school board carried out its actions. Although the Court noted that pervasively vulgar or educationally unsuitable books could properly be removed by school authorities, the same could not be said for books which were being removed solely because of their political orientation and in violation of the school board's own policies for reviewing changes in school curriculum.

Do students have a right to publish and distribute "underground" newspapers at school?

In *Hazelwood School District v. Kuhlmeier,* 484 U.S. 260 (1988) (the same landmark *Hazelwood* case discussed in the introduction to this chapter and in Chapter 1), the United States Supreme Court did not say what standards would be applied to the regulation of non-school-sponsored publications. Traditionally, such publications have been viewed under a balancing test—on one side is the school's legitimate interest in maintaining a safe and orderly educational environment and on the other side are student rights to freely express themselves. The general rule that has evolved over time with regard to off-campus student-produced publications is that the school may impose reasonable time, place and manner restrictions on the *distribution* of non-school-sponsored publications; however, the idea of prior administrator approval of the *content* of the publications is not as clear cut. *Bystrom v. Fridley High Independent School District, No. 14,* 822 F.2d 747 (8th Cir. 1987), *on remand,* 686 F.Supp. 1387 (D.Minn. 1987), *aff'd without opinion,* 855 F.2d 855 (8th Cir. 1988). This latter point was reinforced by the Ninth Circuit Court of Appeals in *Burch v. Barker,* 861 F.2d 1149 (9th Cir. 1988). The court held that "prior restraints are permissible in only the rarest of circumstances" and, as such, requiring that *all* non-school-sponsored publications be submitted to school administrators for prior approval could amount to unconstitutional censoring.

Sexual Harassment

What is the extent of sexual harassment in the public schools and how has Congress sought to prevent students from being sexually harassed?

Essentially, students may face two kinds of sexual harassment while attending public school (see Case Nos. 5 and 6 of this chapter): harassment by a teacher or other adult member of the school staff and harassment by other students. In a recent nationwide survey entitled "Hostile Hallways: The AAUW Survey on Sexual Harassment in America's Schools," the American Association of University Women (AAUW) research found that eighty-five percent of female and seventy-six percent of male secondary-school students who responded to the survey reported having been sexually harassed in some fashion. By far the majority of these students indicated that they were harassed by fellow students rather than by adult members of the school staff.

In 1972, Congress passed Title IX of the Education Amendments to prohibit discrimination on the basis of sex in educational programs that receive federal financial assistance. In *Franklin v. Gwinnett County Public Schools*, 112 S.Ct. 1028 (1992), the United States Supreme Court found that a teacher's sexual harassment of a student constitutes the type of gender-based discrimination that Congress sought to prohibit under Title IX. As a result, the Court concluded that not only may a school district lose its federal funding, but that money damages are also available from a school district which intentionally violates Title IX. In addition, although Title IX actions can only be filed against educational institutions and not individual employees, those same employees may be personally liable for sexual discrimination and harassment under other civil rights legislation (i.e., 42 U.S.C. § 1983). Since Title IX applies to instances of both staff-to-student and student-to-student or peer sexual harassment, the implications are great for educators to take an aggressive and preventive role in ensuring that adequate anti-harassment policies are in place, that all instances of alleged harassment are carefully and fully investigated, and that corrective actions are taken when warranted.

Religious Issues

What are the primary issues at stake with school and religious activities?

The First Amendment to the United States Constitution provides in part that "Congress shall make no law respecting an establishment of religion, or prohibiting the free exercise thereof. . . ." In many respects, the Establishment and Free Exercise Clauses conflict when individual and group religious preferences and interests are involved in a public sector setting. On one hand, the Establishment Clause prohibits school districts from advancing religion or coercing anyone to support religion or to participate in a religious exercise. On the other hand, the Free Exercise Clause prohibits a school district from interfering with an individual's free exercise of his religious beliefs and, in certain instances, requires the accommodation of those personal beliefs.

How has the United States Supreme Court recognized and protected parental rights to control the religious upbringing of their children?

In 1925, the United States Supreme Court held that parents have the right to decide whether to send their children to public or private schools. *Pierce v. Society of the Sisters of the Holy Names of Jesus and Mary*, 268 U.S. 510 (1925). Twenty-seven years later, the Court ruled that children may be released from public school to attend religious instruction classes of their own choice that are conducted away from the public school's grounds. *Zorach v. Clauson*, 343 U.S. 306 (1952). In the early 1960s, the Court held that a state, state board of regents, or local school board may not compose a prayer or select a biblical passage and require that it be recited or read as a part of the school day. *Engel v. Vitale*, 370 U.S. 421 (1962); *School District of Abington Township v. Schempp* and *Murray v. Curlett*, 374 U.S. 203 (1963). More recently, attempts to overcome the Establishment Clause by permitting student volunteers to select or present prayers for morning devotionals or school assemblies have also been ruled impermissible. *Karen B. v. Treen*, 653 F.2d 897 (5th Cir. 1981), *aff'd*, 455 U.S. 913 (1982).

Do these cases imply that students are prohibited from praying privately?

No. As the United States Supreme Court noted in *Tinker v. Des Moines Independent Community School District*, 393 U.S. 503 (1969), a student does not abandon her constitutional rights simply by passing through the "schoolhouse gate"; therefore, she has a right to freely exercise her religious convictions by doing such things as praying quietly and privately or reading a Bible while at school. However, if a student wants to pray out loud or if two or more students wish to pray together, then the "material and substantial disruption" aspect of the *Tinker* case becomes the determinative factor in whether such prayer is permissible (refer to the discussion of *Tinker* in the introduction to this chapter). An additional consideration involves whether this type of prayer activity "invades" the rights of others.

If school prayers are illegal, what about a "moment of silence" during the school day?

In *Wallace v. Jaffree*, 472 U.S. 38 (1985), the United States Supreme Court struck down an Alabama statute authorizing a daily one-minute period of silence in the state's public schools "for meditation or voluntary prayer." The Court found that the clearly sectarian purpose behind the legislation (to encourage prayer in schools) violated the Establishment Clause. However, on the basis of an earlier statute that was not directly involved in the *Wallace* decision, the Court's ruling implicitly acknowledged the propriety of a "moment of silence." Since *Wallace* was decided, a growing number of states have begun to enact "moment of silence" statutes which, at least at this point, have not been explicitly challenged at the United States Supreme Court level. As this book goes to print it appears that Congress may decide to address the school prayer issue in its next session.

What about prayers at graduation ceremonies?

The question of whether a prayer given as part of a high school graduation ceremony violates the Establishment Clause was decided *to some extent* by the United States Supreme Court in *Lee v. Weisman*, 112 S.Ct. 2649 (1992). In *Lee*, the Court held (by a 5-4 majority) that a school district violated the Constitution when the school principal made arrangements for a member of the local clergy to give a brief, nonsectarian prayer at a junior high graduation ceremony. The Court downplayed the school district's argument that attendance at a graduation ceremony was voluntary and, instead, held that the school administrator's involvement in orchestrating the religious exercise created "a state-sponsored and state-directed religious exercise in a public school." *Id.* at 2655.

Why did the response to the previous question state that the United States Supreme Court decided the graduation prayer issue *"to some extent"*?

Shortly after the Court decided *Lee v. Weisman*, the Fifth Circuit Court of Appeals reexamined a graduation prayer case that, in a factual sense, was slightly different from the circumstances in *Lee*. *Jones v. Clear Creek Independent School District*, 977 F.2d 963 (5th Cir. 1992), *cert. denied*, 113 S.Ct. 2950 (1993), involved high school seniors—and not school administrators—who decided to have a nonsectarian and nonproselytizing prayer at their graduation ceremony. The prayer in *Jones* was given by a student volunteer rather than a member of the clergy and, in addition and unlike *Lee*, the school district assumed a more passive role in *approving* the prayer rather than suggesting what it should say. The *Jones* court distinguished the result in *Lee* and held that the graduation prayer did not violate the Establishment Clause. As a result of *Lee* and the fact that the United States Supreme Court declined to grant *certiorari* to consider *Jones*, it is unclear at this time whether *all* or only *some* graduation prayers are unconstitutional. Since *Lee*, this issue has received a great deal of national attention and school districts and courts around the country have taken widely divergent approaches to dealing with the graduation prayer dilemma. It is likely that the United States Supreme Court will again be called upon to more fully resolve this question.

Are prayers or invocations given at school athletic events constitutionally permitted?

In *Jager v. Douglas County School District*, 862 F.2d 824 (11th Cir. 1989), *cert. denied*, 490 U.S. 2431 (1989), the Eleventh Circuit Court of Appeals held that a Georgia school district's practice of having student government officers select nonclergy volunteers from various school clubs and organizations to give pregame invocations at school-sponsored football games violated the Establishment Clause. After a prior adverse judicial ruling, the school district had devised the plan to substitute for the previous custom of having local clergy provide an invocation.

Can a teacher claim a constitutionally protected "free exercise" right to wear religious garb while teaching in the public schools?

A number of states have passed legislation prohibiting teachers from wearing clothing or religious insignia that indicates affiliation with a particular religious order. For example, in

Cooper v. Eugene School District No. 4J, 723 P.2d 298 (1986), *appeal dismissed*, 480 U.S. 942 (1987), the Oregon Supreme Court considered legislation which banned the wearing of religious dress while teaching in the public schools. The court concluded that the state could constitutionally prohibit the teacher in *Cooper* from wearing white clothes and a white turban indicative of her membership in the Sikh religion. The court held that the legislative purpose behind the religious garb statute was intended to maintain religious neutrality and that it would not apply to a teacher who chose to wear such things as a Star of David, a cross, or ethnic or cultural dress.

How have the courts handled the observance of religious holidays in the public schools?

Perhaps the best example of how a court saw fit to resolve the issue of a religious observance in a public school setting is found in *Florey v. Sioux Falls School District 49-5*, 619 F.2d 1311 (8th Cir. 1980), *cert. denied*, 449 U.S. 987 (1980). In *Florey*, the Eighth Circuit Court of Appeals examined a school district's guidelines that would handle holidays such as Christmas which have both a secular and a religious significance. The court concluded that a limited amount of religious symbolism could be incorporated into a school's music, drama and literature curricula so long as the religious themes were presented "in a prudent and objective manner and as a traditional part of the cultural and religious heritage of the particular holiday." *Id.* at 1314.

What happens when students wish to form religious clubs to meet on school premises during noninstructional times?

In response to prior litigation, Congress passed the Equal Access Act, 20 U.S.C. § 4071, in 1984. The Equal Access Act applies only to public secondary schools which receive federal financial assistance. The Act provides that if a school has created a "limited open forum" by allowing one or more noncurriculum-related student groups to meet on school premises during noninstructional time, then it cannot deny equal access to or discriminate against student groups created for religious, political or philosophical reasons. In the most significant case involving the Equal Access Act, the United States Supreme Court held in *Board of Education of the Westside Community Schools v. Mergens*, 496 U.S. 226 (1990), that the school had to allow a Christian club to meet during noninstructional time since it had already created a limited open forum for such other student groups as a chess club, a scuba diving club, and a "peer advocates" club.

May parents choose to educate their children at home?

In recent years there has been an increasing trend toward allowing parents to educate their children at home. Generally, the "home schooling" movement has received legislative and judicial support and appears to have become a viable choice for an increasing number of parents for both religious and non-religious reasons. Most states have legislation that controls home instruction. The statutory restrictions on home schooling range from what can be construed as *permissive* (e.g., permitting children to be taught by a parent or other adult regardless of whether the adult is a certified teacher) or *restrictive* (e.g., allowing instruction only by certified teachers and only under the close supervision and approval of local public school officials). In order to ascertain whether home schooling parents in your school district are in legal compliance, it would be necessary to examine your state's compulsory attendance statutory requirements. In effect, these laws balance the state's interest in creating an enlightened and productive citizenry against the rights of parents to control the upbringing of their progeny.

How has the United States Supreme Court viewed the use of public funds to support parochial school services?

The easiest answer to this question is that the issue is too broad for a simple answer. Although summarizing the large number of cases the Court has decided governing various aspects of public funding for private and/or parochial educational services does not do justice to the scope and breadth of these issues, at least some of the results have settled certain narrow issues. For example, in *Lemon v. Kurtzman*, 403 U.S. 602 (1971), *reh'g denied*, 404 U.S. 876 (1971), the Court declared that a state statute providing for state subsidies to help pay nonpublic school teachers' salaries was unconstitutional even though the funds might only be paid to teachers who taught secular subjects. The Court developed what has come to be known as the three-part "*Lemon* test" for Establishment Clause challenges under the First Amendment: (1) does the statute or governmental policy have a secular purpose?; (2) is its principle effect that it neither advances nor inhibits religion?; and (3) does it avoid fostering an excessive entanglement with religion? If any of these three questions are answered affirmatively, then the challenged legislation or policy is unconstitutional.

In *Wisconsin v. Yoder*, 406 U.S. 205 (1972), the Court held that when a state's compulsory attendance law beyond the eighth grade had a detrimental effect on how an established religious group practiced its religion in a close-knit and traditional community, the compulsory attendance requirements were an unconstitutional infringement on the Amish parents' rights to influence the education of the older Amish children (those Amish students beyond the eighth grade).

In *Stone v. Graham*, 449 U.S. 39 (1980), *reh'g denied*, 449 U.S. 1104 (1981), the Court held that a state statute requiring that privately contributed copies of the Ten Commandments be posted in every public school classroom was unconstitutional since it failed to have a secular purpose (i.e., the first prong of the "*Lemon* test").

More recently, in a case that mixed elements of religion

and special education, the Court held that a public school district must continue to provide a sign-language interpreter for a deaf student who transferred to a sectarian school. *Zobrest v. Catalina Foothills Schools District*, 113 S.Ct. 2462 (1993). The Court rejected the school district's defense premised on the Establishment Clause and, instead, ruled that the service neutrally aided the child without giving a direct financial benefit to the child's parents or parochial school. Further, the Court stated that providing this service did not constitute a governmental participation in religious instruction since the interpreter simply acted as a conduit to assist in the child's communications.

In sum, although this response's "shotgun approach" to mentioning just a handful of the many significant church/state cases decided by the Court cannot fully convey the breadth of the issues involved, it at least provides a sampling of the variety.

Special, Gifted and Bilingual Education

May students be excluded from school because of a handicapping or disabling condition?

No. Beginning with two 1972 cases in Pennsylvania and the District of Columbia, courts have uniformly recognized the rights of disabled children to be admitted to and served by their local public school district regardless of the severity of their particular disabling conditions. In *Pennsylvania Association for Retarded Children v. Commonwealth*, 343 F.Supp. 279 (E.D.Pa. 1972), the court stated that "[A]ll mentally retarded persons are capable of benefiting from a program of education or training. . . ." *Id.* at 296. "It is the Commonwealth's obligation to place each mentally retarded child in a free, public program of education and training appropriate to the child's capacity, within the context of the general educational policy that, among the alternative programs of education and training required by statute to be available, placement in a regular public school class is preferable to placement in a special public school class and placement in a special public school class is preferable to placement in any other type of program of education and training." *Id.* at 307.

In *Mills v. Board of Education of District of Columbia*, 348 F.Supp. 866 (D.C. 1972), the court extended the accessibility of appropriate educational services to *all* disabled students. In addition, the *Mills* court recognized the need for student-specific individualized educational programs and procedural safeguards to ensure compliance. As a direct result of these cases, Congress subsequently enacted federal legislation designed to eliminate discrimination against disabled students. The Vocational Rehabilitation Act of 1973—and § 504 of that act in particular—and the Education for All Handicapped Children Act of 1975 (also commonly referred to as EAHCA, Public Law 94-142, and, since 1990, as the Individuals with Disabilities Education Act or IDEA) were the primary Congressional responses to a perceived need to alleviate discrimination and ensure that *all* students be accorded access to a "free appropriate public education" (FAPE). 20 U.S.C. § 1401(18).

What is the current "hot topic" with regard to special education?

In the last twenty years or so, the extent to which "regular" classroom teachers became involved with "special education" was primarily contingent upon the scope and quality of pull out-type programs for students classified as handicapped or disabled under the EAHCA/IDEA. Students with learning disabilities would be pulled out of their "regular" classrooms and given more individualized instruction in a separate classroom setting elsewhere. Those students with more severe disabilities would spend all or nearly all of their time in segregated programs located in "resource rooms"—and often in separate schools. Today, however, there has been a trend toward keeping special education students in regular classes and supplementing the regular teacher's instruction with the assistance of support personnel and services. This concept, known as "inclusion," finds support in the idea that all students should be "mainstreamed" in a regular classroom as much as possible; however, in reality it takes "mainstreaming" one step further. Instead of finding that the regular classroom is the "least restrictive environment" (LRE) for a particular student for *some* of his educational instruction, under inclusion, many of even the most severely disabled students will remain in a regular classroom setting with massive amounts of special education support staff assistance. The underlying idea behind inclusion is that *all* students (both disabled and nondisabled) will benefit from being educated alongside other students in a "regular" classroom setting, regardless of whether their classmates and peers have disabilities or not. The critical point here is that each disabled student must be evaluated on an individual basis and all placement decisions must hinge on the unique needs and circumstances present in each child's particular situation.

How might inclusion affect "regular" classroom teachers?

It is important to note that the federal special education laws (EAHCA/IDEA) mandating that all students with disabilities are entitled to a free appropriate public education in the least restrictive environment contingent on each student's individualized needs have not changed since they were originally enacted in 1975. The compelling statutory provision mandates that school districts will adopt procedures "to assure that, to the maximum extent appropriate, children with disabilities . . . are educated with children who are not disabled, and that special classes, separate schooling, or other removal of children with disabilities from the regular educational environment occurs only when the nature or severity of the disability is such that education in regular classes with the use of supplementary aids and services cannot be achieved satisfactorily . . . ." 20 U.S.C. § 1412(5)(B). Thus, it isn't a change in the law that has fueled the inclusion movement but rather it is a change in the way the law is interpreted and applied which has stimulated the return of "special" students to the regular classroom. The implications for classroom teachers are profound since in many cases they must now be better prepared and more willing to work with a more diverse group of students (and attendant support personnel) in a regular classroom environment than has traditionally been the case during the last two decades.

Although only a handful of recent cases have been decided in which the courts have adopted a posture favorable to inclusion, the potential implications are significant. For example, in *Sacramento City Unified School District, Board of Education v. Rachel H.*, 14 F.3d 1398 (9th Cir. 1994), *cert. denied*, 114 S.Ct. 2679 (1994), the Ninth Circuit Court of Appeals affirmed a lower court's finding that a mentally retarded 11-year-old student with a measured I.Q. of 44 should remain full-time in a regular second-grade classroom with the assistance of supplemental services provided by a special education consultant and a part-time aide. In its decision, the court adopted a four-factor "balancing test" to determine the student's appropriate placement: (1) the educational benefits of her placement in a full-time regular class; (2) the non-academic (i.e.. social) benefits of such a placement; (3) the effect of such a placement on the teacher and other children in the regular class; and (4) the costs incurred by the school district in mainstreaming the disabled student. On the basis of the evidence presented in a hearing before the lower court, both that court and the Ninth Circuit agreed that Rachel's parents' evidence and arguments for inclusion of their daughter in a regular classroom were more persuasive than the school district's arguments for a placement consisting of part-time special education classes and part-time regular classes. While the rationale that the Ninth Circuit Court of Appeals applied in deciding *Rachel H.* does not necessarily follow that of the other federal circuit courts (e.g., *Daniel R.R. v. State Board of Education*, 874 F.2d 1036 (5th Cir. 1989); *Lachman v. Illinois State Board of Education*, 852 F.2d 290 (7th Cir. 1988), *cert. denied*, 488 U.S. 925 (1988); *Roncker v. Walter*, 700 F.2d 1058 (6th Cir. 1983), *cert. denied*, 464 U.S. 864 (1983)), it does exemplify the continuing and high profile debate over the appropriate placement of disabled students.

How does a student's special education status affect student discipline?

As mentioned in the discussion of *Honig v. Doe*, 484 U.S. 305 (1988) in the "Student Discipline and Control" section of this chapter, the United States Supreme Court was unequivocal in its application of the "stay put" provision under federal special education law. In *Honig*, a California school district suspended two emotionally disturbed students for less than ten days. One of the students had physically attacked a fellow student and the second suspended student had continued to make sexual comments to female classmates after being told not to do so. The school district scheduled expulsion hearings for both suspended students which, in effect, extended the suspensions indefinitely pending the outcome of the expulsion proceedings. Pending the outcome of a statutory review proceeding and absent a court order to the contrary, the "stay put" provision forbids state or local school authorities from unilaterally excluding students classified as "disabled" or "handicapped" for more than ten days on the basis of their dangerous or disruptive conduct *if* such conduct is related to their disabilities.

If "special" education is provided for students with disabilities, what about those students who are "gifted?"

Many states have enacted legislation which either requires or encourages local school districts to address the unique needs of gifted and/or uniquely talented students. Although the definitions of "gifted" or "talented" vary from state to state, the general idea is that students with high potential for intellectual, creative, artistic, leadership or academic performance benefit from enrichment activities designed to nurture fulfillment of that potential. Despite limited federal support for the development of specific educational programs for gifted students during the 1970s and 1980s, it appears that most of that support has dwindled in recent years.

Do students have the right to be taught in their native language?

Yes. In *Lau v. Nichols*, 414 U.S. 563 (1974), the United States Supreme Court held that a school district which receives federal aid must provide special instruction if there are a significant number of non-English-speaking students in the district whose education is severely hampered by the language barrier. *Lau* began in the San Francisco school system which, according to state statute, had a goal of all students acquiring proficiency in English. In this case, the school district failed to offer remedial English language instruction to approximately 1,800 Chinese-speaking students. In a class action suit, the students claimed that the school district's failure to provide special instruction denied them a meaningful opportunity to participate in the public educational program and, as a result, violated the Equal Protection Clause of the Fourteenth Amendment, Title VI of the Civil Rights Act of 1964 (which prohibits the recipients of federal aid from discriminating against students on the basis of race, color, or national origin), and regulations promulgated by the United States Department of Health, Education and Welfare (HEW). Although the Court did not decide the plaintiffs' constitutional claim premised on equal protection, it did rule in their favor on the basis of Title VI and the HEW regulations. Of note, the Court also declined to decide whether bilingual education was the appropriate remedy in this case and, instead, remanded the question of deciding appropriate relief to the trial court.

Case Resolutions

Case No.1: More than just muffins
or
Due process never takes a holiday!
(see page 127)

The court reviewed the school board's decision to impose a two-day academic suspension as well as a year-long social probation and found that this action had a rational basis. The court noted that the law places disciplinary decisions in the hands of "school authorities with general, overall educational responsibilities such as school boards, superintendent and principals, *not* persons insularly involved in only one aspect of the educational process, such as sports." *Manico v. South Colonie Central School District*, 584 N.Y.S.2d 519, 523 (N.Y.App. Div. 1992). In this manner, the best interests of both the student and the institution are well served. The two-day academic suspension and social probation directed by the principal was properly imposed and due process requirements were properly complied with as to that aspect of the student's punishment.

As to the student's suspension from the wrestling team, New York law provides that no hearing is necessary when deprivation is imposed of a "tangential extracurricular privilege"; however, there must be a legal basis for disciplinary action which cannot be arbitrary, capricious nor unreasonable. Further, whatever procedure is adopted must be "basically fair, granting to the student and the person in parental relation to him an *opportunity to appear informally before the person or body authorized to impose discipline*" to discuss the situation—in other words, an administrative hearing. *Id.* at 522.

With regard to the wrestling suspension issue, the school district failed completely to adhere to principles of due process or to protect the student's and parent's rights to be heard. Although it was a holiday season and several school administrators were out of town, the court stated emphatically that "*due process never takes a holiday!*" The final power rests with the school board who should have acted when no one else did—it may not "pass the buck" or "shirk its ultimate responsibility to maximize the potential of each student to serve his community." *Id.* at 523. The school board had an obligation to listen and the student and his parents had a right to be heard.

In addition to placing an "exclamation point" on its discussion of due process considerations, the court further commented that "this athletic director may be a paragon of wisdom; he may be endowed by his Creator with superhuman insight and judgment-making ability. But somewhere there surely must be an athletic director who is not such a paragon, nor so well endowed." *Id.* Interestingly, the Interscholastic Athletic Guide relied upon by the athletic director had never been formally adopted as official policy in the school district; nor did it provide for minimal due process because it did not designate a person or body to determine transgressions of the Guide or to impose punishment. Therefore, the school district had no jurisdiction (or power) respecting the mode in which the extracurricular athletic suspension was imposed, and, as a result, it was arbitrary and capricious.

Case No. 2: Classroom management as an aspect of teaching performance (see page 128)

The critical question in this case is whether the teacher received the benefit of a fair and impartial decision based on the evidence presented. The evidence showed that the principal was an experienced geography teacher while this particular teacher had spent the majority of her time as the library media specialist. The principal admitted that he was predisposed to think the teacher was incompetent, and he was also aware that seventh graders have a difficult time in the transition to junior high school. The principal did not criticize the teacher's lesson plans or method of presentation and, instead, said that she was a fine person who at times did an outstanding job. There was evidence that the teacher had tried to address what the principal observed as deficiencies in her classroom environment (inappropriate behavior, rudeness and responses), but no evidence that the teacher had willfully neglected her duties, particularly in the library. In view of the evidence, the court found that the hearing panel properly determined the credibility of the witnesses and resolved discrepancies in the evidence. Consequently, the hearing panel's decision was *not* clearly erroneous; however, the trial court's decision to reverse the hearing panel *was* clearly erroneous. Thus, the hearing panel's order reinstating the teacher to her former position was revived. *Independent School District 4 v. Orange*, 841 P.2d 1177 (Okla.Ct.App. 1992).

Case No. 3: Procedure to object to discipline of a handicapped child (see page 129)

The federal trial court in Kansas agreed with the parents. However, the Tenth Circuit Court of Appeals reversed after finding that the school's use of the "time-out" room was clearly related to providing an appropriate public education for these particular children. In the court's view, the room was used to avoid sending the children being disciplined out to "roam the streets and goof off." The "time-out" room was an annex of the classroom in which students worked on classroom material and assignments. The Tenth Circuit believes that "[p]roper conduct and education are inextricably intertwined," [cites omitted] and held that "discipline of a child in the classroom, including short-term suspensions and 'time-out' periods, is a matter that relates to the public education of a handicapped child and that therefore falls within the scope of the Education of the Handicapped Act [EAHCA/IDEA]." *Hayes v. Unified School District No. 377*, 877 F.2d 809, 813 (10th Cir. 1989). It followed from this holding that the parents were required to request a hearing and first pursue and exhaust their administrative remedies under the Act before going to court and seeking judicial review.

Case No. 4: Search and seizure (see page 130)

The court recognized that Snyder had a reasonable and constitutionally protected expectation of privacy in his school locker. School policy provided that a student's locker would not be subject to unreasonable search. However, the search in this case did not violate Snyder's Fourth Amendment rights to be free of unreasonable search and seizures. As set forth by the United States Supreme Court, the test for school administrators is "whether the search of the locker was reasonable in all the circumstances." *New Jersey v. T.L.O.*, 469 U.S. 325, 341 (1985). This search *was* legal under these circumstances—in other words, there was reasonable suspicion for the school administrators to conduct the search. By state law, a search warrant is not required for school officials to conduct a search in the school environment if they have reasonable suspicion of wrongdoing and the search is not unduly intrusive. The situation, in this case, did not arise from an anonymous informant but rather from an eyewitness account given by a student to a reliable teacher on whom the principal's reliance was justified. The decision to search the locker, prior to confronting Snyder, was less intrusive than physically searching the student. As to Snyder's other point, there is no rule requiring that a school administrator must furnish Miranda-type warnings since that requirement is only imposed upon law enforcement officials or agents. Finally, the names of the student informant and the teacher who reported the incident to the administrators did not have to be disclosed since Snyder could not show that knowing these identities would have been helpful to him in defending against the criminal charges. *Commonwealth v. Snyder*, 597 N.E.2d 1363 (Mass. 1992).

Case No. 5: Student-to-student sexual harassment under Title IX (see page 131)

The court ruled on numerous claims and defenses asserted in this case and concluded that Title IX provides a private damages remedy for *intentional* discrimination and its scope prohibits "hostile environment sexual harassment." Applying rules from other previously decided cases, it appears that a school district would be liable for intentional sexual discrimination by its agent (i.e., a teacher or counselor)—but this is not necessarily the same as saying the school would be liable for *failure to stop* harassment despite its awareness of the problem. The court concluded that evidence of the school's failure to take appropriate action in this case could be circumstantial evidence of an intent to discriminate and that Jane Doe's claim must be refiled under this theory. The counselor and the principal are not personally liable under Title IX since the act only imposes liability on institutions. However, the counselor and principal both face possible *individual* or *personal* liability under a federal civil rights statute designed to protect against discrimination by those "acting under the color of law." (42 U.S.C. § 1983.) The court also noted that despite compulsory attendance laws, "there is no special relationship between schools and students which would impose a constitutionally required affirmative duty on schools to prevent peer sexual harassment." *Doe v. Petaluma City School District*, 830 F.Supp. 1560, 1578 (N.D.Cal. 1993).

Case No. 6: Sexual harassment by a teacher under Title IX (see page 132)

Title IX of the Educational Amendments of 1972, 20 U.S.C. § 1681(a) states:

> No person in the United States shall, on the basis of sex, be excluded from participation in, be denied the benefits of, or be subjected to discrimination under any education program or activity receiving Federal financial assistance . . . .

The United States District Court for the Northern District of California held that the scope of this mandate forbids the maintenance of a sexually hostile environment in any education program or activity receiving federal financial assistance. Applying the standard of a "reasonable victim" in this case, a jury would be asked to decide whether the daughters who were sexually molested at the ages of ten and twelve years in their own family environment by the music teacher would reasonably be intimidated and fearful of this person's presence at school—enough so as to interfere with their abilities to learn and enjoy all aspects of their education experience. Unfortunately, the judicial opinion in this case does not disclose the ultimate outcome since the court had yet to try the case at this stage in the proceedings. *Patricia H. v. Berkeley Unified School District*, 830 F.Supp. 1288 (N.D.Cal. 1993). Somewhat as an aside, it is also interesting to note that the teacher in this case argued unsuccessfully that he had *not* molested one of the daughters when, in fact, he had *admitted* in writing to "an isolated incident of extremely poor judgment and misconduct" in an earlier administrative hearing before the state's teacher certification commission. *Id.* at 1299. The allegations to which the teacher had admitted his complicity involved placing the hand of the twelve-year-old daughter on his penis, getting into the girl's bed without wearing any clothing, feeling the girl's vaginal area, and—when confronted by the mother—admitting the misconduct and attributing such conduct to his cocaine addiction.

Case No. 7: Play ball? (see page 133)

In this case, it was the IHSAA that took the step that caused harm to the student. Unless its activities—which are entirely dependent on cooperation from the Indiana public school systems—can be considered "state action," the IHSAA is insulated from judicial review in this matter as a voluntary association and private, non-governmental agency. The appellate court went through a thorough analysis to conclude that the IHSAA *was* engaged in state action subject to judicial review. The court's inquiry focused on the relationship of the association to the state; where, as here, the IHSAA membership was located entirely within the state, enforcing IHSAA rules impacts the rights of *all* students enrolled in the public institutions. Therefore, the court concluded that the IHSAA's rule enforcement in this case did constitute state action. Having found state action, the next question is whether participation in interschool sports is protected in some manner under the U.S. Constitution. Applying the "rational basis" test (does a rule bear some rational relation to a legitimate government interest), the court found that the IHSAA scholastic rules were meant to place emphasis on classroom education over participation in extracurricular athletics—definitely a legitimate state interest. Creating a rule regarding the number of classes in which a student must be enrolled is rationally related to attaining the goal of academic achievement. Not counting repeat classes ensures that student athletes will pass enough classes to earn a diploma rather than concentrating too much time on sports. However, even though the rules are rationally related to a legitimate state interest, the court also concluded that they are *overbroad* as applied in this case. Following his illness, it was clearly in the student's best academic interest to repeat his junior year classes; there was no evidence he did so to seek additional playing time and circumvent the IHSAA eligibility rules. The appellate court affirmed the lower court's ruling that the IHSAA erred in making the student ineligible for the spring semester in 1992. At the same time, the court also recognized that the student will ultimately exhaust his eligibility because students can only be eligible for a maximum of eight semesters once they begin high school. *IHSAA v. Schafer*, 598 N.E.2d 540 (Ind.Ct.App. 1992).

Chapter Five

Torts and Liability

Teachers, administrators and school board members have an obligation to provide a safe environment for students while they attend school or when they are involved in school-related activities. Consequently, teachers share a mutual interest in minimizing the risks and reducing the likelihood of student injuries. Teachers have a particularly good reason to be concerned about *liability* (a legal obligation to pay damages for harm caused to another) when a student is injured while under the teacher's care and supervision. Because of the great potential for adverse personal and professional consequences, this chapter deals in large part with the extent to which a teacher may be liable for student injuries. By extension, but to a lesser degree, the chapter also looks at school district liability and other liability-related issues.

Many student injury lawsuits involve allegations of teacher *negligence*. For present purposes, teacher negligence can be defined as conduct in which a teacher fails to exercise reasonable care to protect a student from the risk of harm. The determination of whether a teacher will be found to have been negligent in a given situation will hinge on a variety of factors.

These factors include whether a "reasonably prudent teacher" would have acted as this teacher did under similar circumstances and whether the possibility of likely injury could have been foreseen and appropriate action taken to avoid the injury.

Negligence is one of several types of *tort* actions that may arise in a school setting. A tort is defined as a legal wrong or injury to a person or property, which does not involve a breach of contract, and for which a civil (as distinguished from a criminal) suit can be brought for the recovery of money damages. Tort law is premised on the legal theory that people are liable for the consequences of their actions that result in injury to others.

In addition to negligence, other possible tort actions include: intentional torts (usually involving allegations of assault and battery or false imprisonment); strict liability (when an activity is considered to be particularly hazardous or abnormally dangerous); defamation (written or spoken communication that harms a person's reputation or exposes her to contempt or ridicule); and constitutional torts (when a person alleges he was deprived of his civil rights under either the constitution or other federal law). As a reflection of the relative infrequency with which teachers become involved with most of the tort actions mentioned above, this chapter focuses primarily on negligence issues; however, examples of some of the other types of tort situations are included as well.

Liability is closely related to other legal concepts such as immunity, indemnification, privilege, and monetary limits or "caps" on the amount an injured student may recover in a successful tort action. Each of these "limits" on a teacher or school district's liability in a negligence action depends on the legislative enactment of state statutes designed to protect teachers and their employing districts. The amount and availability of such statutory protections varies from state to state and may be quite extensive or of little use.

Another concept closely identified with liability is insurance to protect a teacher against the personal risk of having to pay damages for certain types of misconduct. Even though a teacher may have been either directly or indirectly responsible for a student's injuries, he may be shielded from personal liability under the protective umbrella of an insurance policy.

It should go without saying that regardless of what measures may be available to relieve someone from personal responsibility for paying damages, a teacher should never consider these measures as an excuse or reason not to exercise reasonable care.

Because each state has its own particular "brand" or variation of tort laws, it is difficult to make valid generalizations in this area of the law. This is particularly true with regard to types of defenses available in tort actions. Consequently, in the event that a teacher becomes involved in a situation with potential liability risks, it is imperative that he obtain the legal advice and expert assistance of a qualified attorney experienced in school law issues and familiar with the particular laws in that state and jurisdiction.

Not surprisingly, much of the litigation in the tort law arena involves cases that challenge the limits and exceptions to liability protections. There are hundreds (and perhaps thousands) of reported cases involving allegations of negligence that illustrate when a teacher may be held liable for damages. Many of these cases rest upon the basic assumption that since most children are subject to compulsory attendance laws and are thus required to attend school, they are entitled to a "safe place" while in attendance or when engaged in school-related activities. Although a teacher is not expected to guarantee that a child will *never* be hurt, the teacher *is* expected to exercise the same standard of care that a reasonably prudent teacher would have exercised under the same or similar circumstances. Thus, a teacher will only be personally liable for monetary damages if the teacher's actions and conduct fail to satisfy the appropriate standard of care.

The following case descriptions and related questions represent situations in which teachers have or have not have been held personally liable for student injuries. These descriptions are taken from reported court cases in several different states. After reading the accounts, ponder the questions to form your own opinions before turning to the case resolutions to see how the cases were actually resolved in the courts. Remember that in tort cases, just a slight variation in the facts or circumstances in a given situation may be critical to a different outcome. To some extent, judicial determinations will vary and may appear to be contradictory because of the differing negligence and liability laws in the fifty states.

Case Descriptions

Case No. 1: Athlete injured during hazing

A freshman high school football player was put through a ritual "hit line" in the back of the bus on the way home from a football game. The coach was driving the bus. The coach and at least one school board member had been aware of the hazing ritual since 1975. On the night in question, the student suffered a broken nose and bruises to his ribs. He incurred medical costs associated with his physical injuries and, in his suit, also alleged emotional distress. He claimed that he had been deprived of his constitutional rights (Fourth Amendment right to be secure in his person and effects against unreasonable seizure and against unreasonable and excessive force, and Fourteenth Amendment rights not to be deprived of life, liberty or property without due process and to equal protection of the law) and that the coach and the school board violated state law as well. Do you agree? Should he be compensated for his injuries?

Case No. 2: Wrongful death?

A high school student who was at football practice suffered heat stroke. The incident occurred about 5:20 p.m. and, although the coaches attempted to administer first aid, they did so by placing a blanket over the player. At 7:15 p.m. the boy was finally taken to the hospital where he later died. His parents brought a wrongful death action against the school district and the coaches. The evidence in the case showed that the coaches did not halt early season practice despite the very hot August temperatures in Louisiana. Prior to this case, Louisiana had repealed the doctrine of governmental immunity in an earlier judicial opinion. Do you think the school district or the coaches were liable? Would medical testimony be necessary to prove the negligence (if any) of the coaches? Does a student who voluntarily goes out for football assume the risk of injury which would exonerate the coaches from tort liability?

Case No. 3: Acting like Superman

A kindergarten student climbed a chain ladder on a playground several times while his teacher watched. As the teacher called the class to line up to return to class, the boy went back for one more climb to the top of the ladder. While descending, he impulsively jumped off and broke his arm. Alleging negligent supervision by the teacher and that the principal had breached his duty to inform the teacher about climbing restrictions on the playground equipment, the student's father sued the school board, the principal and the teacher for damages. Do you think this was a foreseeable, preventable risk if proper supervision had been exercised? Is anyone liable in this situation?

Case No. 4: Gifted students get hurt too

A nine-year-old student, participating in a summer class for gifted and talented children, sustained severe injuries in an accidental explosion during chemistry class. The student was doing an experiment to make sparklers with potassium percholarate, an extremely unstable and highly volatile chemical used in rocket fuel—which is not found in commercially made sparklers. The children were wearing goggles while chemical mixtures were being ignited with a butane lighter. The teacher had a fire extinguisher on a nearby table. School officials were aware that the teacher had planned to do several experiments and that it was to be a "hands-on" experience for the students. Do you think adequate precautions were taken? Should the teacher, his supervisors, or the school district be required to pay damages to the student?

Case No. 5: Excessive corporal punishment?

A sixth-grade boy attended special education classes in Dickinson Independent School District in Texas. He was disruptive and had a history of aggressive behavior. When the teacher sent him to the principal's office for misbehaving, the principal administered corporal punishment. The parents claimed the beating was excessive and that it was witnessed by the teacher, who should have intervened. The child was placed in a psychiatric ward and incurred over $90,000 in expenses. The parents filed a civil rights action against the principal, the teacher, other school officials and the school district alleging that the corporal punishment was done negligently and in violation of the student's substantive due process rights. They also asserted a state law claim against the principal for use of excessive force. The school officials argued that the use of corporal punishment was expressly agreed to by a consent form signed by the boy's mother and was administered in accordance with school policy. Do you think the parents won their suit? Do you think the teacher had a duty to intervene?

Case No. 6: Accidental strangulation?

An eleven-year-old student was absent from the classroom for about twenty minutes for unexplained reasons. He was found next door in the cloakroom, strangled on his bandanna. His parents filed a wrongful death claim and requested damages asserting that the boy's death was a direct result of the teacher's failure to supervise and the principal's deliberate indifference to training and supervision requirements. The teacher and principal were found not liable, and the parents appealed the question of the teacher's liability. Essentially the parents claimed that the student had been deprived of his life without due process since the child was compelled by law to attend school and the teacher failed to provide reasonable care and safety. Do you think the teacher is liable?

Negligence

How did negligence law develop?

Negligence law grew out of our heritage in English jurisprudence. Although the conceptual link between carelessness and fault dates back many centuries, the recognition of negligence as a basis for tort liability coincided with an increase in the number of injuries associated with the Industrial Revolution during the first half of the nineteenth century.

What is the four-part court test for negligence in tort liability cases?

In order to find negligence on the part of a defendant, the following four questions must be answered in the affirmative: (1) Did the defendant owe the plaintiff a duty of care? (2) Did the defendant breach the duty owed to the plaintiff? (3) Was the defendant's conduct in breaching the duty of care the proximate cause of the plaintiff's injury? and (4) Did the plaintiff suffer an actual injury or sustain real damage?

How is the four-part test applied?

In negligence cases, a jury is usually called upon to decide questions of fact pertaining to the case. A judge is responsible for instructing the jury on the applicable law. For example, when a child is injured and a teacher has been charged with failure to provide proper supervision, a jury will first determine whether the teacher owed the child a duty of care prior to and at the time the child was injured. Assuming for the moment that the injury occurred in the teacher's classroom, this question will normally be answered in the affirmative. Next, the jury will consider whether the teacher's conduct failed to conform to the required standard for supervising students under similar circumstances. In other words, the question is whether the teacher did something he should not have done or failed to do something that he should have done. Then the jury will decide if there was a reasonably close causal connection between the teacher's conduct and the child's injury. Finally, the jury will determine whether the student sustained an injury for which damages should be awarded. If all questions are answered in the affirmative, then the judge will instruct the jury to find negligence and to calculate the amount of damages that should be awarded to the student from the teacher to compensate the student for her injuries.

What duties does a teacher owe to his students?

The primary duties a teacher owes his students are to provide adequate supervision, to provide appropriate instruction prior to having the students begin an activity that poses a risk of harm, to maintain equipment and facilities in good repair, and to warn of hazardous conditions and known dangers.

Is a teacher expected to guarantee that no child will be injured?

No. That would impose too high a standard of care. When large numbers of children are brought together in close proximity, it is inevitable that accidents will happen, and students may deliberately or inadvertently injure themselves or each other. When supervision is generally adequate, the teacher in charge will not be held personally responsible. This concept is illustrated in the Colorado Supreme Court's opinion in *Carroll v. Fitzsimmons*, 384 P.2d 81, 83 (Colo. 1963). "There is no requirement that the teacher have under constant and unremitting scrutiny the precise spots wherein every phase of play activity is being pursued; nor is there compulsion that the general supervision be continuous and direct."

How does this concept apply to cases in which students commit suicide?

In cases involving students who commit suicide, courts have often been asked to consider a teacher's involvement and whether or not the suicides might have been prevented. The extent of a school's obligation to shield children from possible dangers is highlighted by comparing two cases involving student suicides. In a 1985 Arkansas case, a third-grader hanged himself in a school bathroom using a nylon cord attached to a wooden bathroom pass. The Arkansas Supreme Court held that the school had taken adequate safety measures and that it was "manifestly futile" to protect students from all types of harm, whether self-inflicted or otherwise. *Gathwright v. Lincoln Insurance Company*, 688 S.W.2d 931 (Ark. 1985). By contrast, in *Eisel v. Board of Education of Montgomery County*, 597 A.2d 447 (Md. 1991), a court held that a student's suicide was foreseeable because two school counselors had evidence of the student's intent. Friends of the suicidal student had reported her statements concerning suicide to the counselors and, in the court's eyes, they had failed to take appropriate action. These two cases emphasize how similar outcomes which developed under slightly different circumstances may have a dramatic effect on the resulting liability.

When does a teacher not owe a duty of care to a student?

In most cases arising in a school setting, it can be presumed that a teacher will owe a duty of care to students. On occasion, though, the usual duty owed by a teacher to a student may be eliminated due to the time and place in which a student is injured. For example, while practicing his golf swing at home, a fourth-grade student injured a younger child. The fourth-grader's teacher had instructed the student as to the safe use of the golf club and had allowed him to take the club home. The parents of the injured child were unsuccessful in their negligence action against the teacher because the court found that no duty was owed by the teacher to the injured child at the time the injury occurred. The at-home golf practice was not supervised by the teacher and simply furnishing the golf club did not create a duty for the teacher toward the injured child. *Brewster v. Rankins*, 600 N.E.2d 154 (Ind.Ct.App. 1992).

What is meant by breach of duty and how does that relate to standard of care?

In the four-part test for negligence, the second prong requires a plaintiff to show that the defendant breached the duty owed to the plaintiff by failing to exercise an appropriate standard of care. Identifying the appropriate standard of care in any given situation is governed by the reasonableness of a person's actions. Courts seek to determine whether a reasonable and prudent person would have acted in the same manner under similar circumstances. In this sense, the "reasonable person" is considered to be a fictional being of normal intelligence, normal perception, and possessing the physical attributes of the defendant. In addition, if the allegedly negligent defendant has had special training, then that person is held to a higher standard of care on the basis of superior skill and knowledge. In a school setting, other factors which affect the duty of care include such things as the age of the students and location of the class (i.e., in a regular classroom or on a field trip). As a rule of thumb, younger and less mature students are generally thought to require greater supervision and more detailed instructions. Also, in classes where the risk of injury in inherently greater due to the type of activity, the teacher's standard of care rises (i.e., an industrial arts or chemistry teacher must satisfy a greater standard of care than most other classroom teachers).

What case illustrates a teacher's breach of duty of care owed to students?

In *Darrow v. West Genessee Central School District*, 342 N.Y.S.2d 611 (N.Y. 1973), a young boy was injured when he ran into another student while playing soccer in physical education class. It was alleged that the teacher breached a duty of care owed to students by failing to warn of the possible danger involved in the activity. Further, it was alleged that the teacher failed to give specific instructions as to all aspects of the game. In an appeal, the court found sufficient evidence of a breach of duty to warrant the trial court giving negligence instructions to a jury.

What is proximate cause?

The third prong of the four-part negligence test looks at whether there is a substantial causal connection between the alleged misconduct and the resulting injury; more specifically, did a teacher's action or failure to act cause an injury or allow it to happen? The relationship between the teacher's behavior and the injury must have been sufficiently close in time and the injury must also have been a foreseeable consequence of the behavior. Foreseeability implies that a teacher both could and should have anticipated the potentially dangerous consequences of her action (or inaction) when taken. Put another way, the question becomes, "Would a reasonable and prudent person in the same circumstance have foreseen that harm might occur?"

What are examples of cases illustrating the effect that an intervening act may have on the concept of proximate cause?

A teacher in New York left the classroom to store instructional materials. A student was injured when another student threw a pencil intended for a classmate. The classmate ducked, and the pencil entered the first student's eye and caused permanent injury. "Whether [tossing the pencil] was done mischievously and heedlessly or wantonly and willfully, or with the serious purpose of returning the pencil to its owner, it was the act of an intervening third party [i.e., the student who threw the pencil] which under the circumstances could hardly have been anticipated in the reasonable exercise of the teacher's legal duty toward the plaintiff." *Ohman v. Board of Education of City of New York*, 90 N.E.2d 474, 475 (N.Y. 1949), *reh'g denied*, 93 N.E.2d 927 (N.Y. 1950). No one could seriously contend that "a pencil in the hands of a school pupil is a dangerous instrumentality. This is one of those events which could occur equally as well in the presence of the teacher as during her absence." *Id.* The teacher owed a duty of care to the student, and by being absent from the classroom she may have breached that duty; however, the proximate cause of the injury was the act of the intervening third party (who threw the pencil) and not the teacher's absence from the room.

More recently in another New York case, a student stole a chemical from his school's science lab. After the chemical was involved in a fire at the student's home which injured the student and damaged the home, the student's father sued the school district for the teacher's alleged negligent supervision and failure to provide adequate warnings. The court found that the student had been warned by the science teacher, but more importantly, it also found that the student's intentional act in stealing the chemical constituted a superseding factor which absolved the school district from any liability since it was not the proximate cause of the physical injuries and harm to property. *Brazell v. Board of Education of Niskayuna Public Schools*, 557 N.Y.S.2d 645 (N.Y.App.Div. 1990).

What is an example of a case in which the alleged cause of the injury was too remote from the injury itself?

In *Person v. Gum*, 455 N.E.2d 713 (Ohio Ct.App. 1983), a teacher sent a second-grade student home for lunch on the student's first day of classes at his new school. The teacher asked the student if he knew how to walk home on his own and the student said that he did. The student's mother had not expected the student to come home for lunch but instead thought that he would eat at school. On his way home, the student was attacked by a dog. When the student ran into the street to avoid the dog, he was hit by a car. When the teacher was sued for negligence, the court focused on whether the teacher's conduct was the proximate cause of harm to the student. In this case, the court held that even if the teacher's conduct was indirectly connected with the student's injuries, the connection was too remote to support a finding of proximate cause. This concept relates to the idea of foreseeability and the "connection" between the alleged negligent act and the resulting injury.

Under what other circumstances might a teacher not be found to have proximately caused a student's injury?

A student was hurt when he bumped heads with another student during a basketball game at school. The injured student's father claimed that the school failed to provide proper supervision for the game. In this case, the court found that this type of injury could have occurred *regardless* of the amount of supervision; thus, under the circumstances, the lack of supervision was not the proximate cause of the injury. The mere presence of a supervising teacher would not have prevented the basketball players from running into each other; "that is one of the natural and normal possible consequences or occurrences in a game of this sort which cannot be prevented no matter how adequate the supervision." *Kaufman v. City of New York*, 214 N.Y.S.2d 767, 768-69 (N.Y.App.Div. 1961).

Should teachers anticipate that children may injure themselves or each other?

Yes. A teacher is expected to have reasonable foresight in anticipating that an injury may occur. For example, in an old Washington case, students had rigged a teeter-board across the playground swing, and children were observed swinging and teetering at the same time. One child was injured when he fell from the board. The child's parents were able to recover damages from the teacher. The court concluded: "If the teacher knew [that students used the teeter-board as they did], it was negligence to permit it; and, if she did not know it, it was negligence not to have observed it." *Bruenn v. North Yakima School District No. 7*, 172 P. 569, 571 (Wash. 1918).

In a case filed many years later in California, a teacher continued to teach outside on the school lawn while a boy played with a knife by flipping it into the ground. The knife hit another student, putting out his eye. The court held that the teacher should have been able to predict that this dangerous practice would result in injury. His failure to stop it amounted to a breach of the duty of care owed to his students. *Lilienthal v. San Leandro Unified School District*, 293 P.2d 889 (Cal. 1956).

What level of foresight is legally adequate?

The law does not require clairvoyance; rather, teachers have a duty to anticipate foreseeable dangers and to take those precautions necessary to protect students entrusted in their care. An Oregon teacher took her young students for an outing at the beach. Anticipating that the students would need greater supervision, the teacher also took along the mothers of some of the children. As the teacher stood with her back to the ocean and posed some of the children on a log in order to take their picture, she failed to notice a large wave coming to shore. The wave knocked the teacher down, and then injured several children when they were pinned under the log. A jury found that the teacher should have recognized the danger and protected her small charges from unusual wave activity along the Oregon coast. Her failure to foresee that such a thing might happen made both the teacher and her school district liable for damages. *Morris v. Douglas County School District*, 403 P.2d 775 (Or. 1965).

By comparison, in another case involving young students, the injury to a student was not foreseeable when a teacher had kindergarten students use toothpicks in a class project. The toothpicks were not considered dangerous instruments that would foreseeably result in injury. *Fuzie v. South Haven School District No. 30*, 553 N.Y.S.2d 961 (N.Y.App.Div. 1990), *aff'd* 575 N.Y.S.2d 451 (N.Y. 1991).

Finally, when a school-sponsored activity takes place in a particularly unusual and hazardous place, school officials are expected to take extraordinary precautions to protect the safety of students. For example, a high school student was killed when she fell through a skylight on the roof of the school while 30 students were on the roof taking photographs for the school yearbook. A court found that general admonitions for the students to be careful were insufficient—explicit instructions about the roof layout, the potential danger and location of the skylight, and exact procedures to be followed were required, plus intensive supervision of the students. Although the teacher gave limited warnings, the student did not hear them, nor did she pay attention to warnings by a fellow student. One teacher supervising 30 students, the teacher's failure to prohibit shooting photos near the skylight, and the fact that the teacher was posing in the photograph rather than supervising students at the time of the incident were found by a jury to constitute negligence. The jury found that the teacher's actions were the proximate cause of the death which was clearly foreseeable under the circumstances. Further, the jury rejected the teacher's defense that the student was comparatively negligent in her own death. (See discussion of comparative negligence in the section beginning on page 195.) *Dade County School Board v. Gutierrez*, 592 So.2d 259 (Fla.Dist.Ct.App. 1991).

Does the kind of instrument that causes a student's injury affect a teacher's potential liability?

It may. In the *Ohman* case cited (on pages 179-180), the teacher was not held to the high standard of foreseeing that a pencil would cause permanent injury to a student. Other cases have had similar results when the instrument causing the injury was a ball, a rock, or the corner of a notebook. Normally, items such as these do not cause injuries, and a teacher is generally entitled to presume that no injury will result despite the presence of such objects. For example, in an early Michigan case, a teacher was aware that an elementary student stood on a chair to water plants with a glass bottle. After the student fell from the chair and was severely cut on the broken bottle, the Michigan Supreme Court ruled that the teacher had not been negligent because children had been watering plants in school classrooms for years without the occurrence of a similar incident. *Gaincott v. Davis*, 275 N.W. 229 (Mich. 1937).

However, a word of caution despite the result in *Gaincott*: although teachers may find some solace in the rationale that simply because an injury involving a certain instrument or object has not happened before, that knowledge will usually not outweigh the teacher's affirmative duty to exercise reasonable care in anticipating potential dangers. Foreseeability is always a key factor.

In what way does time influence the tort liability of teachers?

Injuries may occur either instantaneously or gradually. Normally, those which occur spontaneously and which would probably have occurred regardless of whether a teacher was present or absent do not subject a teacher to tort liability.

A good example is *Carroll v. Fitzsimmons*, 384 P.2d 81 (Colo. 1963), when a student was hit by a rock thrown by an unknown student on the playground. The court found that the injury could have occurred even if the teacher had been standing near the injured child, since it is unlikely that the teacher could have stopped the rock in its flight. The teacher was not negligent.

On the other hand, in those cases in which events build up gradually, a teacher is more likely to be held liable because he should have taken steps under the developing circumstances to stop the situation. *Christofides v. Hellenic E. Orthodox Christian Church*, 227 N.Y.S. 2d 946 (N.Y. App.Div. 1962).

What constitutes legally adequate supervision by a teacher?

There is no absolute rule applicable in all instances because the facts in each case are different. Commonly, two main aspects govern proper supervision—do not create danger by one's own negligent conduct and avoid foreseeable hazards created by others. A teacher's specific responsibility is determined by her job duties, but if supervision in general is adequate, it is not a basis for liability if injuries do occur. For example, a kindergarten teacher did not breach her duty of supervision simply by being with other students when one child fell while swinging on a jungle gym. Teachers are not required to have all students in sight at all times. *Clark v. Furch*, 567 S.W.2d 457 (Mo.Ct.App. 1978).

In another case, a student (who was known to be unruly and who had been required to stay in at recess) injured another student in the classroom. The teacher was monitoring the return of other students from recess while standing just outside the classroom in the hall; a court found that the teacher did not breach a duty to supervise. *Simonetti v. School District of Philadelphia*, 454 A.2d 1038 (Pa.Super.Ct. 1982), *appeal dismissed*, 473 A.2d 1015 (Pa. 1984).

By comparison, however, inadequate supervision was found when a student was injured by falling on rocks and glass on a playground while fighting with another student. In this case, the school district allowed a hazard to exist that could conceivably injure students. *Laneheart v. Orleans Parish School Board*, 524 So.2d 138 (La.Ct.App. 1988).

A teacher cannot ensure that accidents will never happen, but he can reduce hazards by being aware of students' activities and conditions around them. Among things a teacher should do: (1) inspect the area to be supervised for possible hazards such as junk, rusty nails, obstructions, and broken equipment; (2) instruct students about known hazards and warn them of impending dangers; (3) correct unsafe conditions or report all defective equipment or possible nuisance hazards to authorities; (4) separate children into groups so that larger and older students will not injure smaller or younger ones; (5) choose vantage points from which to observe students and then move from point to point; and (6) know where a first aid kit is kept in case it is needed. A teacher is not expected to exercise extraordinary caution, but he should consider whether there is duty to supervise and what degree is reasonably required in the circumstances presented. A teacher should also be familiar with all school safety rules and procedures.

Are standards for adequate supervision and instruction higher in some areas than in others?

Yes, since inadequate supervision and instruction in certain areas (e.g., physical education, industrial arts, science classes) seem to invite more opportunities for risk of harm. For example, the use of faulty or unsafe equipment or requiring students to perform tasks beyond their capabilities substantially increases the risk of liability. An Indiana physical education teacher did not properly prepare a sixth-grade student to perform a vertical jump and the student was injured by hitting a wall while doing the jump. *Dibortolo v. Metropolitan School District of Washington Township*, 440 N.E.2d 506 (Ind.Ct.App. 1982). A New York physical education teacher was found negligent for failing to give students adequate instructions about necessary precautions to take when performing a physical fitness test. *Ehlinger v. Board of Education of New Hartford Central School District*, 465 N.Y.S.2d 378 (N.Y.App.Div. 1983). In another case, a physical education teacher was found negligent for not furnishing a list of exercises requested by the doctor of a student with a back condition about which the teacher should have been aware. *Summers v. Milwaukee Union High School*, 481 P.2d 369 (Or. 1971). A Tennessee shop teacher was negligent for allowing a student to use a drill bit without prior instruction, causing severe injury to another student assisting with the machinery. *Roberts v. Robertson County Board of Education*, 692 S.W.2d 863 (Tenn.Ct.App. 1985).

However, if teachers do give proper instructions and students ignore them, the teacher is usually not responsible. *Izard v. Hickory City Schools Board of Education*, 315 S.E.2d 756 (N.C.Ct.App. 1984). In *Izard*, a shop teacher gave detailed instructions on the safe use of power saws and was not liable when a student subsequently lost several fingers.

How broad is the duty to maintain equipment and facilities?

All school personnel share a common responsibility to keep school facilities reasonably safe. Any known hazards should be corrected or reported. This does not mean every possible danger must be predicted or every minor defect corrected immediately. For example, simply because a student slammed his thumb in a heavy metal door did not make the door such a danger that excessive corrective measures were required. *Narcisse v. Continental Insurance Company*, 419 So.2d 13 (La.Ct.App. 1982). However, when school officials were aware of hazards on the playground which children used after hours, the school district was liable for breaching its duty to maintain the school grounds in a safe condition. *Monfils v. City of Sterling Heights*, 269 N.W.2d 588 (Mich.Ct.App. 1978).

What about duty with respect to "known hazards"?

In certain areas of a school, a reasonable and prudent person should anticipate that an accident might happen. The general rule in such instances is that students are entitled to be warned of the "known hazard" so that they will be on the alert. Students have had such known hazards as buzz saws in the school shop, slippery stairs, shaky railings, and wobbly scaffolding pointed out to them by teachers. When students were later hurt on these hazards, it was held that the teachers had discharged their duties to students by telling them of the hazards. After being adequately warned, the students are on their own. However, failure to notify students and instruct them how to avoid injury on known hazards subjects teachers to the possibility of negligence where a "reasonable and prudent teacher" would have foreseen that a particular condition in the school could cause injury to students. Safety instruction is a part of the standard of care each teacher owes to students; a jury might find that failure to instruct a student about a known hazard amounts to a breach of the duty owed.

What is an example of a teacher's duty to warn against possible consequences of an action which would be foreseeable by a reasonable and prudent teacher?

Several eighth-grade students were preparing for a science exhibit when one was seriously burned after a fellow student struck a match and an open container of alcohol ignited. The question presented to the jury was whether the science teacher should have warned the students that an explosion might occur if a match were to be lit. In addition to not warning of the danger, the teacher was also negligent for keeping alcohol in an open container instead of in a sealed bottle. Thus, the teacher's negligence was the proximate cause of the student's injury. *Station v. Travelers Insurance Company*, 292 So.2d 289 (La. 1974).

Does a duty to protect or supervise students extend beyond the school premises?

Yes, but usually it is not enforced as strictly as is the duty owed to students during school hours and on school property; further, the duty depends on the activity, surrounding circumstances and applicable state law. For example, a thirteen-year-old student on a field trip was hit by a car while crossing a street. Accompanying teachers were exonerated from a negligence charge of acting unreasonably since they had warned the students to be careful, the street was not unusually dangerous and the student was old enough to be responsible. There was no duty found in this case for the teachers to personally escort the students across the street. *King v. Kartanson,* 720 S.W.2d 65 (Tenn.Ct.App. 1986).

In some states, a teacher may receive immunity when acting *in loco parentis* (in the place of a parent) during a field trip. This was the case in *Stiff v. Eastern Illinois Area of Special Education,* 621 N.E. 2d 218 (Ill. App.Ct. 1993), *modified and reh'g denied,* (Ill.App.Ct. 1993), *and appeal denied,* 631 N.E.2d 718 (Ill. 1994), when a teacher was immune under state law for ordinary negligence; however, the school district in the same case was not immune from the suit brought by parents of a child with a disability who was injured on the field trip to a state park. As applied to the school district, the park was not considered public property under that state's immunity law.

If an activity is directed or sponsored by the school, a duty to supervise may continue off premises and even during the summer. This was the case in *Verhel v. Independent School District No. 709,* 359 N.W.2d 579 (Minn. 1984), when a cheerleader injured in a car accident during cheerleading activities received damages from the school district.

Is there a duty to supervise before or after school hours?

This aspect of duty is generally governed by state statute. In the absence of statute, a school district and/or school personnel may be liable for injuries arising from circumstances they are aware of, such as students playing in the schoolyard before supervision started each day. *Chan v. Board of Education of City of New York,* 557 N.Y.S.2d 91 (N.Y.App.Div. 1990). In contrast, state law did not expressly require a school district in Colorado to stop a student from riding his bicycle home after school even though the student did not bring the required notification from home on a given day that he would not be riding the school bus. *Jefferson County School District R-1 v. Justus,* 725 P.2d 767 (Colo. 1986). However, this case was remanded to determine whether the school district might have *assumed* a duty of care based on its practices and procedures in handing out bicycle safety literature and posting a teacher to patrol the bicycle area when the school buses were being loaded.

Finally, a teacher may be found negligent and liable for damages when allowing a student to take home volatile chemicals for a science project without checking further into the student's project. *Simmons v. Beauregard Parish School Board*, 315 So.2d 883 (La.Ct.App. 1975), *cert. denied*, 320 So.2d 207 (La. 1975). In this case, an injury occurred when a student was using the chemicals to build a model of a volcano at home.

Does a teacher's duty encompass providing first aid?

It may. If a student is injured, a teacher should provide assistance in accordance with school policy and any first aid training the teacher may have received. As always, the teacher's actions must be reasonable. In some states, what is known as a "good samaritan" law may also protect teachers from liability when the teacher gives well-intentioned aid in an emergency situation.

What is an "attractive nuisance"?

In simple terms, an attractive nuisance is a physical feature that tends to attract children like a magnet; for example, accessible swimming pools, playground equipment, or other enticements that might lure children into an area where they normally should not go. Cases involving these situations may also touch on a question about duty before or after school hours (discussed above).

A school district should not maintain or allow dangerous or unsafe conditions to exist on school premises. If such dangerous conditions are discovered, they should promptly be rectified and not left unattended. For example, a student was injured on a construction site near a school even though students were warned daily about that hazard. The school district was found to have been negligent because it did not post a teacher to guard against children entering the site. *District of Columbia v. Royal*, 465 A.2d 367 (D.C.App. 1983). Ordinarily, a teacher is not liable for "maintenance of a nuisance" if the teacher has notified appropriate personnel that a hazardous condition exists. It is always helpful if the teacher can prove there was notification via documentation or other written evidence. Some of the other conditions found to be nuisances by courts include: maintaining a junk pile on school grounds, maintaining broken slides and other playground equipment, slippery floors, unprotected stairwells, and jagged holes in fences.

What types of money damages may be awarded to students who are injured if a teacher or school district is held liable?

Several different kinds of damages are sought by injured students as plaintiffs in a lawsuit. The most common type of damages is *compensatory* damages, which compensate an injured party for actual losses. These include medical expenses, lost salary, court costs, or other physical or mental injuries to a person. *Punitive* or *exemplary* damages are awarded when defendants have shown evidence of violence, oppression, malice, fraud, or wanton or reckless disregard for the plaintiff's safety. Punitive damages are intended to prevent or deter defendants from doing the same thing again. *Nominal* (in name only) damages are limited monetary awards (i.e., $1.00) which are given by a court or jury when there is technically little or no actual loss, but the plaintiff nonetheless has been mistreated. Sometimes an amount awarded by a jury may be reduced by court order if the award is found to be excessive in view of the facts (or, in judicial terms, if the size of the award "shocks the conscience of the court"). Monetary damages are the legal system's way of making a plaintiff "whole again," and to compensate a person who has suffered loss to his person, property, or rights through unlawful acts of another.

What cases illustrate the different kinds of damages awarded to injured students?

A new student in a Louisiana school was injured in a game of touch football when he plunged into a ditch overgrown with weeds. No barriers or warning signs were near the ditch. The student was awarded punitive damages of $5,000, while the student's father was awarded actual costs of $651. *Sears v. City of Springfield*, 303 So.2d 602 (La.Ct.App. 1974); *cert. denied*, 307 So.2d 371 (La. 1975). The punitive damages were assessed because the school board had done nothing to reduce danger from the known hazard—the weed-covered ditch. In a particularly sizable tort damage award, another court awarded $4,000,000 to a student, who was injured in a summer playground program jointly sponsored by a school district and the city. *Niles v. City of San Rafael*, 116 Cal. Rptr. 733 (Cal. 1974).

What liability rules govern field trips?

As a rule, the younger the child, the more care is owed the child. Therefore, when you take young children into what may be a potentially dangerous place, you should use reasonable measures to ensure that adequate supervision of that number of students in that age group is being supplied. A teacher should have sufficient personal liability insurance to cover suits by injured students. A teacher should also discuss plans with the principal to make sure that certain steps have been taken to safeguard students. Prior planning with other teachers who have taken this field trip may cause you to take extra precautions while on the trip. Make certain that all necessary paperwork (release or waiver forms, medical forms, etc.) have been completed in advance and are properly filed. Finally, be sure that the transportation (which causes or contributes to many injuries on field trips) is adequate; that is, the school district is fully insured and a safe driver is available. While you are not expected to have extraordinary clairvoyance, you are required to foresee what a normal, prudent teacher might consider a hazard and then to warn students about the situation before going on the trip.

May a teacher be held liable for injuries to students who are on errands for or assisting a teacher?

A teacher may be held liable if, in sending a student on an errand, the child is exposed to a danger which should have been apparent to the reasonable and prudent teacher. In New York, a teacher sent a thirteen-year-old girl on an errand and the girl was raped. In evaluating foreseeability in the case, the court required the plaintiff to show evidence of other incidents which would have led a reasonable teacher to foresee that such consequences might transpire. *Gallagher v. City of New York*, 292 N.Y.S.2d 139 (N.Y. 1968).

A weak, pale lad was working with other boys moving cartons. He complained of a pain in his chest and was told to use "two boys to a carton." When a doctor examined the boy, he said the boy had sustained injury to his heart. The court rendered judgment in the amount of $35,000 against the board of education. The court concluded, "parents do not send their children to school to be returned to them maimed because of the absence of proper supervision or the abandonment of supervision." *Feuerstein v. Board of Education of City of New York*, 202 N.Y.S.2d 524, (N.Y.App.Div. 1960), *aff'd* 214 N.Y.S.2d 654 (N.Y. 1961).

A classroom teacher who also drove a school bus gave the bus ignition key to a fifteen-year-old student who was not licensed to drive. The teacher wanted the student to warm up the bus. The student drove the bus around the block, striking a truck. The truck driver brought an action for damages but was told the State Industrial Commission lacked jurisdiction because the teacher was not operating the bus and the student had no authorization to do so. *Withers v. Charlotte-Mecklenburg Board of Education*, 231 S.E.2d 276 (N.C. 1976).

Finally, in an older case, a New Mexico court ruled that a teacher may be held liable if a student is injured while performing an errand for the teacher even though the injury was the direct result of the student's inexperience and immaturity. *McMullen v. Ursuline Order of Sisters*, 246 P.2d 1052 (N.M. 1952), *overruled in part by Williamson v. Smith*, 491 P.2d 1147 (N.M. 1971).

Defenses Against Charges of Negligence

What defenses are available to teachers facing tort liability for negligence?

Beginning with the four-part test, a teacher may argue that one of the essential elements of a successful negligence claim is missing. For example, possible contentions are that (1) the teacher did not owe a duty of care to a student who was injured; (2) even if a duty was owed, the teacher did not breach the duty; (3) despite the existence of a duty and a breach, the teacher's act was not the proximate cause of the student's injury (either because of an intervening factor which superseded the teacher's conduct, or because the connection between the act and the injury was too remote to have been foreseeable); or (4) the student did not sustain a compensable injury. (See the previous section for examples of negligence claims that lack these elements.) A teacher may also argue that the injury was solely the result of an unavoidable accident. Finally, assuming that an injured student *is* able to show the existence of the four negligence elements, a teacher may have one or more available defenses that might serve to minimize or eliminate the teacher's potential liability. These defenses may or may not be available in every state depending on each state's tort laws. Defenses include: (1) contributory negligence; (2) comparative negligence; (3) assumption of risk; (4) the student's (or student's parents') waiver of liability by signing a release form; and (5) the availability of immunity or other statutory protections which shield a teacher from tort liability.

Will someone be found liable if a student is injured as the result of an accident?

No. By definition, when a "pure" or "unavoidable" accident occurs, no one is at fault under the law. Looking at this from another angle, an event that is completely accidental could not have been prevented by another person's exercise of reasonable care; therefore, without a duty to exercise reasonable care there cannot be negligence (a nonexistent duty cannot be breached).

What is contributory negligence?

In defending against a negligence claim, a teacher may be able to demonstrate that the injured student's own conduct contributed to her injury since it fell below the standard to which a student was required to conform for her own protection. Put another way, a person is expected to act responsibly to protect herself from injury; if she does not, she may be denied an opportunity to recover damages from an otherwise negligent defendant. Whether an injured child can be contributorily negligent in a given situation will usually depend on the age and maturity of the child. For example, if a child is too young to understand the danger of her act, she cannot be held to have contributed to her injury.

However, even an eight-year-old is expected to have a sense of danger with respect to such things as the harm caused by the impact of a moving school bus. A child was injured when he swung up on a moving bus as it pulled into the schoolyard. By the student's own act he contributed to his injury. *Weems v. Robinson*, 9 So.2d 882 (Ala. 1942). The laws governing contributory negligence vary from state to state. In recent years, however, most states have replaced this defense with the doctrine of comparative negligence.

What is comparative negligence?

Unlike the potentially harsh result under contributory negligence (in which an injured person's own negligence will prevent *any* recovery from a negligent defendant), comparative negligence provides for the apportionment of responsibility between the injured party (plaintiff) and one or more defendants. In other words, under a comparative negligence doctrine, *all* of the parties—including the plaintiff—are liable for their respective shares of the plaintiff's loss or injury, and liability is assessed in direct proportion to fault. Although state laws vary as to the specific methods for asking a jury to apply the concept, most states will not allow a plaintiff to recover damages if his own negligence constituted more than one-half of the total amount of negligent conduct.

A 1984 Minnesota Supreme Court case exemplified the concept of comparative negligence. In *Verhel v. Independent School District No. 709*, 359 N.W.2d 579 (Minn. 1984), a high school cheerleader was injured while riding in a van driven by another cheerleader. The van was in an accident with another vehicle and the cheerleader sponsor who knew of the travel plans was not on the trip. School had not yet started for the school year and technically the sponsor's duties had not yet begun. A trial court damage award upheld by Minnesota's highest court held the school district 35 percent liable, the driver of the other vehicle 26 percent liable and the cheerleader driver 39 percent liable for the payment of $200,000 in damages to the injured girl and $14,000 to her father. The cheerleader sponsor was not assigned any degree of comparative negligence.

What is meant by assumption of risk?

Under the doctrine of assumption of risk, an injured person is not allowed to recover damages if the person sustains an injury after voluntarily participating in an activity which is known to be inherently dangerous. In a sense, this doctrine resembles the contributory negligence doctrine in that neither allows for recovery of damages due to the injured person's own conduct. Athletic activities produce a plethora of injuries to students each year. The assumption of risk doctrine may protect coaches and school officials from liability on the grounds that students who voluntarily undertake a hazardous activity or an activity that exposes them to obvious peril assume some risk. However, many states have all but eliminated this defense or made it more difficult to assert. For example, a student athlete injured during football practice did not have a helmet because the school did not have a sufficient number of helmets for all the players. The school argued that the student assumed the risk, but the court rejected the defense by pointing out that there was no evidence the student assumed the risk of participating in football without adequate equipment. *Leahy v. School Board of Hernando County*, 450 So.2d 883 (Fla.Dist.Ct.App. 1984).

In another football case, a student was injured during supervised summer practice where no protective equipment was being used. An opposing team player's hand hit the student's eye causing blindness. Although a lower court dismissed the suit saying the student assumed the risk of injury, the Pennsylvania Supreme Court reversed that ruling and abolished the assumption of risk defense for negligence cases except under very limited circumstances. *Rutter v. Northeastern Beaver County School District*, 437 A.2d 1198 (Pa. 1981).

How effective are waivers of liability signed by parents?

It has been said that most waivers may have public relations value but that they really have very little legal value. Schools often make it a practice to send waiver slips home to parents when students are about to go on field trips or undertake potentially hazardous activities in school. While these waiver slips *may* (the word is used cautiously in this context) exonerate the school of any liability in a negligence suit brought by the parents, they still do not necessarily mean that the student has signed away his own right to sue. For example, even if parents have signed a waiver in the student's behalf, in some cases the student may later sue in his own name. The greatest use of waiver slips is in a communication and documentation sense—a signed waiver slip shows that parents were aware of the impending trip or potentially hazardous activity and, at least to some extent, were willing to acknowledge the risk by allowing the student to be a part of that activity. You should check the law in your own state to determine the legal value, if any, of the liability waiver form. Please note, however, that even if such forms are not given much legal credence in your state, they may still be an important and necessary prerequisite within your school district before embarking on "out of the ordinary" activities with students.

May a teacher plead sovereign immunity as a defense?

No. Sovereign or governmental immunity is premised on the principle that "the king can do no wrong." Under that doctrine, a state—and by extension, the school districts in some states—cannot be sued for negligence unless they consent to be sued or unless the state legislature has specifically stated that districts can be sued for particular events or types of injury. As a result, sovereign immunity generally extends only to governmental units, and not to individuals. For example, in 1976 the Ohio Supreme Court ruled that the immunity of school districts from liability for negligence did not extend to teachers, who must exercise reasonable care in the performance of their duties. *Baird v. Hosmer*, 347 N.E.2d 533 (Ohio 1976). However, after the *Baird* decision came out, Ohio enacted new legislation that superseded *Baird*. It granted general or statutory immunity to employees of political subdivisions (which includes school districts) who act within their discretion and judgment unless it was exercised with malicious purpose.

May a teacher be given personal immunity from liability for negligence?

Yes, although only a handful of states do so. In a Utah case against a teacher who was absent from a physical education class in which a student was beaten by students from other classes, the lawsuit was dismissed on the basis of Utah's Governmental Immunity Law. Even though the injured student's classmates could not locate the teacher when the beating began, Utah law provides immunity to governmental entities and employees (including teachers) as well as to the principal and school district in this type of case. *Ledfors v. Emery County School District*, 849 P.2d 1162 (Utah 1993). Similarly, under Ohio law, a teacher was not liable for administering a paddling in accordance with school policy, and a negligence case against the teacher and principal was dismissed on defendants' motion for summary judgment. The teacher was immune from liability since there was no evidence he acted with a malicious purpose or in a wanton or reckless manner. *Rinehart v. Western Local School District Board of Education*, 621 N.E. 2d 1365 (Ohio Ct.App. 1993).

However, under Montana's amended immunity statute, a teacher was subject to liability for alleged negligent supervision on the playground when a student was struck by a shot put. The court determined that the state's negligence statute did not provide immunity unless the teacher's acts arose out of the discharge of an official duty "associated with legislative acts" of the school board, which was not applicable in this situation. *Hedges v. Swan Lake & Salmon Prairie School District*, 832 P.2d 775 (Mont. 1992).

Rather than providing statutory immunity for teachers, many other states have statutes that require employing school districts to *indemnify* or "hold harmless" its teacher employees. If the teacher is sued for negligence, the school district is required to defend the teacher against a negligence claim if the teacher was engaged in official duties. Further, the school district must pay any damages that may be assessed against the teacher in such litigation. Even in states where indemnification is not required by statute it is permissible for local school districts to voluntarily undertake this obligation for its employees.

Should a teacher obtain insurance coverage for professional liability?

A teacher should not be without adequate professional liability insurance coverage, even during vacation periods. An insurer will soften the blow should you be found personally liable for negligence while on the job. Perhaps the largest risk of "blind-side" liability lies in injury to students who may be transported in a teacher's car. A teacher should become thoroughly familiar with the extent of statutory coverage in his particular state and under his own insurance policy in the event that a student is injured while being driven in the teacher's personal vehicle. This is true regardless of whether a student is being driven home, to a doctor or to a school function such as a ball game or meeting. Further, blanket liability insurance may be available for members of certain teachers' organizations which will provide legal counsel in case you must face a student injury suit.

Should teachers expect the school district's attorney to provide legal representation or counsel against charges of teacher negligence?

Not always. The attorney employed or retained to represent the school district could have a conflict of interest which would prevent that attorney from also representing a teacher (i.e., even if both are named as defendants in a case, the school district and the teacher may not necessarily end up on the same "side" or sharing the same interests if a case goes to trial). In states with collective bargaining, it may be possible to negotiate for the use of the school's attorney with some kind of "hold harmless" clause in the negotiated agreement with the board. In such a case, the school district will come to the legal aid of a teacher who is being sued. If nothing else, a teacher may have to retain legal counsel on a private basis to protect the teacher's individual interest. However, this type of legal counsel may be costly. Chapter 7 expands on legal representation in discussing the attorney-client relationship.

Assault and Battery

What is an "assault"?

Generally characterized as an intentional tort, an assault is a nonphysical act that puts another person in fear of immediate bodily harm. Essentially, an assault is an invasion of a person's peace of mind or her "space" (rather than a physical attack upon her body) such that the victim apprehends immediate harm and knows that the offender has the ability to carry out the harm that is threatened. In most states, an assault may be prosecuted under criminal statutes as well as under civil tort law. Assault may involve words, actions or both.

However, not all verbal attacks are classified as assaults. For example, a parent brought suit against a teacher for intentionally "abusing, attacking, embarrassing, and intimidating" her children. She cited possible injury to their nervous systems, their learning abilities, and their potential earning capacities. The court held that a teacher has the right to chastise a child verbally as well as corporally. Furthermore, a teacher cannot be sued unless there is evidence of malice, which was not shown in this case. *Gordon v. Oak Park School District*, 320 N.E.2d 389 (Ill. 1974).

What is a "battery"?

Unlike an assault, which is nonphysical, a battery involves intentional physical contact that causes bodily injury or is characterized as offensive touching. In a sense, a battery is the consummation of an assault. In most states a battery is subject to criminal prosecution and an injured person may also recover monetary damages under state tort laws.

What motivates most student-initiated suits for assault and battery?

Most assault and battery suits filed against teachers involve either corporal punishment or student discipline. Although some states have statutes that prohibit corporal punishment, most others either say nothing about corporal punishment or have statutes that expressly make it available. Generally, there is a basis for a tort action or criminal prosecution only if the punishment is excessive or unreasonable.

Who determines whether assault or battery occurred?

The existence of an assault or battery is for a jury to decide following legal instructions given by a judge. Factors in the case—age, gender, strength, health, and similar characteristics of the child; the teacher's size, age and general health; the chronological events—are all pertinent. In corporal punishment cases, the critical question is whether the teacher acted reasonably in administering punishment or whether the punishment was excessive, brutal or administered with malice.

Does the Eighth Amendment apply to corporal punishment of students?

No. In *Ingraham v. Wright*, 430 U.S. 651 (1977), the United States Supreme Court held that the Eighth Amendment's prohibition against cruel and unusual punishment applies only to criminals and not to students being disciplined.

> The openness of the public school and its supervision by the community afford significant safeguards against the kinds of abuses from which the Eighth Amendment protects the prisoner. . . . Public school teachers and administrators are privileged at common law to inflict only such corporal punishment as is reasonably necessary for the proper education and discipline of the child; any punishment going beyond the privilege may result in both civil and criminal liability. . . . As long as the schools are open to public scrutiny, there is no reason to believe that the common law constraints will not effectively remedy and deter excesses such as those alleged in this case. *Id.* at 670.

Can a teacher rely on self defense in an assault and battery case?

Yes, if it can reasonably be deduced that a student was about to attack the teacher. A teacher has the same right as any other citizen to protect himself from attack. The rule of thumb is that a teacher can use only that force as is reasonably necessary to end the threat. An example is a case in which a sixty-nine-year-old teacher worked in a "tough" school. Secretly, she armed herself with a "sneeze-gun" that emitted a spray designed to cause the eyes to water and to temporarily put a person "out of commission." When a student in the teacher's class resisted being taken to the principal's office and attacked the teacher, the teacher sprayed the student with the sneeze-gun. The student brought suit for assault and battery against the teacher. The suit failed. The court found that a teacher who had reason to believe that she was about to be assaulted by a student had the right of self-defense. *Owens v. Commonwealth of Kentucky*, 473 S.W.2d 827 (Ky. 1972).

A teacher is generally expected to intervene and attempt to protect students from physical attack by another student or an outsider. If a teacher responds with force that is excessive under the circumstances or continues to use force after a student has submitted or has attempted to flee, a teacher steps outside the protection of acting *in loco parentis* and loses the justification for self-defense.

Defamation

What is defamation?

Defamation is defined as an invasion of a person's interest in her reputation and good name. It involves a communication (by means of either libel or slander, which are discussed below) to a third person which exposes a person to contempt, hatred, scorn or ridicule. It may also cause a person to be shunned or avoided, or it may result in harm to a person's employment or business. Redress for injury to reputation is one of the most cherished legal rights and, contrary to what some people may believe, children and students are not barred from asserting this right.

How do "libel" and "slander" differ?

Libel and slander are the two torts which comprise defamation. In general, libel consists of written statements and slander consists of oral or spoken communications.

Can teachers "defame" their students?

Since teachers come into possession of critical and oftentimes very personal information about students, it is only natural that there is a risk that some of this information might be communicated to others in such a way that a tort action alleging defamation may be justified. Balanced against a student's interest in his own reputation is the need for teachers and school administrators to communicate information about the student's abilities and performance in order to best serve the student's educational interests. The "fine line" between these two interests creates a fertile arena for potential litigation.

Is maintaining the confidentiality of student records an occupational hazard for teachers?

Yes, particularly since 1974 when Congress passed the Buckley Amendment (Family Educational Rights and Privacy Act, P.L. 93-380, commonly known as FERPA) which was designed to protect the privacy of parents and students. As a result of this legislation, school districts are required to prepare guidelines for the release of information about students. These guidelines should be carefully followed by teachers in order to avoid potential liability. Among other things, the act governs access to student records—keeping the records, storing them, and releasing them to interested persons. Parents of students must have access to official records and an opportunity to challenge inaccurate or misleading information. Along these lines, the school district must notify parents and students of their rights on an annual basis. At age eighteen, many of these rights transfer to the student. Due process must be observed in preserving and releasing student records and allowing parents or students to challenge materials to which they object. Although a FERPA violation does not necessarily give rise to a defamation action, it may result in a school district forfeiting federal funds for noncompliance. States may also adopt their own legislation governing access to student records, which may be even more rigorous than FERPA.

What is meant by "privileged communications" and are teachers protected under this principle?

Generally, teachers have what is called a "qualified" or "limited"—but not absolute—privilege to handle and discuss information about their students. Teachers may lose this privilege if they act maliciously or in bad faith. Even though a communication may arguably be defamatory in nature, liability will not attach if the communication is made in the discharge of a public duty and if the information is released to someone having a right to receive the information. Teachers can lose the privilege if they act to "get even" with a student. When a teacher wrote more than one hundred years ago that a student "was tricky and unreliable," she was found to have stepped outside the protection of privileged communications and was held liable in damages for injury to the student's reputation. *Dixon v. Allen*, 11 P. 179 (Cal. 1886). Similarly, a teacher was held liable for describing a student as "ruined by tobacco and whiskey." *Dawkins v. Billingsley*, 172 P. 69 (Okla. 1918).

Is truth a defense to defamation?

Yes. To create liability for defamation, a statement must be both defamatory and false. Consequently, there will be no liability if a defendant in a defamation lawsuit is able to prove that an allegedly defamatory statement is true.

May a teacher be defamed by statements made by parents?

In California, several parents wrote a letter to a principal stating that a particular teacher "displayed an utter lack of judgment and respect, had been rude, vindictive and unjust, misused her authority and had given failing grades to students she did not like." In disallowing the teacher's claim for defamation of character, the court stated: "One of the crosses a public school teacher must bear is intemperate complaint addressed to school administrators by overly solicitous parents concerned about the teacher's conduct in the classroom. Since the law compels parents to send their children to school, appropriate channels for the airing of supposed grievances against the operation of the school system must remain open." *Martin v. Kearney*, 124 Cal. Rptr. 281, 283 (Cal. 1975).

Can parental criticism of a teacher's work be considered "privileged"?

Yes, so long as certain conditions are met. In *Segall v. Piazza*, 260 N.Y.S.2d 543 (N.Y.App.Div. 1965), the court held that certain statements were privileged even though they were proved to be false and despite the fact that the parent who wrote them in a letter to the teacher's principal thought they were true. Since the parent was not motivated by ill will or malice but only by an interest in her son, the court did not find that she had stepped outside her normal right to criticize the teacher. She had gone through channels, had kept her son's interests central in her letter, and had acted in good faith. The fact that the teacher had been denied a promotion because of the letter and had demonstrated a resulting loss of income was not grounds for recovery of damages but only an "unfortunate misunderstanding" according to the court.

In a more recent case, a Michigan court reached a similar result when a teacher brought a defamation action against a father who wrote a letter to the school principal accusing the teacher of treating his child unfairly, unprofessionally and insensitively.

The court recognized the father's qualified privilege to communicate his interest in his child's well-being with someone (the principal) who shared a corresponding interest in the student's well-being. *Swenson-Davis v. Martel*, 354 N.W.2d 288 (Mich.Ct. App. 1984), *appeal denied*, (Mich. 1984)[citation unavailable].

Educational Malpractice

What is educational malpractice?

An educational malpractice claim is an attempt to use tort law to seek compensation when a student who has been through an educational program has failed to attain a certain level of achievement. In order for a student (or, more likely, a former student) to prevail in an educational malpractice lawsuit, it would be necessary to satisfy all of the basic elements of a traditional negligence action. In other words, a student/plaintiff must show that: (1) a school district and/or particular teacher(s) owed the student a duty that is recognized under the law; (2) the standard of care required by this duty was breached; (3) the school district's or teacher's breach of this duty was the proximate cause of injury to the student; and (4) the student suffered an actual injury or harm.

Should teachers be concerned about being sued for educational malpractice?

The simple answer is "yes" because it is always costly—emotionally even if not financially—to defend a lawsuit. However, a more accurate response to the question would be, "be concerned but not overly so." Although a large number of negligence-based educational malpractice claims have been filed over the years in various courts around the country, the plaintiffs bringing the suits have uniformly met with little success. In fact, with the exception of several special education-related cases involving issues such as misclassification and inaccurate diagnostic testing, there have not been any reported educational malpractice suits that could be characterized as truly successful. This is due to two primary reasons: (1) it is not exactly certain what constitutes effective schooling—but even if it were, numerous other non-school factors affect how (or if) a particular student will learn; and (2) assuming that schools and teachers *can* breach a duty owed to students, public policy considerations dictate that schools and teachers not be held accountable for *guaranteeing* a certain level of student academic proficiency. To do so would place an unacceptable burden on the educational system in general and individual educators in particular. The bottom line is this: Educational malpractice is not a recognized cause of action under the laws of most states. Although certain circumstances may give rise to a change in the law, at this time most teachers need not live in fear of being liable for an educational malpractice claim filed by a student (or former student).

Which cases exemplify educational malpractice claims?

One of the first educational malpractice claims was asserted in *Peter W. v. San Francisco Unified School District*, 131 Cal.Rptr. 854 (Cal. 1976) in which an 18-year-old graduate of the district's school system claimed he was not provided with the basic academic skills he should have acquired during twelve years of school attendance. More specifically, educators had failed to diagnose his reading disabilities, placed him in classes which were beyond his capabilities and allowed him to graduate without being able to read at the eighth-grade level as required by state law. An appellate court dismissed the student's negligence claims based on grounds of budget restrictions and public policy principles which included: (1) the difficulty to establish a standard of care by which to measure educators' conduct; (2) that there is no reasonable degree of certainty the student suffered harm as defined by the meaning of negligence law; and (3) that no identifiable connection between the educators' conduct and the alleged injury establishes a causal link between the two. In other words, three of the four negligence elements were not present in this student's educational malpractice claim. Finally, the court refused to recognize educational malpractice claims because it would expose educators to tort claims by "disaffected students and parents in countless numbers." *Id.* at 861.

A similar result was reached by a New York court which relied on the *Peter W.* case to support its refusal to recognize an educational malpractice claim in that state. In *Donohue v. Copiague Union Free School District*, 418 N.Y.S.2d 375 (N.Y. 1979), a student graduated with inadequate reading and writing skills for which he needed additional tutoring. He claimed the school district was negligent for having failed to educate him as required by the state constitution. In dismissing the claims, the court noted that "the failure to learn does not bespeak the failure to teach." The student did not allege that his classmates also did not learn, so the court concluded that other factors caused this student's failure to learn. Again, public policy prevailed as evidenced by the court's concern that "[r]ecognition in the courts of this cause of action [educational malpractice] would constitute blatant interference with the responsibility for the administration of the public school system lodged by the Constitution and statute in school administrative agencies." *Id.* at 378. However, this court did not foreclose the possibility that a legal duty could be imposed on schools and educators as professionals, similar to that duty imposed on doctors, lawyers, engineers and other professionals. Even if a duty element existed, and the duty was breached, it would still be a demanding challenge to show the causation link to an injury given the many collateral factors involved in the learning process. In both of these cases the student/plaintiffs failed to recover damages from their respective school districts.

Child Abuse

Do teachers have a duty to report suspected child abuse?

Yes. State statutes in all fifty states require school personnel to report known or suspected child abuse or neglect. This even applies to abuse by other school employees. For example, a kindergarten teacher reported aides for abuse when they put a child's hand under hot water making him scream and blistering his hand. *Morris v. State*, 833 S.W.2d 624 (Tex.Ct.App. 1992), *cert. denied*, 113 S.Ct. 1387 (1993). Each state's statutes define the concepts of abuse and neglect; the definitions and statutory obligations to report that are imposed on teachers and other educators differ from state to state. Your building principal should have the applicable statutes for your state available for you to review. In addition, your school district should have in place a well-crafted procedure for all school personnel to report suspected abuse (for example, the designation of one person in each building to take reports of suspected abuse, to complete all the necessary documentation and memorialize the report, and then to pass the information along to the proper state agency or authorities for timely investigation).

Does a teacher need to have absolute knowledge that abuse has occurred?

No, not usually. Most state statutes speak in terms of "suspected" abuse or that someone has a "reason to believe" that abuse or neglect has occurred. As long as a report is filed in good faith and in a timely fashion with the proper agency, the statutes will provide a teacher with immunity from liability regardless of whether he had "absolute" knowledge or certainty and regardless of whether the abuse or neglect actually occurred.

Does a teacher who reports suspected child abuse face liability for filing a report?

Under the laws in most states, the only time a teacher faces possible liability is if she *fails* to report suspected abuse or neglect. This liability may be either civil liability, criminal liability, or both (i.e., fines, imprisonment, or both). It may also be possible for an employing school district to sanction or discipline a teacher for failing to file a timely report.

Constitutional Torts

What is a constitutional tort?

Following the end of the Civil War, Congress sought to provide legal redress to southern African-Americans who, because of race, had been mistreated by the government. Consequently, the Civil Rights Act of 1871 was enacted by Congress. It contained a short and fairly straightforward provision which opened the door for the recovery of damages from government agencies, officials and employees who deprive others of rights protected by the Constitution or other federal laws. Perhaps the most important portion of that legislation is presently found in Title 42 of the United States Code in section 1983 (42 U.S.C. § 1983). That section reads:

> Every person who, under color of any statute, ordinance, regulation, custom, or usage, of any State or Territory, subjects, or causes to be subjected, any citizen of the United States or other person within the jurisdiction thereof to the deprivation of any rights, privileges or immunities secured by the Constitution and laws, shall be liable to the party injured in an action at law, suit in equity, or other proper proceeding for redress.

In layman's terms and as applied in a school setting, "§ 1983" protects an individual's constitutional and civil rights by providing an avenue to sue school boards, individual school board members, school administrators and teachers for mon-

etary damages following the denial or deprivation of a protected right. In the last thirty years or so, civil rights legislation—and particularly § 1983—has become a well-traveled
route in school-related litigation. Simply put, individuals often
bring "§ 1983 suits" against school personnel, school officials,
and/or the school district itself for the alleged denial of such
things as the individual's rights to due process, equal protection of the laws, or freedom of speech. The prerequisite to
holding someone liable under § 1983 is that the person must
have acted with some kind of authority (i.e., "under color of
state law") on behalf of the governmental agency.

May teachers have constitutional tort liability?

Yes. Teachers and other school district employees may be personally liable for violating the constitutional or statutory
rights of students and others they interact with in the course
of their employment. However, if sued under a § 1983 claim,
teachers (and other school district employees) may assert a
"qualified good faith immunity" defense. Essentially, this defense requires that the defendant must be able to show that he
did not *knowingly* violate a "clearly established statutory or
constitutional right" of another person. *Harlow v. Fitzgerald*,
457 U.S. 800 (1982). In other words, the defendant will need to
show that a "reasonable person" in the defendant's same position would not have known that the action that was taken
would violate one of the plaintiff's "clearly established" rights.
If the defendant can satisfy this standard, then he is entitled to
immunity from liability under the "qualified good faith immunity" defense.

What is an example of a case illustrating the "qualified good faith immunity" defense?

In *Jefferson v. Yselta Independent School District*, 817 F.2d 303
(5th Cir. 1987), a second-grade teacher used a jump rope to tie
a young female student to a chair, allegedly as a means of im-

proving the student's behavior. The student was the only child in her classroom who was tied to a chair and the "treatment" was part of an instructional technique imposed by school policy. She was kept tied to the chair for the better part of two school days during which time she was denied access to the restroom. As a result of her treatment, the student's parents filed a § 1983 constitutional tort claim against the teacher, the school principal and the school district seeking damages for mental anguish, humiliation and an impaired ability to study productively.

At trial, the court rejected the teacher's "qualified good faith immunity" defense because the teacher's alleged actions violated one or more of the student's protected rights of which the teacher should have been aware. For example, the parents claimed that their daughter's Fifth and Fourteenth Amendment rights to substantive due process were violated in that the student was not free from bodily restraint. On appeal to the Fifth Circuit Court of Appeals, that court agreed with the trial court that a "reasonable teacher" should and would have know that tying a second-grade student to a chair for two days would violate the student's constitutional rights.

It is significant that the teacher in this case was not expected to have exact knowledge of "the law" as it relates to proper instructional techniques; rather, the key is that a reasonable teacher would know (or "feel") that tying a second-grade student to a chair and denying her access to go to the restroom "just isn't right." In the court's words, the standard is that "the teacher [is expected to] be aware of general, well-developed legal principles"—*not* that the teacher necessarily be familiar with specific constitutional laws governing bodily restraint or proper instructional techniques. Put another way, a teacher in this type of situation will lose a good faith immunity defense claim if the evidence shows a "callous indifference" to an individual's constitutionally or statutorily protected rights.

Do school districts also have constitutional tort liability?

Yes. Although § 1983 refers to "person[s]" acting with governmental authority, the United States Supreme Court has interpreted that statutory provision to include governmental entities such as school districts. *Monnell v. New York City Department of Social Services*, 436 U.S. 658 (1978). Thus, a school district may be liable for § 1983 damages; however, in order to be successful in such a suit against a governmental agency, a plaintiff will have to be able to prove that the wrong committed was either the result of an official governmental policy or unwritten "custom." The government will not be held liable simply because it employs someone who violated another person's protected rights; rather, liability will only attach if the government itself acted more "directly" to cause the harm by vesting "final" policy-making authority in an employee who then proceeded to misuse that authority. The "policy or custom" aspect of governmental liability is a complex and heavily litigated aspect of constitutional tort law.

What are the present trends in constitutional tort litigation involving schools and teachers?

In the last few years, there have been a great many § 1983 claims brought by students who have been physically or sexually assaulted by other students or, in some cases, by teachers or other school personnel. Although schools have been fairly successful in avoiding liability for student-on-student instances of abuse, they have not avoided liability in some cases alleging teacher-on-student misconduct. Despite the fact that some of these situations may involve elements of traditional tort law (i.e., battery, negligent hiring and negligent supervision), many lawsuits are premised in terms of civil rights (i.e., discrimination under Title VII of the Civil Rights Act of 1964; gender discrimination under Title IX of the Educational Amendments of 1972) or constitutional violations in order to avoid immunity protections which the defendants might otherwise be able to claim under state tort law.

What kinds of damages can be sought under a § 1983 claim?

Often, a plaintiff in a § 1983 claim seeks monetary damages to compensate for an injury incurred as the result of a violation of the injured person's federally protected rights. In order to obtain compensatory damages a plaintiff must be able to show actual injury (which may include mental suffering); otherwise, without a showing of actual injury, all that a plaintiff can hope to recover for an impairment of civil rights will be nominal damages. In cases seeking nominal damages, it is often "the principle of the thing" that is at stake—even though there was no actual injury, the plaintiff is "trying to right a wrong." If the plaintiff is successful and prevails by winning an award of nominal damages, it is likely that he will also be awarded costs and attorney's fees associated with the lawsuit. Other types of damages which may be sought include punitive damages; however, punitive damages are only available from individual defendants and not from governmental entities. Finally, not all of the claims filed under § 1983 seek monetary damages; rather, many seek injunctive relief. In requesting an injunction, a plaintiff will attempt to convince a court that certain unlawful action should be stopped or "enjoined" so as to prevent harm or further injury.

Does the usual liability insurance policy (i.e., homeowners, automobile or professional association) cover constitutional tort actions?

No. Liability insurance coverage is generally limited to common negligence. However, there is a type of insurance that covers "wrongful acts of school officials" (sometimes called "deprivation of civil rights insurance") that is a distinctly separate type of indemnity coverage. If an insured teacher is ever found liable for a constitutional tort and required to pay damages for wrongful acts, the insurance company will provide indemnity—either by paying attorney's fees or any damages which are awarded in court or agreed to in a pre-trial settlement.

Case Resolutions

Case No. 1: Athlete injured during hazing (see page 172)

To recover on his constitutional claims, the student must show he was deprived of a constitutional right by a person "acting under color of state law." There was no evidence in this case to support the plaintiff's contention. A failure by the school board and the coach to halt the "hit line" does not amount to an abuse of due process; nor does due process entitle every individual under care of state authorities to protection from physical injuries except in certain circumstances. In this case, the injuries were incurred in conjunction with the student's *voluntary* participation on the football team, an extracurricular activity. Even if the student could show that the coach and school board owed him a constitutional duty of protection, the coach is protected by qualified immunity. No court has found that school officials are constitutionally required to protect students from assaults by fellow students during extracurricular activities, even if, as here, the officials were aware of the activity. The court emphasized that:

> The Constitution of the United States is, and must be, a document of grandeur and wisdom which secures and protects the most fundamental and sacrosanct rights of our people. To extend the protections of the Constitution to the most mundane fracases of everyday life cheapens and trivializes not only the Constitution itself, but those rights and privileges which are protected under it, as well.

The federal court also dismissed the plaintiff's state law claim but noted that such claims could be refiled in an appropriate state court action. *Reeves by Jones v. Besonen*, 754 F.Supp. 1135, 1141 (E.D.Mich. 1991).

Case No. 2: Wrongful death (see page 172)

The school district was held liable for a $42,000 judgment for wrongful death due to the negligence of the coaches. During the trial, expert testimony by members of the medical profession was introduced which indicated that when a person sustains a heat stroke, every effort should be made to stop the accumulation of heat, not to conserve it. Once the process of heat stroke reaches a certain high level in the body, the damage becomes irreversible—much like boiling an egg. The record supported the plaintiff's contention that the coaches were negligent in not immediately seeking medical aid. The court said that all that had to be done to establish negligence was to prove that it was more likely than not that the deceased player would have survived with prompt and reasonable medical attention. (Would it make sense to claim that a student out for football would assume the risk of receiving *this* type of medical "treatment" from "reasonable" coaches?) *Mogabgab v. Orleans Parish School Board*, 239 So.2d 456 (La.Ct.App. 1970); *cert. denied*, 241 So.2d 253 (La. 1970).

Case No. 3: Acting like Superman (see page 173)

The teacher was found not to have been negligent in her supervision of the children. She testified that the student was agile, coordinated and active and easily climbed the ladder. She was not apprehensive while watching him. Indeed, the student himself said he had climbed that type of ladder before. He failed to follow instructions to line up, and in fact, he did not *fall* off the ladder, but rather he jumped because he "wanted to act like Superman." The principal did not breach his duty to inform the teacher about climbing rules because there was no rule applicable to kindergartners using the equipment. Without negligence on the part of the teacher or the principal, the school board in this case was not liable either. *Hunter v. Cado Parish School Board*, 627 So.2d 772 (La.Ct.App. 1993).

Case No. 4: Gifted students get hurt too (see page 173)

The student and his parents sued the District of Columbia Public Schools, who, in turn, sued the director of the summer program and the chemistry teacher, and all were found negligent. The school district was liable because its employee (the principal) knew the teacher planned to do a dangerous activity with young children. Only a student counselor who helped distribute some of the materials was not found negligent. The jury awarded $8,000,000 to the student for pain and suffering, and $1,000,000 for past and future medical expenses. (Part of the medical expense award for future damages was later reversed on appeal as being too speculative, and $1,000,000 awards to each parent for loss of parent-child consortium were also reversed.) The teacher was declared bankrupt during the trial and was dismissed from the case. However, the director of the program had to pay the school district a portion of the damage award given to the student. *District of Columbia v. Howell*, 607 A.2d 501 (D.C. 1992).

Case No. 5: Excessive corporal punishment? (see page 174)

The federal appellate court dismissed the parent's civil rights claims after concluding that there was no substantive due process violation. Whether the punishment was excessive was remanded for consideration by a Texas state court. The Fifth Circuit Court of Appeals quoted *Ingraham v. Wright*, 525 F.2d 909, 917 (5th Cir. 1976), *aff'd*, 430 U.S. 651 (1977):

Paddling of recalcitrant children has long been an accepted method of promoting good behavior and instilling notions of responsibility and decorum into the mischievous heads of school children.

Corporal punishment is not a deprivation of due process rights unless it is "arbitrary, capricious, or wholly unrelated to the legitimate state goal of maintaining an atmosphere conducive to learning." Texas law allows *reasonable* corporal punishment, and, in this case, the student's mother consented to its use. Because Texas law prohibits abuse of students, there is no substantive due process violation because no arbitrary state action exists. Further, Texas law does not create a duty for teachers to intervene in corporal punishment administered by fellow educators. *Fee v. Herndon*, 900 F.2d 804 (5th Cir. 1990), *cert. denied*, 498 U.S. 908 (1990).

Case No. 6: Accidental strangulation (see page 174)

There was no deprivation of due process simply because the child was required to attend school under compulsory attendance laws. Though this was a tragic situation, the due process clause does not transform every injury where a state employee is present into a constitutional violation. Thus, the teacher was not liable for a constitutional deprivation of due process. *Maldonado v. Josey*, 975 F.2d 727 (10th Cir. 1992), *cert. denied*, 113 S.Ct.1266 (1993).

Chapter Six
Collective Bargaining

In comparison with those employed in private enterprise, collective bargaining has been somewhat late in coming to teachers and other public sector employees. In fact, even though many states presently provide an express statutory basis entitling teachers to negotiate with school districts over terms and conditions of employment, a small number of states—including Texas and North Carolina—prohibit the practice altogether. In between these two extremes, a sizable group of states implicitly condone the practice where teachers and school boards voluntarily "meet to confer" about employment issues. Because states may exercise legislative discretion as to how much or how little public sector bargaining they wish to cultivate, this chapter provides an overview of bargaining concepts and frequent points of contention. You will have to become familiar with the laws in your state and the practices, if any, within your particular school district in order to fully comprehend the personal and professional implications of collective bargaining on your teaching career.

A brief background about the history of collective bargaining in this country is helpful to set the stage for an appreciation of where the practice is in the mid-1990s. Private employees won the right to bargain in 1935 when Congress passed the National Labor Relations Act (NLRA) in response to bloody labor-management wars that had been ongoing for years. This legislation, commonly known as the Wagner Act, was an initial step in placing restrictions on what had previously been unfettered employer power. Among other things, the Wagner Act recognized the right of private sector employees to strike. In regulating employer activities, this legislation helped swing the pendulum of power in the direction of employees. However, the act specifically excluded government employees from coverage.

Twelve years later Congress amended the National Labor Relations Act by passing the Labor Management Relations Act, also known as the Taft-Hartley Act. The Taft-Hartley Act was intended to "even up" the employer-employee relationship by placing limits on certain union activities and imposing a requirement for good faith bargaining on both sides. Over the years Congress has continued to modify this legislation and today the NLRA serves as a model for many aspects of public sector bargaining.

Following a series of United States Supreme Court cases interpreting the "right of assembly" provision in the First Amendment, teachers began in earnest to form teachers' organizations after World War II. However, it was not until the late 1950s and early 1960s that public employees—and particularly public school teachers—began to enjoy much in the way of bargaining rights and power. In 1959, Wisconsin enacted legislation authorizing public sector collective bargaining. The United Federation of Teachers won the right to represent New York City's teachers in negotiations with the city school district in 1961. The following year, President Kennedy signed an executive order that extended bargaining rights to federal employees. Although this did not affect public school teachers directly, it gave additional support to public employees seeking bargaining rights at the state and local levels.

Much has been written about why teachers showed so much union-like militancy during the 1960s. Perhaps Victor Hugo summed up the concept best when he wrote in 1877, "Greater than the tread of mighty armies is an idea whose time has come." Seeing their counterparts in the private sector sit down with management and bargain over wages, hours and employment conditions must have been at least part of the reason that teachers sought empowerment to finally take a seat at the bargaining table.

It was not until the New York City teachers' ground-breaking accomplishments in 1961 that traditionally blue-collar organized labor fully realized the potential for unionizing teachers and other white-collar public sector workers. Before the 1960s were over, most of the major cities and many of the smaller ones in this country had embraced some sort of negotiating relationship with teachers' unions and associations. The American Federation of Teachers (AFT) and the National Education Association (NEA) had engaged in a bitter fight for power. Although both groups sought to represent teachers, their organizational philosophies were different. For example, the AFT endeavored to represent teachers as "members" while the NEA sought to retain a practice purporting to represent children as "clients." Although conceptually distinct, the separate focuses were not conducive to an "either-or" mentality. Consequently, over time both organizations made adjustments to move closer toward a philosophical center. Today, a substantial majority of all public school teachers in this country belong to either the NEA (with over two million members) or the AFT (with over 850,000 members).

Case Descriptions

Case No. 1: Out you go!

The year was 1917. The Chicago Board of Education adopted a resolution prohibiting its teachers from belonging to the Chicago Federation of Teachers, a teachers' union. In making up its mind to enact the resolution, the school board had decided that membership in the union "was inimical to proper discipline, prejudicial to the efficiency of the teaching force, and detrimental to the welfare of the public school system." Several teachers who were already members were subsequently dismissed from their jobs simply for that reason. Could the school board legally enact such a regulation or was it unconstitutional on its face? Was this not a biased opinion by the school board, rather than a proven fact?

Case No. 2: Guidelines for bargaining

The Norwalk Teachers' Association (NTA) represented 298 of the 300 teachers employed in Norwalk, Connecticut. In April 1946, a dispute arose over salaries and as a result, 230 NTA-affiliated teachers turned down the contracts proffered by the school board and refused to return to work. After further negotiation, however, the teachers went back to work following the school board's acceptance of the NTA as the exclusive bargaining agent for the teachers. In the meantime and because the parties could not agree on the extent of the NTA's power, they asked the Connecticut state courts to look at several issues. The issues related to the teachers' rights to organize as a labor union, to use a strike or work slowdown as a means of enforcing employee demands, to enter into written contracts with a school board, and to mediate and arbitrate disputes. The guidelines set down in this case became the model in many other states until those states got around to enacting legislation to control bargaining by governmental employees. What common points of law were laid down in this case which still apply in the absence of legislation either permitting or requiring (but not prohibiting) bargaining between teachers and school boards?

Case No. 3: Duty to negotiate in good faith

In 1989, the school board and the education association began negotiating for a collective bargaining agreement to cover the 1989-92 school years. A final agreement was signed in 1990 and teacher contracts were issued funded by monies previously appropriated by the city council. Subsequently, the new collective bargaining agreement was submitted to the city council for approval of budget items. The council rejected the items.

The school board met in emergency session and voted to rescind the teacher contracts, reissue new contracts to the teachers (though with lower salaries than required in the agreement) and to request the education association to renegotiate. The school board then notified the association's negotiator of these actions. The association filed an unfair labor practice charge with the state's Public Employee Labor Relations Board. The charge was dismissed and the parties were ordered to return to the negotiating table. The association appealed, arguing that the city council knew how the first year of the agreement would be funded and that this implied the council's ratification of the disputed budget items as well as additional years' items. The association also contended that by sending contracts directly to the teachers the school board violated its duty to negotiate in good faith with the association's exclusive representative. What do you think?

Case No. 4: How public is a grievance?

In response to voter rejection of an earlier budget, the school board offered a reduced budget which eliminated some of the allocations for sports activities. Three teachers complained about this in a letter, which was printed on school stationery and sent to voters in the school district. The school board condemned the action by the teachers, and the teachers then filed a grievance under the contract between the school board and the education association. Upon request, the grievance was heard in executive session and the school board rejected the teachers' claim. The school board acted formally in open session to deny the grievance. Later, a member of the community requested to see the file and was denied access by the superintendent. The school board also voted to deny the request to see the underlying documents on the grounds that the records were exempt from disclosure because they dealt with a personnel matter. Do you think these documents should be available to the public?

Case No. 5: Unfair labor practices

Since 1976, a vocational agriculture teacher had taught under a series of limited contracts. The latest five-year contract expired in 1984. Then, upon the recommendation of the principal and superintendent, the teacher was issued a two-year probationary contract. The teacher's duties included visiting his students' places of employment during the school year and in the summer; however, the administrators believed the teacher had failed to provide an accurate work schedule to accomplish this task. An evaluation, performed just prior to issuance of the probationary contract, showed that the teacher needed improvement in certain areas but that he was effective in most areas. The teacher was informed that at the end of the two-year period he would either be offered a continuing contract or he would be nonrenewed. Citing the teacher association's collective bargaining agreement with the school district, the teacher filed a grievance stating that the school board's failure to offer a continuing contract, rather than a probationary contract, violated the agreement. The matter went to arbitration, and an arbitrator found that the agreement had not been violated.

Consequently, during the two-year probationary period, the teacher's evaluations were acceptable with few areas being marked as "needing improvement." His new principal recommended he be given a continuing contract. However, the new superintendent (his former principal) recommended that he be nonrenewed. The school board agreed with the superintendent and declined to renew his contract. The education association then filed an unfair labor practice challenge alleging the teacher's nonrenewal was due to his filing the grievance, and that as a result the school board was motivated to retaliate against the teacher for exercising his protected rights. The State Labor Relations Board found an unfair labor practice, and concluded that the teacher had apparently improved and received satisfactory ratings. The labor board ordered that the teacher be reinstated and awarded back pay. The school board appealed. Who won?

Case No. 6: Another illustration of good faith negotiations

The education association and the school board entered negotiations for a new master contract. The parties spent a great deal of time reaching agreement on the ground rules for their negotiations. Eventually, the association agreed to limit negotiating sessions to two two-hour sessions, and, in turn, the school board agreed to negotiate about leave items as part of salary. After a break in negotiations, proposals and counterproposals were exchanged. The school board's proposal did not address the leave items despite the fact that its proposal was characterized as a "final offer." In subsequent sessions, the school board presented several more "final offers." No agreement was ever reached. Alleging that the school district had failed to negotiate in good faith, the association sought a court order to compel the school board into further negotiations. The association's request was dismissed. What do you think constitutes "good faith" and how would you define "negotiations?"

Case No. 7: Are teachers ever authorized to strike?

In 1981, about one-half of the teachers in a school district went on strike. The teachers were members of the education association, and the strike's purpose was to compel the school district to recognize the association as the exclusive bargaining agent for the teachers. The teachers sought to force the school board to negotiate a master contract with the association with an underlying motive of improving salaries and working conditions.

Before the strike, the school district held meetings with the teachers and made proposals, but ultimately refused to recognize the association. An impasse in the dispute resulted. The association then notified the director of the state division of labor that a labor dispute existed. The school district countered that it would take legal action to oppose any intervention by the director and that he had no jurisdiction over the district. The director declined to exercise jurisdiction after concluding that it would not serve a useful purpose.

After the strike began, the school district notified the teachers that their contracts were in jeopardy because their actions could be considered an abandonment of their employment without approval by the school board. Some of the teachers then returned to work. The school board then offered hearings for the remaining striking teachers, who denied they had abandoned their employment. Only one teacher attended the hearings and returned to work. The rest were discharged by the school board who determined the teachers had "voluntarily terminated" their employment and abandoned their contracts by striking. Two lawsuits were filed: first, the school board sought to enjoin (halt) the strike and obtain damages resulting from the teachers' actions, and second, the education association filed suit contending that the school board violated the teachers' rights under state law, and it sought damages for unlawful dismissal. The question is—do public employees have a right to strike in some states? Should public employees have such a right?

How Collective Bargaining Works

What is collective bargaining?

Collective bargaining has been described as "a knocking together of heads to get a meeting of the minds"; however, it is actually far more subtle than that. Collective bargaining is an orderly way of resolving matters of dispute between employer and employee without resorting to outright physical confrontation, court action, or flipping a coin. Collective bargaining essentially rests on several fundamental principles: the employees' right to organize (derived from the constitutionally protected freedom of association found in the First Amendment); the right to be represented by a single bargaining agent (to "speak with one voice"; *all* employees are represented by the bargaining agent regardless of affiliation status); the right to strike or submit to binding arbitration; the right to bilateral and good faith negotiations over appropriate subjects; and the right to create a binding contract which supersedes the rights of individuals to bargain separately. Of these principles, the right of public sector employees to strike has been substantially curtailed by legislation in most states.

Is public sector collective bargaining handled the same way in all states?

No. As was suggested in the introduction to this chapter, each of the fifty states has the legislative discretion to decide how much, if any, collective bargaining it wants its employees to enjoy. Some states prohibit public sector bargaining entirely; other states allow bargaining only by specific employee groups (often, police and fire fighters are the only groups of state employees given statutory authority to bargain); a third group of state statutes says nothing about bargaining and it is thus left to the discretion of each governmental agency or political entity (including school districts) in the state to decide whether to bargain with its employees; a fourth group provides a statutory basis for public employees to "meet and confer"; and finally, a fifth group of states have statutorily established strict and extensive procedures for bargaining which control most aspects of the negotiating process.

If it is optional, should local school boards choose to bargain with teachers over the terms and conditions of employment?

Arguably, a great deal can be gained from a mutually voluntary continuing dialogue between a local school board and its teachers. By involving teachers in the planning, focusing and balancing of interests and objectives, collective bargaining is a proactive way for a school board to ascertain what its teachers are thinking. When done in a positive light, bargaining may serve to encourage teachers to take ownership in decisions being made as well as instill a sense of justice derived from an understanding of *why* such decisions were made. In many ways, collective bargaining has much in common with the contemporary trends toward site-based (or campus-level) management and site-based decision making presently in vogue in many states across the nation.

Do both sides need to have fairly equal negotiating strength if collective bargaining is going to work?

In most cases, meaningful negotiations cannot take place unless both parties are approximately equal in their bargaining power. As mentioned earlier, Congress intended the Wagner and Taft-Hartley Acts to equalize or balance the latent power on each side of the bargaining table. History has shown that negotiations will be little more than a sham unless power is somewhat equal.

What is the model for collective bargaining in public education?

The idyllic model for productive collective bargaining is the negotiating table where equals face each other across the table; if the parties are unequal when they come to the table, the law will attempt to make them so. For example, when the Wagner Act was first passed, management was stronger than labor. Congress restricted management's power by requiring employers to bargain with laborers and by defining certain "unfair labor practices" which were prohibited—such as firing workers for being active in unions. In the private sector, the right to strike is and always has been a formidable "bargaining chip" that labor could hold over management's head. However, since most states which allow public sector collective bargaining also expressly prohibit teachers from striking, a *legal* strike by teachers is frequently out of the question.

How does collective bargaining differ between the public and private sectors?

With few exceptions, the primary focus in private sector labor-management negotiations is economic—employees usually want to be paid better wages and to receive better benefits while employers hope to insure profitability for stockholders. If negotiations fail, employee strikes and employer lockouts may serve to stimulate action or compromise. For the most part, national labor laws govern private sector bargaining and both sides must abide by such laws in the negotiating process. In contrast (and perhaps somewhat altruistically), the focal point in public sector bargaining is not as directly economic in nature; rather, it is that the public (i.e., students) will benefit from the government service of a free and quality public education. As a result, the most effective sanctions available in the private sector—strikes and lockouts—are generally not available when negotiations between school boards and teachers' associations fall apart since students are always "caught in the middle."

What are the basic ground rules under which collective bargaining is usually conducted?

There are four basic rules: (1) the parties must agree in advance to bargain in good faith; any departure from good faith can be construed as an unfair labor practice and may be subject to sanction; (2) the parties must give something in exchange for what they want in return *(quid pro quo)*; (3) there must be some way to resolve impasses when they occur; and (4) the final agreed-upon details must be reduced to a writing which then becomes binding on the parties during the duration of the agreement. These principles are discussed in the following questions.

What is meant by "bargaining in good faith?"

Good faith bargaining means that both sides agree before bargaining begins to bring everything out in the open, to deal fairly with the other side, and to honestly seek to reach a meeting of the minds on the points which separate the two sides. Failure to act appropriately can be construed as an unfair labor practice for which the perpetrating party may be penalized or sanctioned. Those states with statutes governing teacher-school board bargaining often list certain "unfair labor practices" such as creating intentional delay or the failure to "level" with the other side. In the event of "bad faith" bargaining, an offended party may be able to secure a "cease and desist" order from a statewide labor board which governs collective bargaining in that state. The parties' shared commitment to bargain in good faith is mutually beneficial; the alternative usually consists of stalemate, confusion, delay and disrespect.

What is meant by the term *quid pro quo*?

Quid pro quo is a Latin term meaning "something for something." In theory, any offer must be honored either by acceptance or with a counter-offer from the opposite side. This approach is viewed as the best way to avoid impasse. In reality, however, it is not unusual for a teachers' group to seek many gains and for the employing school district to take a completely defensive position without making too many demands or concessions of its own.

What are various methods the parties may use to resolve an impasse?

Although there are a multitude of variations, essentially three basic methods are used to resolve an impasse. First, the parties may use a mediator to facilitate the reopening of discussion. A mediator is an independent third party who does not have decision-making power but, instead, is called upon to help the parties reestablish lines of communication. Any "suggestions" the mediator makes are non-binding. For example, after hearing the arguments presented by both sides, the mediator might say, "Why don't you consider the following as a way out of the impasse. This would be a fair settlement for the following reasons: . . . "

A second method involves using a fact finder. Among other things, a fact finder attempts to verify the accuracy and merit of various assertions being made by the parties. For example, a fact finder might attempt to discover whether the school board's budget calculations justify its assertion that it cannot meet the wage and benefit demands being made by the teachers. Fact finders, like mediators, usually do not have any type of enforcement authority to compel action.

Finally, the third method of resolving an impasse involves arbitration. Arbitration may be "interest" arbitration (arbitration of disputes over what the terms of new or renewed contracts shall be) or "grievance" arbitration (disputes over whether the employer or an employee has violated a term or provision in the existing agreement). Grievance arbitration is commonly written into collective bargaining agreements as the last step in most grievance procedures. Arbitration may be either advisory (nonbinding) or binding (in which the parties agree in advance that they will be bound by the arbitrator's decision—assuming that there is no law to the contrary. Some courts have held that binding arbitration violates the state's constitution as an unlawful delegation of power *(School Board of the City of Richmond v. Parham*, 243 S.E.2d 468 (Va. 1978)) while courts in other states have reached exactly the opposite conclusion when interpreting different statutory language *(City of Biddeford v. Biddeford Teachers Association*, 304 A.2d 387 (Me. 1973)).

What is generally included in a completed collective bargaining agreement?

All of the things that the parties agreed to during the negotiation process should be reduced to writing. Some of the more critical items that are typically included in a finalized agreement are a description of grievance procedures and the specific terms of the agreement with regard to salaries, benefits and leave policies. The document should also address the employees' rights to communicate with members using such things as school bulletin boards and teacher mailboxes.

What is meant by "managerial prerogatives"?

In a public school setting, "managerial prerogatives" are the school board powers that cannot be delegated or bargained away. For example, the state legislature vests the local school board with authority to determine educational policy for the welfare of students in the school district; such authority is nonnegotiable and cannot be a subject for bargaining with a teachers' association or union. By contrast, employee salary and working conditions usually fall within the category of permissible bargaining topics. Most states with fairly extensive collective bargaining statutes usually spell out with some exactitude the extent to which a local school board can "give away the store." It should be noted, however, that the distinction between permissible and impermissible topics for bargaining is not always clear and, as a result, frequently serves as a point of dispute during negotiations.

What is an example of a case illustrating the "managerial prerogatives" concept?

In *Kenai Peninsula Borough School District v. Kenai Peninsula Education Association*, 572 P.2d 416 (Alaska 1977), the Alaska Supreme Court was asked to decide the propriety of teacher association input in or influence over educational policies established by a local school board. The court concluded that while the question of "what is bargainable" is not precisely clear, the basic control that a school board must exercise over educational policies cannot be shifted to the teachers' union. The court felt that a legislative mandate that teachers and school boards "meet and confer" provides school boards with valuable input without forcing boards to relinquish their decision-making power.

How the Rules are Enforced

Can unilateral or one-sided action by one of the parties be considered an unfair labor practice?

Yes, although it is important to keep in mind that a school board must be free to exercise such managerial prerogative as it needs to keep the enterprise running. Since the essence and spirit of collective bargaining involves bilateral decision making, the common position is that any unilateral action on things outside the managerial prerogative is tantamount to an unfair labor practice.

May a school board enter an "agency shop" or "fair share" agreement with a teachers' union?

Like all unions, teachers' associations need dues-paying members to show strength and remain viable as the "voice" speaking on behalf of all teachers. Consequently, such groups seek to encourage membership and financial support by enlisting employer cooperation. This type of cooperative arrangement is most often accomplished via either an "agency shop" or a "fair share" agreement. If an employing school district is an "agency shop," it will require that all employees pay dues to the union for the privilege of being represented at the bargaining table but individual employees are not compelled to actually become members (as they would be in a "union shop").

An alternative to "agency shop" is the "fair share" arrangement in which nonmembers pay a service fee to help defray the union's bargaining costs. In deciding *Abood v. Detroit Board of Education*, 431 U.S. 209 (1977), *reh'g denied*, 433 U.S. 915 (1977), the United States Supreme Court upheld the "agency shop" concept. However, the court's ruling was limited in the sense that service fees could only be collected insofar as they pertain to collective bargaining and contract administration— not for influencing political outcomes. The Court remanded the case on the issue of how nonmember employees who had been required to pay service fees could obtain refunds for that portion of their dues which had gone toward improper activities.

Tangential issues related to mandated union service fee contributions continue to reappear in court challenges. For example, the United States Supreme Court recently declined to review a Ninth Circuit Court of Appeals ruling in *Grunwald v. San Bernardino City Unified School District*, 994 F.2d 1370 (9th Cir. 1993), *cert. denied*, 114 S.Ct. 439 (1993). Several nonmember teachers claimed that the school district's temporary pre-refund retention of certain fees collected from nonmember teachers and held in an escrow account violated the teachers' rights of association under the First Amendment. The Ninth Circuit concluded that the delay between the time when fees were collected and when the nonmember teachers received their refunds was not excessive. The teachers in *Grunwald* were entitled to refunds for that portion of their service fees which normally would have gone toward nonrepresentational activities (i.e., contributions to political candidates).

One further note—the union-favoring result that the United States Supreme Court reached in *Abood* does not mean that every state *must* allow agency shop arrangements. For example, Maine's Supreme Court interpreted that state's collective bargaining statute so as to prohibit the collection of service fees. *Churchill v. School Administrator District No. 49 Teachers Association*, 380 A.2d 186 (Me. 1977). The court held that the forced payment of a service fee was "tantamount to coercion toward membership."

Are "union shops" illegal in public education?

They are in many states. By definition, a "union shop" agreement requires all new employees to join the union within a designated period of time after securing employment. "Union shops" have traditionally been a private sector phenomena; the limited headway such agreements may have made in the public sector have been curtailed in recent years with "right-to-work" legislation enacted in many states. Further, when asked to interpret collective bargaining statutes, state courts have declared that local school boards exceed their powers when they adopt resolutions requiring that all teachers join a union as a condition of employment. *Benson v. School District No. 1 of Silver Bow County*, 344 P.2d 117 (Mont. 1959), *reh'g denied*, (Mont. 1960).

What is an example of a school board entering into an agreement to do something illegal?

In *Cumberland Valley Education Association v. Cumberland Valley School District*, 354 A.2d 265 (Pa. 1976), Pennsylvania's statutes limited teachers on full-year sabbatical leave to one-half of their regular salary. When a school board was challenged for agreeing to provide full pay during a half-year sabbatical, a state court found that the collectively bargained provision was null and unenforceable. The court held that the state's constitution and statutes precluded the school board from doing something other than what was expressly permitted by statute. In other words, the school board could not "contract around" or circumvent existing state laws which already addressed the particular issue.

May school boards agree to binding arbitration?

They may in some states; however, they are usually not required to do so unless compelled by state law. Since most public sector employers view binding arbitration with disfavor, they are generally not very willing to agree to the process. Although binding arbitration may serve to even out the balance of power between the parties, it is often viewed as eroding the school board's managerial prerogative.

What items are negotiable between teachers and school boards?

Although the answer to this question will vary from state to state, the "scope" of negotiable items generally falls under the heading of "wages, hours and conditions of employment." Some state statutes spell out exactly which items are (or are not) negotiable; however, most do not mandate bargaining over specific items and, instead, leave the decision as to the appropriateness of certain items to the discretion of the parties.

Another way of looking at this is in terms of mandatory, permissive and prohibited subjects for negotiation. If a particular subject is mandatory, then the parties must engage in good faith bargaining or risk the possibility of sanctions. Permissive items will be negotiated only if both sides agree to negotiate. Prohibited items cannot be negotiated since they generally fall within the "managerial prerogatives" or educational policy aspect of the school board's authority. Although it is impossible to list all of the appropriate subjects that may be negotiable (beyond the relatively familiar and expected items such as salary and benefits), several of the more common and perhaps more controversial subjects are discussed in the following questions.

Is class size a valid item for negotiation?

As is often the case in this area of the law, the appropriate response is "it depends on the state." Teachers have long claimed that class size should be mandatorily negotiable as a "condition of employment." In contrast, school boards have traditionally objected that class size touches fundamentally on educational policy and thus is not a proper subject for negotiation. In between these two extremes are states which have found that class size is a permissive subject for bargaining. *Fargo Education Association v. Fargo Public School District*, 291 N.W.2d 267 (N.D. 1980). Still other courts have drawn even narrower lines; for example, in *Beloit City School Board v. Wiscon-*

sin Employment Relations Commission, 242 N.W.2d 231 (Wis. 1976), the Wisconsin Supreme Court concluded that class size is a permissive subject for bargaining but that the *impact* of class size on the teachers' conditions of employment is a mandatory subject for negotiation. More recently, the Oregon Supreme Court reversed a finding that class size was subject to mandatory bargaining since the state's employment relations board erred when drawing that conclusion without having examined the full impact of class size on other conditions of employment. *Tualatin Valley Bargaining Council v. Tigard School District 23J*, 840 P.2d 657 (Or. 1992).

May teachers bargain away a right?

Yes. As an example, several English teachers objected when the school board banned ten books which the teachers had formerly used in their classes. The teachers objected on the grounds that the school board's actions violated principles of academic freedom supported by the First Amendment. The collective bargaining agreement between the school board and the teachers included the provision that, "The board shall have the right to determine the processes, techniques, methods and means of teaching any and all subjects." In ruling for the school board, the court concluded that whatever the scope of the constitutional protections in this case, such protections do not present a legal impediment to the freedom to contract. "Thus, a teacher may bargain away the freedom to communicate in her official role in the same manner as an editorial writer who agrees to write the views of a publisher or an actor who contracts to speak the author's script. One can, for consideration, agree to teach according to direction." *Cary v. Board of Education*, 427 F.Supp. 945, 956 (D.Colo. 1977), *aff'd* 598 F.2d 535 (10th Cir. 1979).

Teacher Strikes

Is it legal for teachers to go on strike?

It is arguable whether true collective bargaining can exist if employees do not have the right to withhold services. Today, however, most states have statutes that expressly prohibit teachers from striking. Even in those states that permit teacher strikes, the teachers are allowed to do so only after they have satisfied a number of pre-strike conditions. Although these conditions vary from state to state, they generally include some or all of the following provisions: (1) teachers must exhaust all mediation or fact-finding opportunities; (2) the existing collective bargaining agreement must have expired; (3) a pre-established period of time must have elapsed; (4) the teachers must have provided the school board with written notice of their intent to strike; and (5) the teachers must be able to show evidence that the proposed strike will not constitute an immediate danger to public health or safety. The teachers' failure to satisfy any one or more these (or other applicable) conditions may result in a strike being "illegal."

What is an example of a legal teachers' strike?

Case No. 7 in this chapter provides an example in which teachers legally had a right to strike.

By contrast, what is an example of a case in which striking teachers failed to satisfy a pre-strike "condition"?

In *Jersey Shore Area School District v. Jersey Shore Education Association*, 548 A.2d 1202 (Pa. 1988), the Pennsylvania Supreme Court looked at statutory language pertaining to public employees and whether a strike would create "a clear and present danger or threat to the health, safety or welfare of the public." In effect, the court was balancing two statutory provisions—the right of teachers as public employees to strike (after meeting certain criteria) against the requirement that school districts provide 180 instructional days each year for all students. On the cumulative basis of a combination of factors and evidence presented by the school board, the court held that the school days "lost" to a teachers' strike could not simply be "made up" without the risk of students suffering substantial harm. Consequently, the court upheld a lower court's issuance of an injunction enjoining the teachers from striking.

May teachers resign "en masse" in order to enforce their demands?

No, because such a mass resignation amounts to a strike even though it may not be called that in so many words. A New York Court determined that the tactic of "mass resignations" was, in essence, a strike. *Board of Education of the City of New York v. Shanker*, 283 N.Y.S.2d 432 (N.Y.Super.Ct. 1967), *aff'd* 286 N.Y.S.2d 453 (N.Y. 1967). Similarly, work stoppages (*Warren Education Association v. Adams*, 226 N.W.2d 536 (Mich.App. 1975)), refusing to report for work at the beginning of the school year (*Pinellas County Classroom Teachers' Association, Inc. v. Board of Public Instruction*, 214 So.2d 34 (Fla. 1968)), and refusing to perform extracurricular duties (*Board of Education of City of Asbury Park v. Asbury Park Education Association*, 368 A.2d 396 (N.J.Super.Ct.App.Div. 1976), *modified, aff'd in part, dismissed in part*, 382 A.2d 392 (N.J. 1977)) all represent situations in which courts found that teacher actions constituted a strike.

May a school board penalize teachers for striking illegally?

Yes. Depending on the circumstances in a given situation and the laws in a particular state, the penalties for teachers who strike illegally may encompass a wide-range of actions including termination (*Hortonville Joint School District No. 1 v. Hortonville Education Association*, 426 U.S. 482 (1976)) and paying for the costs incurred by the school district for substitute teachers during a strike (*National Education Association v. Lee County Board of Public Instruction*, 467 F.2d 447 (5th Cir. 1972)). In addition to having penalties imposed on illegally striking teachers, school boards may also go to court to seek an injunction to halt an illegal strike and get the court to order the teachers back to work. Teachers who violate an injunction may be found in contempt of court and subject to fines and/or jail time. *In re Block*, 236 A.2d 589 (N.J. 1967). Although the requirements for obtaining injunctive relief vary from jurisdiction to jurisdiction, it will generally be necessary for the school board to show that irreparable harm or injury will result if the injunction is not issued.

May a teachers' group invoke "sanctions" against a school district in lieu of a strike?

It depends on how the "sanctions" may be construed. For example, when a school board declined to renew the contracts of three nontenured teachers—one of whom happened to be the president of the local teachers' association—the local, state and national-level organizations invoked "sanctions" against the school district. These "sanctions" involved sending notices to undergraduate teacher education institutions asking candidates not to apply for employment in the school district. The New Jersey Supreme Court held that the purpose of the action was to support a refusal of others to work and thus to withhold services which the district needed in order to meet its obligation to educate students. In this light, the "sanctions" amounted to "the usual concerted refusal to work," that is, a strike. The association was ordered to undo what harm it had done by sending disclaimer letters to all those to whom the earlier "sanction" letters had been sent. *Board of Education of Union Beach v. New Jersey Education Association*, 247 A.2d 867 (N.J. 1968).

Case Resolutions

Case No. 1: Out you go! (see page 222)

The resolution by the school board was upheld. The court stated that:

> The board of education has the power to make and enforce any rules that it sees proper . . . The board has the absolute right to decline to employ or re-employ any applicant for a position as teacher for any or no reason. No person has the right to demand that he or she shall be employed as a teacher. The board is the best judge of whether or not to employ or re-employ. [The resolution] was an exercise of the discretionary power of the board which the courts will not overthrow.

In effect, the court concluded in no uncertain terms that those who chose to teach in Chicago in 1917 took their employment conditions as set forth by the school board and not as they might otherwise prefer them to be. *People ex rel. Fursman v. City of Chicago*, 116 N.E. 158, 160 (Ill. 1917).

Case No. 2: Guidelines for bargaining (see page 223)

The *Norwalk* guidelines are frequently used to help control bargaining in those states lacking legislation on this point. Beginning with Wisconsin in 1959 (when the first state bargaining laws for teachers were enacted), the influence of the *Norwalk* guidelines began to wane. However, these five points of law are still commonly recognized: (1) public school teachers have the right to organize and be active in their unions; (2) a school board is permitted, but not legally required, to negotiate with a teachers' organization; (3) a school board may agree to arbitrate with teachers, but only on those issues that do not erode the sovereignty of the board; (4) a school board may not agree to a closed shop (where only members of the union may work); and (5) public school teachers may not strike to enforce their demands unless there is special permission given to do so by the legislature. *Norwalk Teachers Association v. Board of Education of City of Norwalk*, 83 A.2d 482 (Conn. 1951).

Case No. 3: Duty to negotiate in good faith (see page 223)

The court reversed and remanded the Labor Relations Board's directive to return to the bargaining table. When the city council voted to appropriate money, it was not aware of what the budget items would be for the first year of the collective bargaining agreement, let alone for additional years. A municipal body can only be bound on a multi-year contract if it knew with specificity about the items for *each* year. Further, the school board violated its duty to negotiate in good faith with the association's exclusive representative by dealing directly with the teachers. The contracts sent to the teachers stated that the contracts would be amended as appropriate when the association and the school board reached a new agreement. In the meantime, the teachers were required to sign their contracts "at once" or risk losing their jobs. Effectively, if the contracts were signed, the school board would have little incentive to negotiate further and agree to higher wages; instead, the school board would be encouraged to prolong the process. The second round of contracts sent to the teachers were declared invalid and the Labor Board decision was reversed and remanded for remedies appropriate under New Hampshire statutes. *Appeal of Franklin Education Association,* 616 A.2d 919 (N.H. 1992).

Case No. 4: How public is a grievance? (see page 224)

Under the state's Public Records Act, right of access to public records is liberally construed in favor of open access with few exceptions. The school district is a public agency to which disclosure laws apply, and the grievance and the school board's subsequent decision are public records. Even though the labor contract provision between the school board and the association permitted grievances to be heard confidentially, that agreement did not override or circumvent the provisions in the Public Records Act. The personal documents exception is not so broad that it protects the content of all so-called personal documents about personnel matters. The term "personal documents" is interpreted to apply only when the privacy of the individual is involved (if the documents reveal "intimate details of a person's life, including any information that might subject the person to embarrassment, harassment, disgrace, or loss of employment or friends") or if it is so personal that the information would normally not be shared with strangers. Under this definition, the documents in this case were not personal. (However, since it was requested, a court will examine the documents to make sure they are not exempt.) *Trombley v. Bellows Falls Union High School District*, 624 A.2d 857 (Vt. 1993).

Case No. 5: Unfair labor practices (see page 225)

The teacher received reinstatement and back pay. There was substantial evidence in the record to support the determination that an unfair labor practice occurred. The fact that the teacher received good evaluations and that his current principal recommended a continuing contract are evidence of a discriminatory motive behind the decision not to renew the contract. Further, the teacher had improved in setting and adhering to work schedules. In applying Ohio's legal standards to evaluate the school board's motivation, the court held that an unfair labor practice occurs when "an employer takes an action regarding an employee that is motivated by antiunion animus." Considering all the evidence and focusing on the employer's intent, the evidence clearly supported the determination that an unfair labor practice had occurred. *State Employment Relations Board v. Adena Local School District Board of Education*, 613 N.E.2d 605, 614 (Ohio 1993).

Case No. 6: Another illustration of good faith negotiations (see page 226)

Both sides have a duty to negotiate in good faith in teacher contract negotiations. The teachers' association argued that the school board refused to include the leave items as part of salary and that this showed evidence of bad faith. "Negotiation" does not compel a party to agree to a proposal or make a concession. The school board's position was that they offered additional salary concessions to keep the leave items out of the master contract. The school board was not compelled to accept the association's proposals about leave items or to include them—thus, they did "negotiate" the leave items. Even limiting the time allotted to the sessions was not bad faith since agreements had been reached historically in a reasonable time and the association had agreed to the time limits. Moreover, after additional sessions were held, the education association negotiators walked out and shortly thereafter brought suit despite the school board's continued willingness to attempt further negotiations. In assessing "good faith," courts do not look at isolated actions, but rather at the overall conduct of a negotiating party to determine if it actively engaged in the bargaining process with an open mind and sincere desire to reach an agreement. Viewing the overall conduct of the school board here, the court affirmed that negotiations had been done in good faith. *Belfield Education Association v. School District 13*, 496 N.W.2d 12 (N.D. 1993).

Case No. 7: Are teachers ever authorized to strike? (see page 226)

Under the law in some states, public employees have a "qualified" right to strike subject to explicit executive and judicial controls. In other words, a strike may be authorized, but it is strictly regulated. For example, the Colorado Industrial Relations Act provides a regulatory scheme covering both public and private employers and employees. It grants a right to strike, but places conditions on the right. Public employees must accept that state authorities may intervene in disputes with public employers whenever the interests of the community as a whole require that intervention. Colorado is one of few states that deals with its public and private labor relations in the same manner by not prohibiting strikes by public employees. Public sector disputes, however, are subject to the authority of the director of the division of labor who will attempt to avoid legal proceedings by voluntary arbitration, mediation or conciliation of the dispute. No strike is authorized as long as the director maintains jurisdiction over a dispute. A strike is permitted after jurisdiction terminates if the employees deem it in their best interests.

In this case, the court soundly rejected the school district's argument that the director of labor relations had no jurisdiction over public labor disputes or over the school district. The court observed that human needs of public employees are identical to the needs of private employees, and Colorado recognizes the right of both to strike. The court also noted that sometimes the disruption by private sector strikes (e.g., coal miners strikes) may be more adverse to the public than disruptions in public services. This legislatively-created right to strike, subject to supervision, is designed to promote labor peace and thereby serve the public interest.

Finding that the strike was lawful, the court then discussed whether it was abandonment by the teachers of their employment under the Teacher Tenure Act. The court found that since the purpose of the strike was to gain a concession from the employer and enjoy that benefit, the strike did not constitute termination of the employment relationship. In fact, the teachers in this case notified the school district of their intent to return to their classrooms. Thus, for the school district to have terminated the teacher contracts, it would have been necessary for the school board to follow procedures for involuntary dismissal instead of concluding the strike was a voluntary termination. *Martin v. Montezuma-Cortez School District RE-1*, 841 P.2d 237 (Colo. 1992), *reh'g denied*, (Colo. 1994) [citation unavailable].

Chapter Seven

The Teacher's Role in the Attorney-Client Relationship

One of our most highly-prized rights as Americans is the right to be represented by legal counsel. In a very real sense, the civil rights movement can be characterized as an attempt to achieve that "fundamental" right for every individual.

Over the years, large groups of American citizens—the poor, the aging, children, and racial and ethnic minorities to name a few—have been directly or indirectly deprived of recourse for alleged wrongs. Frontier justice was often the law of the six-gun; property was passionately protected by law while individual rights and minority interests might be ignored. On occasion, the legal principle behind trial by jury would be dispensed with in the interest of "winning the West."

In more recent times, justice has been delayed (at best) or denied entirely due to clogged court calendars. Due in part to the alleged inadequacy of their legal representation, some would argue that suspects in criminal cases have ostensibly been considered guilty unless and until they could prove their innocence. Prisons held felons without thought to their rehabilitation. Mental patients and the infirm were institutionalized for life with little attention given to therapy, treatment or, in some cases, even basic human dignity. The history of justice in America has too often meant justice for those who could afford it, and denial of justice for those who could not. The advent of nonprofit legal service agencies and other donated legal aid has helped to overcome some, but certainly not all, of these problems.

Although most people are familiar with the maxim that everyone is expected to know the law and ignorance of the law cannot be used as a defense, the intricate and ever-growing web of law crisscrossing our everyday lives makes such a straightforward standard somewhat foreboding. As a result, we all need—and must prepare for—our own legal defense or suffer potentially dire consequences. This is as it should be. Common sense tells us that we must get competent legal advice at the time we stand before the bar of justice. Perhaps even better advice is to keep informed of legal requirements so as to take proactive steps to minimize risks and avoid the prospect of ever having to appear in court.

In a 1963 Florida case, the United States Supreme Court overruled several earlier court decisions and declared that any individual faced with *criminal* charges is entitled to be represented by legal counsel regardless of that individual's ability to hire and pay for an attorney. *Gideon v. Wainwright*, 372 U.S. 335 (1963). The case involved a man charged with misdemeanor theft who was denied counsel under Florida law. Citing the Fourteenth Amendment, the unanimous Supreme Court held that the right to counsel is "fundamental and essential to a fair trial." *Id.* at 340. The Court emphasized that a person who under our adversarial system of justice is "hailed into court, who is too poor to hire a lawyer cannot be assured a fair trial unless counsel is provided for him . . . .The right of one charged with crime to counsel may not be deemed fundamental and essential to fair trials in some countries, but it is in ours." *Id.* at 344. Thus, the Supreme Court recognized that the guarantee of counsel provided for in the Sixth Amendment applied to all capital as well as non-capital criminal cases in the state and federal courts.

By comparison, most litigation faced by teachers is civil rather than criminal; as such, the right to counsel is generally not an issue unless the court is convinced that fundamental fairness cannot be obtained without counsel. This is a very rare occurrence. Although everyone has the right to plead his own case, cases in which this was done tend to show that a layman is at a distinct disadvantage against trained attorneys. The only reasonable alternative is to arrange for legal representation and thus reduce the odds against being overwhelmed while under pressure by the complexity of the law and the procedural aspects of being in court. Of course, if you are the plaintiff, your first act should be to consult with counsel and begin preparations to file your lawsuit. On the other hand, if you have been sued and are now a defendant, do not delay in seeking legal advice. Otherwise, deadlines may pass without your knowledge which may affect you adversely in presenting your defense to the charges.

One other note of caution: simply be aware that, like a math teacher who may not be very good at teaching French or biology, not all attorneys are experts in all areas of the law; rather, they often tend to specialize. Ask around to find out who has handled "school law" cases or seek a referral from your local bar association or education association. (For example, your attorney friend down the street who helped with a traffic ticket or who wrote your will may not be the ideal person to handle your wrongful job termination claim or defend you in a student injury case.)

The body of law that constitutes "school law" is not static. State and federal legislatures are constantly reviewing, modifying and adding statutes and laws that affect many facets of education. National, state and local regulations and policies that supplement the legislation help create a framework for school operations on a daily basis. Courts and the judicial branch get involved when disputes arise which are not resolved by the legislation or regulations and which must be litigated to reach a solution.

Once you have become aware of your rights and responsibilities (which can be accomplished in some small part by reading the earlier portions of this book), you must then attempt to keep up with future developments. Stories in newspapers, professional journals, and attendance at conventions and seminars where school law is discussed can help you stay current with changes in your legal status. Perhaps your school can host an in-service program on school law as part of a site-based staff development activity. Taking a class on school law offered by a local university is certainly one of the best ways to become informed of legal issues impacting education and your role as a teacher. With the technological advances being made in multiple-site course availability via satellite and telecommunications, it may also be possible to "attend" school law classes even in rural or remote locations.

The other equally important step consists of availing yourself of legal counsel in case you must go into litigation. Your professional union or association may provide general advice, or you may contact your state department of public instruction (most have full-time legal advisers). Finally, in a worst case scenario, you should have in mind a competent attorney trained and experienced in school law who can come to your assistance when litigation looms on the horizon. "Forewarned is forearmed" applies to educational law, and should be a preventive consideration even if you don't anticipate any lawsuits in the near future. Keep the name and phone number of a competent lawyer handy and use it when legal action is forthcoming.

Depending on the circumstances, you may or may not be able to rely on legal counsel retained by the board of education in the school district in which you are employed. This is because the school board or the school district itself may conceivably become your adversary in a court action. Although there has been some talk at the national level of providing legal insurance (much like health, hospital and dental insurance) as one of the fringe benefits of your membership in a professional association, that idea has not yet received widespread acceptance. Thus, you should take it upon yourself to become legally literate and when a problem arises know what to do until you talk to an attorney. The following cases illustrate the need for close liaison with legal counsel.

Case Descriptions

Case No. 1: When in Rome . . .

An unmarried female teacher from New York obtained a teaching position in Union Center, South Dakota (pop. 100). Housing was scarce in the community so the teacher lived in a trailer near the school. All went well until her boyfriend moved in with her, causing the school board to hold a conference with the teacher. The school board felt the teacher's lifestyle would have a detrimental effect on her pupils in the small community. (She was a capable teacher and popular with her students.) The teacher replied that what she did with her time outside school was her own affair, and that to dismiss her would violate her constitutional rights to privacy and freedom of association. The board, however, produced a petition with 140 names of citizens from the surrounding area protesting the teacher's conduct. Should the teacher's right to privacy and association outweigh a parental right to influence the upbringing of children? Should the local school board be able to dismiss this teacher for immorality?

Case No. 2: Conduct for a disciplinary proceeding

In 1990, a tenured teacher was suspended *with* pay pending the outcome of disciplinary proceedings. Three years later, the school board terminated her pay *without* giving her any prior notice or opportunity to be heard. The teacher claimed violation of due process. The school board justified terminating her pay on grounds that she acted in *bad faith* by seeking numerous, unnecessary adjournments to the disciplinary proceedings and, by doing so, she forfeited her rights to employment benefits. Do you think the teacher was obstructing the proceedings? Should she be allowed to explain why she sought many adjournments? Or was the school board justifiably exasperated and thus authorized to act as it did?

Case No. 3: Illegal drug possession (or procedure to the max!)

A tenured junior high teacher was arrested and charged with distributing marijuana. The assistant superintendent confirmed the arrest and charges, spoke with the teacher, and later notified the teacher by letter that he was suspended without pay. The assistant superintendent offered to meet with the teacher to discuss his future employment status. The criminal charges were subsequently dismissed when the teacher became an informant for the police department. Nonetheless, the school board terminated the teacher's employment on the basis of his criminal conduct. The teacher requested a hearing; before that occurred, his criminal record was *expunged* (wiped clean) by court order. The school board held the hearing—no evidence was allowed about the charges against the teacher or his record, but a detective who arrested the teacher did testify. A hearing officer who presided over the hearing recommended reinstatement but the school board voted to terminate. Subsequently, the teacher filed a § 1983 civil rights action alleging a constitutional violation of his due process rights and requesting damages and reinstatement. The school board obtained *summary judgment* at the trial court level (meaning the board won on points of law without having to go to trial) on most of the issues. However, the court found irregularities in the hearing and ordered the school board to hold another hearing— the result of which was to affirm the earlier termination decision. Once again the court was asked to rule and this time the court held that the teacher was denied due process at the first hearing and should receive compensatory damages and attorney fees on that issue only. Next, the school board argued it was immune from liability under the Eleventh Amendment and thus could not be sued by the teacher. The teacher appealed on several grounds including that the school board was not immune, that he should have received a pre-suspension hearing, and that his post-suspension pre-termination hearings did not comply with due process protections. What hearings and procedures do you think the teacher should have received, and do you think the appeals court will affirm the decision for the school board or will it agree that the teacher was denied due process? Regardless of the outcome, with all of these legal maneuverings, do you think it was necessary for the teacher to have been represented by legal counsel?

Case No. 4: A multitude of claims (or just sex discrimination)

A non-tenured teacher taught under a series of short-term contracts from 1978 until 1989. She had received generally satisfactory evaluations but there were also numerous parental complaints about her performance. She attended but did not complete teacher enrichment courses. In 1988, she became pregnant by artificial insemination and sought a leave of absence. Her supervisor had previously recommended she not be retained, and school administrators expressed concerns about the problems of being an unwed parent. While she was on maternity leave, the school board voted not to renew her contract, claiming this was based on her being a poor teacher, complaints by parents of her unfairness toward some students and her demonstrated lack of professionalism. She filed a discrimination claim with the Equal Employment Opportunity Commission (EEOC), was unsuccessful, and received a "right to sue" letter so that she could proceed with filing a lawsuit against the school district. She then filed a complaint asserting numerous claims: violation of Title VII (which forbids sex discrimination because of "pregnancy, childbirth or [other] related medical conditions"), § 1983 civil rights claims for denial of procedural and substantive due process, privacy and equal protection laws, and additional pendant state claims of intentional or reckless infliction of emotional distress, breach of contract, tortious interference with contract, wrongful discharge and sex discrimination. Can you think of anything the teacher missed? Do you think she prevailed?

The Attorney-Client Relationship

Is it desirable that teachers handle their own legal problems?

No, of course not. You are the expert in the field of education whereas an attorney should be an expert in the field of law. The first question to be asked when a problem arises is whether this is an educational or a legal problem. Many problems judged to be legal are simply educational or psychological problems, and should never be brought into the courtroom for adjudication. With respect to the education of those under your care and supervision, you should know enough law to avoid doing something which you should not do; conversely, you should also know enough law so that you do not neglect to do something that you are obligated to do. The suggestions outlined near the end of this chapter will assist you in placing yourself in a favorable position—to be legally literate and to keep up with changes in the law which affect how students are taught and how schools are managed. Your yardstick should be that of fundamental fairness in dealing with students and others. You should remember that the courts will balance your right and obligation to maintain a safe and peaceful school and classroom with others' constitutionally protected rights to such things as privacy, freedom of speech, freedom of religion and freedom of association.

How can an attorney help the educator?

An attorney is primarily a legal advisor and advocate for her client. A successful attorney is generally skilled in fact-finding, decision making and conflict resolution. While the attorney is usually not an educator trained in the theories of how children learn, she can provide a valuable service to educators during a legal dispute by assisting them in making the best of what may be an unsettling situation by helping them continue their lives and occupations in as normal a setting as possible. However, to do this as expeditiously as possible, it is necessary that the attorney be well informed with accurate facts and evidence. It is also helpful if the teacher does not muddle the situation by doing or saying things which may complicate the case and ultimately delay or preclude a satisfactory resolution.

What should the teacher's relationship be with his attorney?

The attorney is your legal representative in matters having to do with the law. This might suggest a "team" relationship, since you are pooling your knowledge of education and the facts and circumstances in a troublesome situation with your attorney's knowledge of the law. Regardless of whether you are bringing a claim as a plaintiff or defending yourself from charges brought by others, in order to increase your chances for success it is necessary that you make contributions to your case which will enable your attorney to provide the best representation. For example, you should disclose to your attorney all facts (both favorable and unfavorable) about your role in the disputed matter. If your attorney so advises, you should keep objective documentation of conversations and events that might bear on the disputed matter. Keep in mind, however, that the documentation you prepare may have to be provided to the opposing side in the event of litigation. Also maintain confidentiality and do not talk to others—principally the media—about the disputed matter. This may present a difficult challenge—particularly if the "other side" attempts to "try" its case in the media. Your relationship with your attorney should be close enough for mutual trust and respect so that together, working as a team, you can see that your rights are vindicated before the law.

Is a legal resolution the only way to resolve a dispute over educational matters?

It is an attorney's stock in trade to resolve legal issues. However, some critics of the proliferating litigation in education have said that educators did not have any legal problems until attorneys became involved. You should recognize what is a purely educational problem and learn to deal with it within the educational context. Even those problems that seem to hinge on a person's constitutional rights, as outlined in the earlier chapters of this book, might be mitigated if someone does not decide that the only answer is to "sue the bastards." There are many (and more advantageous) ways of resolving most differences than to take them into court. Hasty or ill-advised litigation is costly, takes an inordinate amount of time, and may force the loser to pay damages as well as the other side's litigation costs. In addition, litigation almost always takes a toll in terms of physical stress and emotional anxiety. Such avenues as filing a grievance or using fact-finding, mediation or arbitration are often much more productive than going to court. In almost all circumstances, going to court should ordinarily be the last resort.

How can a teacher find an attorney skilled in school law?

Attorneys in many states cannot advertise. However, in those states where they can, it might be possible to look at these ads and find someone who "looks good." More importantly, remember that even where attorneys can advertise, many excellent attorneys choose not to do so. You may also wish to contact the local, county or state bar associations as they may keep lists of attorneys who specialize in certain areas of law. If you belong to a union or association, they may advise you as to who is familiar with and up-to-date on school law. In addition, you might want to ask other teachers who have recently been involved in litigation for advice and guidance. Not all attorneys are familiar with or wish to engage in school-related cases. Since the hunt for a credible, competent attorney may take some time, it is always important to begin this search as soon as problems arise in which legal counsel might be needed. Even if you end up not actually needing to retain legal counsel, the information you accumulate may eventually be useful to you or your colleagues.

What services can a skilled school law attorney provide the teacher?

First, an experienced attorney can provide you with some predictability about the course of events in your search for justice. This means that an attorney may be able to help you weigh the benefits and risks of selecting and following different courses of action. However, keep in mind that regardless of your attorney's advice and counsel, as the client *you* (not your attorney) will make "final decisions" from among the available alternatives. Second, an attorney might help you in establishing policy and in formulating rules that can be followed safely in your work. An attorney who is familiar with the case law in your jurisdiction can help in making policy related to a particular problem with the assurance that it is likely to be the safest alternative in a given situation. Third, the attorney can provide you with crisis counseling. However, if you wait until a crisis has gotten out of hand before you consult an attorney, you may have waited too long and "counseling" may offer little solace.

Precautions to Take to Avoid Litigation

In summary, what are some precautions you can take to avoid litigation?

Be aware and be prepared! You spent considerable time, money and effort to become a teacher; yet, you may not be prepared for an event that could jeopardize your entire career. A good procedure is to assess your position from time to time using these questions:

1. Am I firm and do I have reasonable limits in my teaching—and do the students know what those limits are?
2. Am I caring and do I look out for the interests of the children as if I were a surrogate parent?
3. Am I fair and do I realize that children will make mis-

takes—and that one of the functions of the school is to provide life-like experiences where children can learn that democracy works and that inappropriate behavior has its limits?

4. Do I use common sense?
5. Do I anticipate and confront potential problems head on rather than hoping they will go away if I simply ignore them?
6. Do I look around and see how other teachers do things productively and successfully?
7. Do I keep my building principal and other school administrators informed of dangerous situations and conditions around the school—and do I watch to see that these problems are resolved?
8. Do I ask questions and seek the advice of those who have accurate and dependable information which will allow me to make informed decisions?

These are good operational principles by which to teach. If you can answer all of these questions in the affirmative, you have taken an excellent first step in reducing the chances that you will become involved in a legal dispute.

Case Resolutions

Case No. 1: When in Rome . . . (see page 251)

An attorney might have advised the teacher that constitutional rights are never absolute—only circumstantial and conditioned upon the facts in each particular case. When the dismissed teacher lost at the federal district court level, she appealed to the Eighth Circuit Court of Appeals. The Eighth Circuit upheld the lower court, declaring that "the state is entitled to require teachers to maintain a properly moral [sic] scholastic environment" in view of the independent "interest in the well-being of youth" as well as its interest "in preserving the right of parents to control the upbringing of their children." These rights (of the state) are to be weighed against the teacher's right to privacy. In denying her damages and attorney's fees, the court noted that even if the Constitution does "afford [the teacher's] lifestyle some protection," under *Pickering v. Board of Education*, 391 U.S. 563 (1968), the school board must "balance the interests of the teacher against its own legitimate government interests." *Sullivan v. Meade County Independent School District*, 530 F.2d 799, 806 (8th Cir. 1976).

Case No. 2: Conduct for a disciplinary proceeding (see page 251)

The school board's actions infringed upon the teacher's right to due process. As a tenured employee in New York, she could only be removed "for cause." Thus, she had a property right in continued employment, salary and benefits which could not be terminated without due process. An employee must be given opportunity for a hearing *before* being deprived of a significant property interest "except . . . where some valid governmental interest . . . justifies postponing the hearing until after the event." Here, the teacher's interest in receiving her salary outweighed the board's interest in suspending her pay because of bad faith. In fact, the board's allegation of bad faith was suspect because it failed to allow the teacher to explain why the adjournments were needed; in addition, the hearing panel had previously agreed to all the adjournments. *McCreery v. Babylon Union Free School District*, 827 F.Supp. 136 (E.D.N.Y. 1993).

Case No. 3: Illegal drug possession (or procedure to the max!) (see page 252)

The Tenth Circuit Court of Appeals agreed with the teacher only on the issue that the school board did not have immunity from suit under the Eleventh Amendment. The court reached this conclusion after deciding that the school district is not an arm or alter ego of the state. However, the court did not agree that the teacher was denied due process in his first hearing—he had the opportunity to correct any false information before he was suspended. Further, he received post-suspension, pre-termination due process. The school board complied with the requirements that the teacher was entitled to *notice* of the charges, *explanation* of the evidence against him, and an *opportunity* to present his side of the story. The fact that the teacher did not request a post-suspension, pre-termination hearing did not change the fact that he was offered a hearing.

However, the court did find that the teacher was denied due process in his second post-termination hearing because the board should not have been allowed to present evidence of the arresting officer's testimony after the teacher's records had been expunged of the criminal charges and sealed by court order. The case was *remanded* (sent back) for yet another due process hearing. *Ambus v. Granite Board of Education*, 975 F.2d 1555 (10th Cir. 1992), *aff'd, cause remanded, on rehearing en banc, modified*, 955 F.2d 992 (10th Cir. 1993), *appeal after remand, Ambus v. Utah State Board of Education*, 858 P.2d 372 (Utah 1993) (Ambus also sought damages via state court and was similarly successful).

Case No. 4: A multitude of claims (or just sex discrimination) (see page 253)

The teacher got past the initial hurdle toward a final goal of having a jury decide her claims since the trial court found that there were conflicting reasons why the teacher's contract was not renewed. The trial court denied summary judgment to the school board on several of the claims (meaning the case would go to trial so a jury could decide who to believe). Under her protected privacy interest, the teacher had a right to become pregnant by artificial insemination. The defendants were not entitled to qualified good faith immunity from liability for damages because reasonable school officials should have known that actions imposed against a woman on the basis of an unwed pregnancy induced by artificial insemination would violate a woman's privacy rights.

In addition, contract issues (she did not receive an evaluation prior to nonrenewal as required by school policy) and, under state law, sex discrimination issues remained. However, the trial court also found several issues which would not go before a jury: there was no procedural due process violation (the teacher was not tenured and thus had no property interest); there was no evidence of emotional distress manifest by such conduct as the teacher's need to consult medical or psychological experts for assistance; and the teacher was not wrongfully discharged (her contract was simply "not renewed"). *Cameron v. Board of Education of Hillsboro, Ohio School District*, 795 F.Supp. 228 (S.D.Ohio 1991).

After the remaining issues were tried to a jury, the jury returned a verdict for the school board. At the trial, testimony was allowed about parental complaints against the teacher. This evidence showed that the motivating factor for the school board to dismiss the teacher was grounds other than sex discrimination. When the jury weighed the credibility of all the evidence, it concluded that the teacher's nonrenewal was based on her teaching performance and not on other discriminatory or unconstitutional factors. The court denied the teacher's motion for a new trial. *Cameron v. Board of Education of Hillsboro City School District*, 820 F.Supp. 336 (S.D.Ohio 1993).

Appendix A

Amendments to the United States Constitution

Amendment I [1791]

Congress shall make no law respecting an establishment of religion, or prohibiting the free exercise thereof; or abridging the freedom of speech, or of the press; or the right of the people peaceably to assembly, and to petition the Government for a redress of grievances.

Amendment II [1791]

A well regulated Militia, being necessary to the security of a free State, the right of the people to keep and bear Arms, shall not be infringed.

Amendment III [1791]

No Soldier shall, in time of peace be quartered in any house, without the consent of the Owner, nor in time of war, but in a manner to be prescribed by law.

Amendment IV [1791]

The right of the people to be secure in their persons, houses, papers, and effects, against unreasonable searches and seizures, shall not be violated, and no Warrants shall issue, but upon probable cause, supported by Oath or affirmation, and particularly describing the place to be searched, and the persons or things to be seized.

Amendment V [1791]

No person shall be held to answer for a capital, or otherwise infamous crime, unless on a presentment or indictment of a Grand Jury, except in cases arising in the land or naval forces, or in the Militia, when in actual service in time of War or public danger; nor shall any person be subject for the same offence to be twice put in jeopardy of life or limb; nor shall be compelled in any criminal case to be a witness against himself, nor be deprived of life, liberty, or property, without due process of law; nor shall private property be taken for public use, without just compensation.

Amendment VI [1791]

In all criminal prosecutions, the accused shall enjoy the right to a speedy and public trial, by an impartial jury of the State and district wherein the crime shall have been committed, which district shall have been previously ascertained by law, and to be informed of the nature and cause of the accusation; to be confronted with the witnesses against him; to have compulsory process for obtaining witnesses in his favor, and to have the Assistance of Counsel for his defence.

Amendment VII [1791]

In Suits at common law, where the value in controversy shall exceed twenty dollars, the right of trial by jury shall be preserved, and no fact tried by jury, shall be otherwise re-examined in any Court of the United States, than according to the rules of the common law.

Amendment VIII [1791]

Excessive bail shall not be required, nor excessive fines imposed, nor cruel and unusual punishments inflicted.

Amendment IX [1791]

The enumeration in the Constitution, of certain rights, shall not be construed to deny or disparage others retained by the people.

Amendment X [1791]

The powers not delegated to the United States by the Constitution, nor prohibited by it to the States, are reserved to the States respectively, or to the people.

Amendment XI [1798]

The Judicial power of the United States shall not be construed to extend to any suit in law or equity, commenced or prosecuted against one of the United States by Citizens of another State, or by Citizens or Subjects of any Foreign State.

Amendment XII [1804]

The Electors shall meet in their respective states and vote by ballot for President and Vice-President, one of whom, at least, shall not be an inhabitant of the same state with themselves; they shall name in their ballots the person voted for as President, and in distinct ballots the person voted for as Vice-President, and they shall make distinct lists of all persons voted for as President, and of all persons voted for as Vice-President, and of the number of votes for each, which lists they shall sign and certify, and transmit sealed to the seat of the government of the United States, directed to the President of the Senate;— The President of the Senate shall, in the presence of the Senate and House of Representatives, open all the certificates and the votes shall then be counted;—The person having the greatest number of votes for President, shall be the President, if such number be a majority of the whole number of Electors appointed; and if no person have such majority, then from the persons having the highest numbers not exceeding three on the list of those voted for as President, the House of Representatives shall choose immediately, by ballot, the President. But in choosing the President, the votes shall be taken by states, the representation from each state having one vote; a quorum for this purpose shall consist of a member or members from two-thirds of the states, and a majority of all the states shall be necessary to a choice. And if the House of Representatives shall not choose a President whenever the right of choice shall devolve upon them before the fourth day of March next following, then the Vice-President shall act as President, as in the case of the death or other constitutional disability of the President.—The person having the greatest number of votes as Vice-President, shall be the Vice-President, if such number be a majority of the whole number of Electors appointed, and if no person have a majority, then from the two highest numbers on the list, the Senate shall choose the Vice-President; a quorum for the purpose shall consist of two-thirds of the whole number of Senators, and a majority of the whole number shall be necessary to a choice. But no person constitutionally ineligible to the office of President shall be eligible to that of Vice-President of the United States.

Amendment XIII [1865]

Section 1. Neither slavery nor involuntary servitude, except as a punishment for crime whereof the party shall have been duly convicted, shall exist within the United States, or any place subject to their jurisdiction.

Section 2. Congress shall have power to enforce this article by appropriate legislation.

Amendment XIV [1868]

Section 1. All persons born or naturalized in the United States, and subject to the jurisdiction thereof, are citizens of the

United States and of the State wherein they reside. No State shall make or enforce any law which shall abridge the privileges or immunities of citizens of the United States; nor shall any State deprive any person of life, liberty, or property, without due process of law; nor deny to any person within its jurisdiction the equal protection of the laws.

Section 2. Representatives shall be apportioned among the several States according to their respective numbers, counting the whole number of persons in each State excluding Indians not taxed. But when the right to vote at any election for the choice of electors for President and Vice President of the United States, Representatives in Congress, the Executive and Judicial officers of a State, or the members of the Legislature thereof, is denied to any of the male inhabitants of such State, being twenty-one years of age, and citizens of the United States, or in any way abridged, except for participation in rebellion, or other crime, the basis of representation therein shall be reduced in the proportion which the number of such male citizens shall bear to the whole number of male citizens twenty-one years of age in such State.

Section 3. No person shall be a Senator or Representative in Congress, or elector of President and Vice President, or hold any office, civil or military, under the United States, or under any State, who having previously taken an oath, as a member of Congress, or as an officer of the United States, or as a member of any State legislature, or as an executive or judicial officer of any State, to support the Constitution of the United States, shall have engaged in insurrection or rebellion against the same, or given aid or comfort to the enemies thereof. But Congress may by a vote of two-thirds of each House, remove such disability.

Section 4. The validity of the public debt of the United States, authorized by law, including debts incurred for payment of pensions and bounties for services in suppressing insurrection or rebellion, shall not be questioned. But neither the United States nor any State shall assume or pay any debt or obligation incurred in aid of insurrection or rebellion against the United States, or any claim for the loss or emancipation of any slave; but all such debts, obligations and claims shall be held illegal and void.

Section 5. The Congress shall have power to enforce, by appropriate legislation, the provisions of this article.

Amendment XV [1870]

Section 1. The right of citizens of the United States to vote shall not be denied or abridged by the United States or by any State on account of race, color, or previous condition of servitude.

Section 2. The Congress shall have power to enforce this article by appropriate legislation.

Amendment XVI [1913]

The Congress shall have power to lay and collect taxes on incomes, from whatever source derived, without apportionment among the several States, and without regard to any census or enumeration.

Amendment XVII [1913]

Section 1. The Senate of the United States shall be composed of two Senators from each State, elected by the people thereof, for six years; and each Senator shall have one vote. The electors in each State shall have the qualifications requisite for electors of the most numerous branch of the State legislatures.

Section 2. When vacancies happen in the representation of any State in the Senate, the executive authority of such State shall issue writs of election to fill such vacancies: *Provided*, That the legislature of any State may empower the executive thereof to make temporary appointments until the people fill the vacancies by election as the legislature may direct.

Section 3. This amendment shall not be so construed as to affect the election or term of any Senator chosen before it becomes valid as part of the Constitution.

Amendment XVIII [1919]

Section 1. After one year from the ratification of this article the manufacture, sale, or transportation of intoxicating liquors within, the importation thereof into, or the exportation thereof from the United States and all territory subject to the jurisdiction thereof for beverage purposes is hereby prohibited.

Section 2. The Congress and the several States shall have concurrent power to enforce this article by appropriate legislation.

Section 3. This article shall be inoperative unless it shall have been ratified as an amendment to the Constitution by the legislatures of the several States, as provided in the Constitution, within seven years from the date of the submission hereof to the States by the Congress.

Amendment XIX [1920]

Section 1. The right of citizens of the United States to vote shall not be denied or abridged by the United States or by any State on account of sex.

Section 2. Congress shall have power to enforce this article by appropriate legislation.

Amendment XX [1933]

Section 1. The terms of the President and Vice President shall end at noon on the 20th day of January, and the terms of Senators and Representatives at noon on the 3rd day of January, of the years in which such terms would have ended if this article had not been ratified; and the terms of their successors shall then begin.

Section 2. The Congress shall assemble at least once in every year, and such meeting shall begin at noon on the 3rd day of January, unless they shall by law appoint a different day.

Section 3. If, at the time fixed for the beginning of the term of the President, the President elect shall have died, the Vice President elect shall become President. If the President shall not have been chosen before the time fixed for the beginning of his term, or if the President elect shall have failed to qualify, then the Vice President elect shall act as President until a President shall have qualified; and the Congress may by law provide for the case wherein neither a President elect nor a Vice President elect shall have qualified, declaring who shall then act as President, or the manner in which one who is to act shall be selected, and such person shall act accordingly until a President or Vice President shall have qualified.

Section 4. The Congress may by law provide for the case of the death of any of the persons from whom the House of Representatives may choose a President whenever the right of choice shall have devolved upon them, and for the case of the death of any of the persons from whom the Senate may choose a Vice President whenever the right of choice shall have devolved upon them.

Section 5. Sections 1 and 2 shall take effect on the 15th day of October following the ratification of this article.

Section 6. This article shall be inoperative unless it shall have been ratified as an amendment to the Constitution by the legislatures of three-fourths of the several States within seven years from the date of its submission.

Amendment XXI [1933]

Section 1. The eighteenth article of amendment to the Constitution of the United States is hereby repealed.

Section 2. The transportation or importation into any State, Territory, or possession of the United States for delivery or use therein of intoxicating liquors, in violation of the laws thereof, is hereby prohibited.

Section 3. This article shall be inoperative unless it shall have been ratified as an amendment to the Constitution by conventions in the several States, as provided in the Constitution, within seven years from the date of the submission hereof to the States by the Congress.

Amendment XXII [1951]

Section 1. No person shall be elected to the office of the President more than twice, and no person who has held the office of President, or acted as President, for more than two years of a term to which some other person was elected President shall be elected to the office of President more than once. But this Article shall not apply to any person holding the office of President, when this Article was proposed by the Congress, and shall not prevent any person who may be holding the office of President or acting as President, during the term within which this Article becomes operative from holding the office of President or acting as President during the remainder of such term.

Section 2. This article shall be inoperative unless it shall have been ratified as an amendment to the Constitution by the legislatures of three-fourths of the several States within seven years from the date of its submission to the States by the Congress.

Amendment XXIII [1961]

Section 1. The District constituting the seat of Government of the United States shall appoint in such manner as the Congress may direct:

A number of electors of President and Vice President equal to the whole number of Senators and Representatives in Congress to which the District would be entitled if it were a State, but in no event more than the least populous State; they shall be in addition to those appointed by the states, but they shall be considered, for the purposes of the election of President and Vice President, to be electors appointed by a State; and they shall meet in the District and perform such duties as provided by the twelfth article of amendment.

Section 2. The Congress shall have power to enforce this article by appropriate legislation.

Amendment XXIV [1964]

Section 1. The right of citizens of the United States to vote in any primary or other election for President or Vice President, for electors for President or Vice President, or for Senator or Representative in Congress, shall not be denied or abridged by the United States, or any State by reason of failure to pay any poll tax or other tax.

Section 2. The Congress shall have power to enforce this article by appropriate legislation.

Amendment XXV [1967]

Section 1. In case of the removal of the President from office or of his death or resignation, the Vice President shall become President.

Section 2. Whenever there is a vacancy in the office of the Vice President, the President shall nominate a Vice President who shall take office upon confirmation by a majority vote of both Houses of Congress.

Section 3. Whenever the President transmits to the President pro tempore of the Senate and the Speaker of the House of Representatives his written declaration that he is unable to discharge the powers and duties of his office, and until he transmits to them a written declaration to the contrary, such powers and duties shall be discharged by the Vice President as Acting President.

Section 4. Whenever the Vice President and a majority of either the principal officers of the executive departments or of such other body as Congress may by law provide, transmit to the President pro tempore of the Senate and the Speaker of the House of Representatives their written declaration that the President is unable to discharge the powers and duties of his office, the Vice President shall immediately assume the powers and duties of the office as Acting President.

Thereafter, when the President transmits to the President pro tempore of the Senate and the Speaker of the House of Representatives his written declaration that no inability exists, he shall resume the powers and duties of his office unless the Vice President and a majority of either the principal officers of the executive department or of such other body as Congress may by law provide, transmit within four days to the President pro tempore of the Senate and the Speaker of the House of Representatives their written declaration that the President is unable to discharge the powers and duties of his office. Thereupon Congress shall decide the issue, assembling within forty-eight hours for that purpose if not in session. If the Congress, within twenty-one days after receipt of the latter written declaration, or, if Congress is not in session, within twenty-one days after Congress is required to assemble, determines by two-thirds vote of both Houses that the President is unable to discharge the powers and duties of his office, the Vice President shall continue to discharge the same as Acting President; otherwise, the President shall resume the powers and duties of his office.

Amendment XXVI [1971]

Section 1. The right of citizens of the United States, who are eighteen years of age or older, to vote shall not be denied or abridged by the United States or by any State on account of age.

Section 2. The Congress shall have power to enforce this article by appropriate legislation.

Appendix B
Table of Cases *

Abood v. Detroit Board of Education, 431 U.S. 209 (1977), *reh'g denied*, 433 U.S. 915 (1977), **234**, **235**

Acanfora v. Board of Education of Montgomery County, 491 F.2d 498 (4th Cir. 1974), *cert. denied*, 419 U.S. 836 (1974), **48**

Adler v. Board of Education of City of New York, 342 U.S. 485 (1952), *overruled in part by Keyishian v. Board of Regents of the University of the State of New York*, 385 U.S. 589 (1967), **115**

Ambach v. Norwick, 441 U.S. 68 (1978), **96**

---

* Case citations were valid at the publication date of this book. However, readers are reminded that recent cases, in particular, may be subject to modification, reversal or other action through an appeal to a higher court or subsequent legislation.

Pages where these cases are discussed follow each citation in bold.

Appendix C

States in the Federal Judicial Circuit Courts of Appeal

28 U.S.C. §41

FIRST CIRCUIT	SECOND CIRCUIT	THIRD CIRCUIT
Maine	Connecticut	Delaware
Massachusetts	New York	New Jersey
New Hampshire	Vermont	Pennsylvania
Rhode Island		

FOURTH CIRCUIT	FIFTH CIRCUIT	SIXTH CIRCUIT
Maryland	Louisiana	Kentucky
North Carolina	Mississippi	Michigan
South Carolina	Texas	Ohio
Virginia		Tennessee
West Virginia		

SEVENTH CIRCUIT	EIGHTH CIRCUIT	NINTH CIRCUIT
Illinois	Arkansas	Alaska
Indiana	Iowa	Arizona
Wisconsin	Minnesota	California
	Missouri	Hawaii
	Nebraska	Idaho
	North Dakota	Montana
	South Dakota	Nevada
		Oregon
		Washington

TENTH CIRCUIT	ELEVENTH CIRCUIT	FEDERAL CIRCUIT
Colorado	Alabama	All federal judicial
Kansas	Florida	districts
New Mexico	Georgia	
Oklahoma		
Utah		
Wyoming		

DISTRICT OF
COLUMBIA
District of
Columbia

Glossary

Certiorari

A higher court's discretion to review an appeal from a lower court. For example, certiorari on an appeal is granted or denied by a vote of the nine justices on the United States Supreme Court.

Civil rights

Fundamental personal rights guaranteed by the Constitution (for example, freedom of speech). Also refers to a significant body of antidiscrimination legislation which may be litigated under a commonly used statute—42 U.S.C. § 1983 (see below).

Common law

Judge-made law dating back over centuries and incorporating recognized customs, prior judicial principles, and other rulings emanating from either the judicial or executive branches of government. It is applied to decide a case if there is no statute enacted or other controlling law.

Compensatory damages

A monetary award made to a plaintiff who has suffered a legal wrong; a civil remedy designed to make the injured party "whole."

Constitution

The fundamental document of a political body which establishes the governmental structure and sets forth basic principles under which society will operate.

Defendant Person being sued against whom recovery is sought in a civil suit, or the accused in a criminal case.

De facto In fact. For example, *de facto* segregation is segregation that exists because of housing patterns or other factors, but does not result from the action of a state or governing body.

De jure By law. *De jure* segregation is segregation accomplished by law or from the action of a state or governing body.

De novo A fresh review of a matter, or a second look without reference to a prior proceeding on the same matter.

Discovery Method of ascertaining relevant information about a suit in order to assist in preparing for trial or proposing a settlement. It includes requesting the opposing party to furnish documents and respond to questions, both in writing and in oral depositions.

Dismissal Generally refers to the termination of employment prior to the end of a contract or expected period of employment.

Id. Indicates a reference immediately prior to this one.

Indemnify To "make good" for another or secure them against loss. Also referred to as "hold harmless."

Injunction A court order forbidding (or enjoining) some act or the continuation of some act.

In loco parentis In the place of a parent.

Jurisdiction A court's power or authority to make a decision on a matter in controversy. (For example, a state court in New Hampshire has no "jurisdiction" to decide a dispute about land located in Wyoming.)

Jurisprudence The pursuit of ascertaining legal principles which legal rules are based upon.

Liability A legal obligation to pay damages for harm caused to another.

Negligence Conduct in which a person fails to exercise reasonable care to protect another from risk of harm, or failure to do what others would do under similar circumstances. (May lead to being a defendant and to liability.)

Nominal damages Limited monetary award (e.g., $1.00) given by a court or jury in a case where there is little or no actual loss but the plaintiff has proven mistreatment.

Nonrenewal Usually refers to the situation in which a probationary or non-continuing contract teacher is not given an employment contract for the following school year.

Plaintiff Person who complains and files a civil lawsuit.

Probationary A teacher who has not attained tenure or continuing contract employment status.

Punitive damages	A monetary award designed to punish a wrongful defendant in a civil lawsuit; also referred to as exemplary damages.
Remanded	Sent back for further action.
Section 1983	A provision in the Civil Rights Act of 1871 (42 U.S.C. § 1983) passed by Congress which provides that any person who acts under color of state law to deprive another individual of rights secured by the federal constitution or laws is subject to personal liability.
Statute	An act passed by Congress or a state legislature requiring or prohibiting something.
Summary judgment	A court decision that essentially means a party wins judgment on points of law without having to go through a trial (in other words, there is no genuine dispute about the facts of a case, and under the applicable law, one party is entitled to prevail without further litigation).
Tenure	A statutory right that confers permanent or continuing employment status on teachers.
Title VII	A part of the Civil Rights Act of 1964 passed by Congress which prohibits employers from discriminating against employees on the basis of race, color, religion, sex or national origin. This provision covers hiring, promotion, compensation, fringe benefits and other terms and conditions of employment.
Title IX	A provision in the Education Amendments of 1972 passed by Congress which

prohibits gender discrimination against participants in or beneficiaries of federally funded educational programs.

Tolled   To stop temporarily.

Tort   A legal wrong or injury to a person or property which does not involve breach of contract and for which a civil (as opposed to a criminal) suit can be brought for the recovery of money damages.

Ultra vires   Beyond the scope of authority.

Index